PERENNIALS

BY JANET H. SANCHEZ AND THE EDITORS OF SUNSET BOOKS

SUNSET BOOKS · MENLO PARK, CALIFORNIA

PERENNIALLY SATISFYING

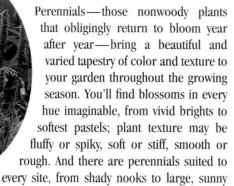

Perennials—those nonwoody plants that obligingly return to bloom year after year—bring a beautiful and varied tapestry of color and texture to your garden throughout the growing season. You'll find blossoms in every hue imaginable, from vivid brights to softest pastels; plant texture may be fluffy or spiky, soft or stiff, smooth or rough. And there are perennials suited to every site, from shady nooks to large, sunny borders to containers that can grace a deck or patio.

This book offers an introduction to the fascinating world of perennials. The first chapter, "Perennials in the Garden," covers choosing and combining these plants—a creative outlet for gardeners everywhere. "Planting and Caring for Perennials," the second chapter, teaches you the basics of successful cultivation, from planting to pruning to propagation. Finally, an extensive encyclopedia of perennials includes over 140 plants, providing descriptions and cultural information for each.

We are grateful to the many dedicated amateur and professional growers who have guided us in the preparation of this second edition of *Perennials*. Our special thanks go to John R. Dunmire of Los Altos, California, for assistance with the manuscript and to Randy and Kara Stephens-Flemming of Petaluma, California, for creating the garden designs.

SUNSET BOOKS

Vice President and General Manager: Richard A. Smeby
Editorial Director: Bob Doyle
Production Director: Lory Day
Art Director: Vasken Guiragossian

Staff for this book:

Managing Editor: Marianne Lipanovich
Sunset Books Senior Editor, Gardening: Suzanne Normand Eyre
Copy Editor and Indexer: Rebecca LaBrum
Photo Researcher: Tishana Peebles
Production Coordinator: Patricia S. Williams
Special Contributors: Lisa Anderson, Bridget Biscotti Bradley, Barbara Brown, Jean Warboy
Proofreader: Susan Brown

Art Director: Alice Rogers
Illustrator: Erin O'Toole
Additional Illustrations: Jenny Speckles
Computer Production: Joan Olson, Linda Bouchard

PHOTOGRAPHERS:

Scott Atkinson: 3 middle, 30-31, 97 bottom; **Max E. Badgley:** 40 bottom left; **Marion Brenner:** 64 left, 77 bottom right; **David Cavagnaro:** 8 top left, 10 bottom left, 11 top right, middle left, middle right, 50 top left, 51 top, 52 top left, bottom right, 55 bottom right, 56 top, 57 top, bottom; 58 bottom left, 62 bottom, 67 top, 70 top, 75 left, 76 bottom, 78 top left, bottom left, 82 middle bottom, 86 bottom, 90 top right, 91 bottom, 97 top, middle, 99 top, 101 top, 104 top left, 110 top left, 112 bottom, 116, 119 bottom right, 121 top; **R. Todd Davis:** 12 top left, bottom left, 14 bottom, 67 bottom, 78 right, 82 bottom, 93 bottom right, 96 left; **Alan & Linda Detrick:** 10 top left, 51 bottom, 58 bottom, 59 left, 61 bottom right, 72 bottom left, 74 top, 87 left, 92 middle, 100 middle, 107 left, 110 bottom left; 111 bottom, 118 bottom; **Derek Fell:** 3 top, 4-5, 7 top right, 8 top right, 36 right, 95 bottom, 99 middle, 105 bottom, 111 top, 114 right, 117 left; **William E. Ferguson:** 41 middle left; **Lynne Harrison:** 7 left, 8 middle right, 11 bottom left, 28 bottom, 52 middle left, 53 bottom right, 58 top left, 60 bottom, 65 top right, 68 right, 75 top right, 76 top, 80, 83 top, 84 top left, bottom left, 88 middle, 89 top, 102 top, 103 top, 109 top, 113 bottom, 114 top left, 117 top right, bottom right, 118 top, 119 left, back cover top left; **Philip Harvey:** 24 bottom; **Saxon Holt:** 3 bottom, 8 bottom right, 10 top right, 17 top left, top right, 25, 32, 46-47, 50 left, 54 right, 63 top right, 65 bottom right, 71 bottom, 83 bottom, 85 top, 89 bottom, 90 top left, 91 middle, 92 top, 96 top right, 100 top, 101 bottom, 106, 107 top right, bottom right, 110 right, 112 top, 120; **Lee Valley Garden Tools:** 38; **Charles Mann:** 1, 2, 12 top middle, top right, bottom right, 14 top, 21 top left, 23 bottom, 29 top, 48, 49 top, 53 left, 54 left, 55 left, 56 bottom, 63 bottom right, 68 top left, bottom left, 72 top left, right, 73 bottom, 74 bottom, 77 left, top right, 81 left, 82 middle top, 84 right, 87 top right, 88 bottom, 90 bottom, 91 top, 93 left, 94 bottom, 95 top, 98, 102 bottom, 108 left, back cover right; **Jim McCausland:** 23 top; **Baldassare Mineo:** 81 top right; **Jerry Pavia:** 6 top, middle left, bottom, 7 middle right, 9 middle, bottom, 11 top left, 13 top, bottom right, 16 top, bottom left, bottom right, 17 bottom, 29 middle, 35, 53 top right, 55 middle right, 61 top right, 63 left, 64 right, 65 left, 66 top, 75 bottom right, 79 bottom right, 88 top, 92 bottom, 99 bottom, 115, 121 bottom, back cover bottom left; **Norman A. Plate:** 6 middle right, 24 top, 34, 37, 42, 66 bottom; **Susan A. Roth:** 85 bottom; **Chad Slattery:** 86 top; **Randy & Kara Stephens-Flemming:** 70 bottom, 101 middle; **K. Bryan Swezey:** 93 top right; **Michael S. Thompson:** 8 bottom left; 10 middle right, bottom right, 13 bottom left, 16 middle, 27 top, middle, 28 middle, 29 bottom, 36 left, 57 middle, 59 top right, bottom right, 60 top, 61 left, 62 top, 69, 71 top, 79 left, top right, 81 bottom right, 82 top, 87 bottom right, 94 top, 96 bottom right, 100 bottom, 103 bottom, 104 bottom left, 105 top, 108 right, 109 bottom, 113 top, 114 bottom left; **Ron West/Nature Photography:** 40 top left, top right, bottom right, 41 left, middle right, right; **Tom Woodward:** 9 top, 21 top right; 27 bottom, 28 top, 49 bottom, 50 bottom left, 55 top right, 62 top right; **Cynthia Woodyard:** 21 bottom, 73 top, 104 right, 119 right.

Cover: *Trollius.* Photograph by Charles Mann. Border photograph (*Aster novae-angliae* 'Purple Dome') by R. Todd Davis.

CONTENTS

PERENNIALS IN THE
GARDEN

Welcome to the world of perennials! It's a realm offering an incredible array of plants, with blossoms in every color of the rainbow and bloom seasons including spring, summer, fall—and even winter, in some climates. Many of these plants also have beautifully textured or colored leaves, bringing yet more interest to the garden. In size, perennials range from diminutive mounding sorts to towering 8-footers. Their adaptability is broad, too; you'll find choices for hot, dry expanses, damp and shady cool spots, and everything in between.

Choosing the right perennials for your garden and deciding where to put each one is an enjoyable task—but given the range of possibilities, it can also be a confusing one. This chapter aims to make the process clearer. We review typical planting areas, including the time-honored beds and borders; discuss the importance of exposure and soil type; and review some basics of garden design, including color schemes, plant texture, season of bloom, and plant size and spacing. Four sample plans offer combinations of perennials suited to specific sites; these are followed by pointers for creating your own designs.

Drifts of elegant bearded iris draw the eye through a rich tapestry of color
in this large perennial border.

Lavender *(Lavandula)* and other billowy perennials line a walkway.

The world of perennials includes plants suited to every site. Shown above is a group of sun lovers, among them tall yellow mullein *(Verbascum)* and white feverfew *(Chrysanthemum parthenium)*. Below, ferns and epimediums share a shady bed.

WHAT ARE PERENNIALS?

Regarded by many as the stars of the garden, perennials are nonwoody plants that return to grace the landscape year after year. They complement the garden's other elements—adorning the framework typically provided by trees and shrubs (both with woody stems), offering a longer-lived presence than the fast-growing annuals and biennials that provide almost instant color but live for only 1 or 2 years.

The general category of perennials encompasses plants with varying habits of growth. Some, such as hosta and peony *(Paeonia),* die down to the ground at the end of each growing season, then reappear at the start of the next; these are often referred to as "herbaceous" plants. Others, including Shasta daisy *(Chrysanthemum × superbum)* and coral bells *(Heuchera),* go through winter as low tufts of leaves, ready to grow when spring arrives. A third type of perennial is truly evergreen, with foliage that persists almost unchanged throughout the winter months.

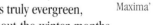

Paeonia 'Festiva Maxima'

Thrift *(Armeria maritima)* and yucca are two familiar examples.

These broad distinctions, however, only hint at the incredible diversity perennials have to offer. There are choices to flourish in almost any part of your garden—sunny or shady, moist or dry. Some perennials are suited to cold-winter regions, others to milder areas; a surprising number grow in a wide range of climate zones. You'll find flowers in every color imaginable, and foliage too provides a wonderful range of colors and textures. In size, these plants range from low mounds to giants reaching 8 feet or taller. Bloom times cover spring, summer, and autumn, and a few perennials can even bring color to the garden in winter.

WHERE TO PLANT PERENNIALS:
BEDS, BORDERS, AND OTHER CHOICES

Perennials are the traditional mainstay of beds and borders. Among beds, the so-called "island" bed, a planting area surrounded by lawn, paths, or paving, shows off perennials especially well. Because it's visible from all sides, an island can showcase many plants; it may contain trees and shrubs in addition to perennials. Other potential perennial beds might include a corner near the front door, edged by the house wall and a front path; the strip of ground between sidewalk and curb; and plantings along a driveway or path. And foundation plantings of low shrubs gain color and interest when assorted perennials are planted in front of them.

Borders, dating back to Victorian times, are typically wide rectangular beds backed by a hedge or wall and fronted by an expanse of lawn or a paved walkway. Within the border, perennials are arranged as an artist might compose a painting, with attention not only to complementary flower colors but also to bloom season, leaf color and texture, and plant height. A variation on this theme is the "mixed" border, which includes plants other than perennials: small trees, flowering shrubs and vines (especially roses), and a few evergreen shrubs to provide interest when most of the other plants are dormant.

Whether mixed or composed entirely of perennials, borders vary in their degree of formality. Highly formal plans feature plants arranged by height, with the shortest in front and the tallest at the rear; fairly large groups of each kind of perennial are used, giving the planting an orderly appearance. In less formal borders, drifts of perennials weave together, with a few taller plants accenting the front; the edges may be curved instead of straight. The least formal border is the cottage garden, an exuberant free-for-all of perennials and whatever else the gardener desires: vegetables, herbs, annuals, bulbs, shrubs, trees.

Creative gardeners find many other ways to use perennials. More and more often, high-maintenance sweeps of lawn are

TOP: Bordered by sweeps of lawn, this island bed can be viewed from all sides.

BOTTOM: A cottage-style garden fills a front yard with color.

being abandoned in favor of pocket-handkerchief plots of grass combined with large perennial borders and beds. You can even replace an entire front lawn with a mix of perennials and other plants. Perennials provide charming accents for vegetables in a kitchen garden; they can be planted in a cutting garden to provide season-long bouquets (our plant encyclopedia, pages 46–121, indicates good choices for cut flowers). Finally, perennials are colorful, long-blooming choices for containers, whether you opt for terra-cotta urns or raised beds built around a deck. See page 25 for more information on growing perennials in containers.

Planted along a path, daylilies (*Hemerocallis*) and other perennials invite close-up inspection.

In this mixed border, low-growing moss pink *(Phlox subulata)* and white evergreen candytuft *(Iberis sempervirens)* enhance the springtime blossoms of a dogwood tree.

TOP: This mixed border features pink foxgloves *(Digitalis)* and roses.

BOTTOM: Low-growing perennials soften the edges of a stone path.

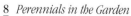

RIGHT: Blooming salvia, yarrow *(Achillea),* and balloon flower *(Platycodon grandiflorus)* create waves of color in a perennial border.

LEFT: The soft flower spikes of aromatic catmint *(Nepeta)* form a mound of lavender blue at the foot of a wooden garden bench.

DESIGNING WITH PERENNIALS

Whether you're planting a grand traditional border or a small bed near the front door, putting together a perennial garden is an enjoyable learning process. You'll discover that creating pleasing combinations of plants involves more than simply choosing those you like best; some amount of analysis is required. To begin with, evaluate potential sites for their exposure (sun or shade), soil type, and available moisture; this will make it easier to select plants likely to thrive where you want them to grow. Next, consider the ornamental aspects of each plant—its texture, foliage and flower color, overall size and form, and season of bloom—and how these characteristics relate to aspects of design such as contrast and repetition, scale, and plant groupings.

Penstemon × gloxinioides 'Garnet'

TOP: Perennials such as pink Mexican evening primrose *(Oenothera speciosa)*, Santa Barbara daisy *(Erigeron karvinskianus)*, and spiky New Zealand flax *(Phormium)* flourish in a sunny site.

BOTTOM: Western bleeding heart *(Dicentra formosa)* and a host of hostas thrive in a sheltered, shady location.

CONSIDERING YOUR SITE

Because there are perennials adapted to most conditions, it's never necessary to "fight the site" by choosing plants that aren't well suited to it. Besides, selecting plants that naturally prefer what a site has to offer will help you create a good-looking garden with less effort and less input of scarce resources. The encyclopedia on pages 46–121 notes the conditions in which each plant flourishes. As you make your choices, keep the following factors in mind.

SUN AND SHADE. Survey the proposed site to determine how much sun it receives each day. A sun-loving plant located in shade will usually bloom sparsely and may also become tall and leggy, requiring staking. Likewise, plants that need shade fare poorly in full sun; they'll scorch and may even die. Some perennials do well in either sun or light shade, often depending on the climate: that is, a plant that succeeds in full sun where summers are cool often prefers light shade in hot climates, especially in the afternoon.

SOIL CONDITIONS. To a certain extent, soil can be amended to make it more hospitable to the perennials you want to grow (see pages 32–33), but there's a limit to how much you can really change it. With this in mind, try to choose plants that like the basic soil texture in the planting area—don't set out types that must have light, sandy soil in heavy clay, for example. Likewise, if you're planting a perennial

Many plants with gray or gray-green leaves are adapted to hot, sunny areas with fairly dry soil. Shown here are yarrow *(Achillea),* catmint *(Nepeta),* lavender *(Lavandula),* and lamb's ears *(Stachys byzantina).*

that's particular about soil pH (its acidity or alkalinity), aim to locate it where the existing conditions suit it (though you can adjust soil pH to some degree; see page 32). The same rules hold for areas where soil is naturally wet or dry. For extremely damp locations, focus on moisture-loving perennials (see page 35 for ideas). For dry-soil sites, choose among plants adapted to drought (see page 23); keeping water-loving types healthy in such spots would involve applying lots of extra water, a wasteful practice that may even be prohibited in areas where water use is restricted.

COLD HARDINESS. Most gardeners wisely select perennials adapted to the average amount of winter cold their region receives. If you want to experiment with plants that are only marginally hardy in your area, look for extra-warm microclimates within your garden—spots that are sheltered from wind and cold and that hold heat, such as courtyards or beds near a south-facing wall.

CONSIDERING TEXTURE

Variety in texture is an important element in creating perennial plantings with long-lasting interest. Consider not only the texture of individual plant parts—flowers, stems, and foliage—but the way these combine to lend each plant an *overall* texture. Some plants, for example, have a "lightweight" look; these include airy, delicate baby's breath *(Gypsophila paniculata),* lacy, billowing *Artemisia* 'Powis Castle', and wispy toadflax *(Linaria purpurea).* Bergenia, hosta, and ligularia, in contrast, are solid-looking and heavier in texture. A number of perennials get a fluffy, feathery appearance from their finely divided leaves; astilbe, yarrow *(Achillea),* columbine *(Aquilegia),* corydalis, lavender cotton *(Santolina),* and most ferns are good examples.

Flowers have their own textures. Globe thistle *(Echinops)* and sea holly *(Eryngium)* bear blossoms with a spiky look, while the blooms of purple coneflower *(Echi-*

TOP: *Phlomis russeliana*
BOTTOM: *Miscanthus sinensis*

TOP: *Artemisia abrotanum*
BOTTOM: *Eryngium planum*

nacea purpurea) have a bristly center that contrasts with the softer petals surrounding it. Evening primrose *(Oenothera)* flowers are silky and smooth all over.

Foliage offers fascinating textural contrasts, often inviting the passerby to stop and touch. Many sedums have almost waxy leaves; some kinds of hosta have a puckered, seersucker-like leaf surface, while the foliage of lamb's ears *(Stachys byzantina)* and crown pink *(Lychnis coronaria)* is soft and woolly. The leaves of lady's-mantle *(Alchemilla mollis)* have an unusual pleated-looking surface; the foliage of some mulleins *(Verbascum)* and phlomis is rather rough or prickly.

THE IMPORTANCE OF FOLIAGE

Planning for satisfying, long-lasting foliage combinations is just as important and interesting as working out designs with flowers: bloom time typically lasts for a just a few weeks to a month (up to 8 weeks or so at the outside), but foliage is highly visible all season long. As you put together your plan, consider not only texture (see above) but color as well—besides every possible shade of green, you'll find a variety of other colors. Among the many perennials featuring gray to silver foliage are yarrow *(Achillea)*, lavender *(Lavandula)*, Russian sage *(Perovskia)*, and lamb's ears *(Stachys byzantina)*. Blue fescue *(Festuca glauca)* and some hostas have bluish leaves. Offering attractive purple to bronze foliage are, among others, 'Fanal' astilbe, 'Palace Purple' coral bells *(Heuchera)*, some forms of calico aster *(Aster lateriflorus)*, and 'Matrona' sedum. Yellow to chartreuse foliage brightens golden feverfew *(Chrysanthemum parthenium* 'Aureum') and 'All Gold' Japanese forest grass *(Hakonechloa macra)*. Variegated leaves add still more color variety, and they often outshine flowers, especially in some forms of coral bells *(Heuchera)*, hosta, New Zealand flax *(Phormium)*, and lungwort *(Pulmonaria)*.

TOP: *Canna* 'Pretoria'
BOTTOM: *Pulmonaria* 'Spilled Milk'

TOP: *Heuchera* 'Cascade Dawn'
BOTTOM: *Hakonechloa macra* 'Aureola'

Leaf shape and size vary dramatically, giving further scope for intriguing designs. Think of the contrasts between the short, narrow leaves of pink *(Dianthus)*, the hand-shaped foliage of peony *(Paeonia)*, the tiny, threadlike leaf segments of threadleaf coreopsis *(Coreopsis verticillata)*, the bold 2-foot-long leaves of colewort *(Crambe cordifolia)*, and the heart-shaped foliage of epimedium—and these are just a few examples.

PLANT FORM AND SIZE

Combining different shapes adds spice to a planting. Perhaps most distinctive are perennials with an overall spiky appearance, such as red-hot poker *(Kniphofia)*, New Zealand flax *(Phormium)*, gayfeather *(Liatris)*, and yucca. Daylily *(Hemerocallis)* and many sorts of ornamental grasses have a softer and more arching outline, while baby's breath *(Gypsophila paniculata)* and lady's-mantle *(Alchemilla mollis)* are rounded or trailing in form.

Contrasts in foliage shape and texture add lasting interest to this planting.

Euphorbia myrsinites (right) has a low, rounded form that makes it ideal for edging a border, while gayfeather *(Liatris spicata,* far right) adds vertical punctuation to a design.

TOP: The firm, rounded flower heads of *Sedum spectabile* offer a pleasing contrast to the soft, featherlike spikes of fountain grass *(Pennisetum).*

BOTTOM: Lady's-mantle *(Alchemilla mollis)* is another excellent choice for the edge of a border.

Baby's breath *(Gypsophila paniculata)* forms a large yet airy mound of blossoms.

Many perennials change their shape rather dramatically through the season, especially when in flower. For example, mullein *(Verbascum),* delphinium, and perennial sunflower *(Helianthus)* start out as low mounds of foliage, but soon produce tall flowering stems that give the plants a narrow, upright form. Speedwell *(Veronica)* and catmint *(Nepeta)* are fairly low and flat early in the season, but when in flower they are taller, with a more rounded look.

Size is another element to consider. Check each plant's approximate height (see the encyclopedia on pages 46–121), keeping in mind that the same plant may grow somewhat taller or shorter depending on soil conditions and climate. Paying attention to the perennials growing in your own and nearby gardens will help you learn more about ultimate sizes in your region.

For relatively narrow or small beds or borders, it's usually best to stick with lower-growing species, since very tall ones tend to look out of proportion. In larger plantings, on the other hand, be sure to include some plants of a goodly size to avoid a too-flat look.

For the most part, gardeners place taller perennials behind lower ones, simply to avoid blocking a good view of all the plants. There are exceptions, however. A few tall perennials have a filmy, open appearance and, in small numbers, are quite effective right at the front of a bed or border. Such "see-through" choices include upright, 3- to 6-foot-tall *Verbena bonariensis* and a couple of ornamental grasses: giant feather grass *(Stipa gigantea),* with airy, open flower stems to 6 feet high, and blue oat grass *(Helictotrichon sempervirens),* with slim blossoming stems held a foot or two above 2- to 3-foot clumps of narrow blue leaves. Tall plants can also be used among shorter ones in the foreground of a planting to provide contrast in both height and form. Think of drifts of catmint *(Nepeta)* and threadleaf coreopsis *(Coreopsis verticillata)* punctuated by a clump of red-hot poker *(Kniphofia).* A few substantial perennials are effective as single specimens planted in a noticeable spot—at the end of a border or near a bench, for example. Among these are acanthus, colewort *(Crambe cordifolia),* goatsbeard *(Aruncus dioicus),* canna, hibiscus, ornamental rhubarb *(Rheum palmatum),* and yucca.

Goatsbeard *(Aruncus dioicus)* is an imposing, shrublike perennial, effective planted as a single specimen.

Verbena bonariensis (far left) and giant feather grass *(Stipa gigantea,* left) are tall plants, but both have a filmy, open, see-through structure that makes them fine choices for the front of a border.

PERMANENT PERENNIALS: PLANTS THAT GROW BEST IF NOT MOVED OR DIVIDED

The following perennials are most successful if not disturbed, especially once they are mature.

Aconitum (Monkshood)

Adenophora (Lady bells)

Aruncus dioicus (Goatsbeard)

Baptisia (False indigo)

Crambe cordifolia (Colewort)

Dictamnus albus (Gas plant)

Eryngium (Sea holly)

Gaura lindheimeri (Gaura)

Gypsophila paniculata (Baby's breath)

Paeonia (Peony)

SPACING PERENNIALS

Plant size is, of course, connected to the question of appropriate spacing between plants, an issue that's sometimes vexing for new and seasoned gardeners alike. As a rule of thumb, space low-growing, front-of-the-border types (those that grow up to a foot tall) 8 to 12 inches apart; midsize plants (those that reach 1 to 2½ feet high) 15 to 24 inches apart; and tall growers about 3 feet apart. If you want your perennials to fill in more quickly, space them more closely, but bear in mind that you'll need to divide them in a few years, as they become crowded. You can also use annuals between more widely spaced perennials to cover the ground and provide color while the perennials are growing to their full size.

Because most perennials are easy to move, any mistakes in spacing (or in any other aspect of plant choice, for that matter) can usually be corrected with little trouble. The perennials listed at left, however, are difficult to move or recover slowly (or not at all) after transplanting. It's best to place these in their intended permanent location, with enough room to accommodate them at maturity.

GROUPING PERENNIALS

Most small and medium-size perennials look best set out in groups of three or more of the same kind; planting just one of each sort lessens the planting's impact and can lead to a hodgepodge appearance. For a natural-looking arrangement, stagger the plants within each group rather than lining them up in rows. Larger perennials are usually planted singly—except in the largest borders, which offer enough space for groups. Examples of such good-sized plants include false indigo *(Baptisia)*, baby's breath *(Gypsophila paniculata)*, and New Zealand flax *(Phormium)*, as well as big ornamental grasses like eulalia grass *(Miscanthus sinensis)*. Whatever the size of plant, repetition in several places helps unify the composition and draw the eye through the planting, whether you're setting out three or four large specimens at intervals or repeating drifts of the same plant.

When you're planting a number of the same (or closely related) perennials, you'll find that setting them out in groups provides more impact than "scattering" them individually throughout a planting. Shown here are several cultivars of hosta and astilbe.

CONSIDERING COLOR

Whether you envision a bed filled with flamboyant reds, oranges, and yellows or a serene border of restrained pinks and blues, learning about color and the words used to describe it will help you achieve your goals. For gardeners, the artist's way of looking at color is most relevant and familiar, though of course there are other approaches (physicists, psychologists, and botanists, for example, all have differing interests and viewpoints).

Containing colors related to those in a rainbow or electromagnetic spectrum, the basic painter's color wheel holds six pure *hues*—colors containing no white, black, or gray. Three of these—red, yellow, and blue—are *primary* hues; the other three—green, orange, and violet—are *secondary* hues. Primary hues are so called because they cannot be produced by any mixture of other colors; secondary hues result from various mixtures of the primary hues.

The basic wheel can be expanded to make a more complex wheel including further pure hues intermediate between the primary and secondary hues—yellow-orange, yellow-green, blue-green, and so forth. (In actuality, of course, the number of such gradations is infinite.) As shown at lower right, this larger wheel also illustrates *value:* the relative lightness or darkness of a color. Add white, and a hue becomes lighter than the pure hue; this is called a *tint.* Add black, and it becomes darker; this is a *shade.* Only one tint and one shade are shown here for each hue, but many more exist.

Saturation or intensity, another attribute of color, describes the brightness or dullness of a hue. When gray is added to a pure hue, it becomes less saturated. The colored bars below illustrate the progressive desaturation of green and red, as more and more gray is added.

The color wheel can be divided into *warm* and *cool* hues by drawing a line between green and yellow-green on one side, between red and red-violet on the other. The warm colors include yellow, orange, chartreuse, and red; among the cool ones are green, blue, and violet. Warm colors tend to be stimulating and dynamic; cool colors produce a feeling of quiet and calm. Warm colors advance visually, while cool ones recede.

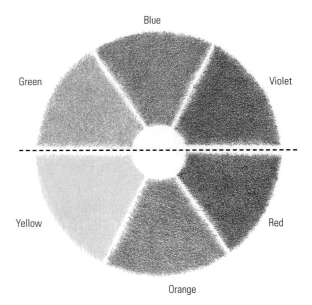

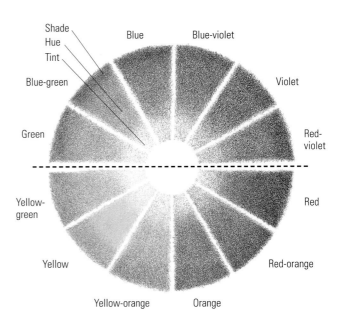

TOP: The basic color wheel is made up of six pure hues. The dotted line divides warm hues below from cool ones above.

BOTTOM: A more complex color wheel includes intermediate hues and illustrates *tints* (made by adding white to a pure hue) and *shades* (created by adding black).

LEFT: As more and more gray is added, the pure (fully saturated) hues green and red become progressively less saturated.

Examples of desaturated foliage color are found in the bronzed leaves of *Euphorbia amygdaloides* 'Rubra' (top) and the silvery gray ones of *Artemisia* 'Powis Castle' (bottom).

COLOR SCHEMES. When you plan perennial combinations, you can use color in various ways, creating schemes that feature contrasting or harmonious colors as well as those that emphasize a single color.

Contrasting schemes feature colors from opposite sides of the wheel. Those directly opposite each other, called complementary colors, contrast the most strongly: red and green, yellow and violet, blue and orange. Such sharp contrasts are effective focal points, giving punch to a planting: Think of a bright yellow daylily *(Hemerocallis)* flowering in front of pure violet salvia, or orange geum with blue speedwell *(Veronica)*. Remember that leaves are just as important as flowers: fire-engine red Oriental poppies *(Papaver orientale)* set in front of a mass of green foliage also provide a complementary combination. Note that contrasting pairs of pure hues can make for disquieting compositions if overused. For a calmer look, you can use one color sparingly, as an accent for greater amounts of its complement.

Another way to soften contrasts is to use tints and shades of the chosen colors. Pair a pale, creamy yellow daylily with soft lavender salvia, for example, or choose a salvia in deep violet (a shade) for yet another contrast. Similarly, a light pink Oriental poppy offers a toned-down contrast to green foliage. Varying the saturation of one member of the pair (that is, choosing a grayer color) also changes the contrast. The highly saturated red of the Oriental poppy looks quite different when it is backed not by bright green, but by the grayed (less saturated) foliage of silver king artemisia *(Artemisia ludoviciana albula* 'Silver King').

Harmonious schemes, also known as analogous schemes, feature colors adjacent (or nearly adjacent) on the color wheel, such as blue, blue-violet, and violet. These colors are harmonious because they share a pigment (blue, in the above example). A trio of perennials offering this sort of harmony might include catmint *(Nepeta),* penstemon, and a cranesbill such as *Geranium himalayense.* To enliven groups of perennials in closely related colors, vary the values by adding tints or shades, and use a small amount of a complementary color.

To vary color contrast, vary color value. At right, the pairing of blue dephiniums with bright golden yarrow *(Achillea* 'Coronation Gold') provides maximum contrast, since the blossom colors are close to pure hues. A softer contrast is shown at far right, in the combination of Russian sage *(Perovskia)* in a lighter blue (a tint) with golden coneflower *(Rudbeckia).*

LEFT: A harmonious scheme in cool colors features violet speedwell *(Veronica)* and pink bee balm *(Monarda)*.

BELOW: Coneflower *(Rudbeckia)* and another bee balm cultivar illustrate harmonious hot colors.

Monochromatic schemes are centered on one hue and include all the various tints, shades, and variations in saturation found in that hue. All-blue plantings are popular, featuring every possibility from indigo to soft powder blue. Deep, rich shades, such as dark red with plum and purple, offer another intriguing monochromatic scheme. And though white is not, strictly speaking, a hue (it may be defined as achromatic or lacking color), the all-white garden is a classic of garden design.

Of course, monochromatic plantings are not truly monochromatic: other colors from foliage are always present. Even a peaceful all-green garden includes colors from bark, soil, walkways, and surrounding structures. And indeed, most monochromatic schemes benefit from a contrasting splash of another color. If you opt for such a plan, it's also wise to pay special attention to foliage and to plant texture, form, and size.

Shown at left is a largely monochromatic color scheme. A bit of contrasting color makes such schemes more effective; to illustrate the influence of contrast here, cover the white blossoms with your finger.

A SUNNY GARDEN WITH HOT COLORS

PLANT LIST

A. **Achillea 'Rodney's Choice'.** Yarrow (1)

B. **Achillea tomentosa.** Woolly yarrow (1)

C. **Calamagrostis × acutiflora 'Karl Foerster'** ('Stricta'). Feather reed grass (2)

D. **Carex elata 'Aurea'.** Bowles' golden sedge (4)

E. **Clematis tangutica.** Golden clematis (vine) (2)

F. **Coreopsis grandiflora 'Early Sunrise'** (3)

G. **Euphorbia × martinii** (3)

H. **Gaillardia × grandiflora 'Goblin'** (5)

I. **Geum chiloense 'Mrs. Bradshaw'** (5)

J. **Helenium 'Moerheim Beauty'.** Sneezeweed (2)

K. **Hemerocallis 'Stella de Oro'.** Daylily (3)

L. **Hemerocallis 'Flasher'.** Daylily (5)

M. **Hemerocallis 'Red Rim'.** Daylily (3)

N. **Imperata cylindrica 'Red Baron' ('Rubra').** Japanese blood grass (7)

O. **Lobelia cardinalis.** Cardinal flower (1)

P. **Penstemon × gloxinioides 'Firebird'** (3)

Q. **Penstemon × gloxinioides 'Burgundy'** (3)

R. **Rheum palmatum 'Atrosanguineum'.** Ornamental rhubarb (2)

S. **Rudbeckia fulgida sullivantii 'Goldsturm'.** Coneflower (3)

T. **Thymus × citriodorus 'Lime'.** Thyme (7)

A SUNNY GARDEN
WITH COOL COLORS

Though both are intended for sunny areas, the plans shown on these two pages illustrate different approaches to designing with color. On the facing page, a dynamic blend of yellows and reds creates a lively, stimulating mood; a golden-blossomed vine *(Clematis tangutica)* on the trellis behind the perennials continues the theme. The plan on this page, in contrast, paints a subtler picture, thanks to an emphasis on cool colors—blue, lavender, pink, and white, enlivened with splashes of darker pink. In both plans, ornamental grasses add texture and movement to the composition.

To see which perennials in our encyclopedia prefer sunny conditions, check the at-a-glance information preceding each entry. For a list of perennials by flower color and season of bloom, see pages 26–29.

PLANT LIST

A. **Adenophora confusa.** Common lady bells (5)

B. **Aster novi-belgii 'Professor Anton Kippenberg'.** New York aster (1)

C. **Boltonia asteroides 'Snowbank'** (1)

D. **Calamagrostis × acutiflora 'Overdam'.** Feather reed grass (3)

E. **Campanula portenschlagiana.** Dalmatian bellflower (3)

F. **Campanula persicifolia 'Telham Beauty'.** Peach-leafed bluebell (3)

G. **Chrysanthemum × superbum 'Tinkerbell'.** Shasta daisy (4)

H. **Delphinium × belladonna 'Volker-frieden' ('People of Peace')** (3)

I. **Dianthus × allwoodii 'Horatio'.** Allwood pink (4)

J. **Echinacea purpurea 'Magnus'.** Purple coneflower (3)

K. **Festuca amethystina 'Superba'.** Large blue fescue (3)

L. **Geranium × riversleaianum 'Russell Prichard'.** Cranesbill (3)

M. **Iris, Siberian, 'Ego'.** Siberian iris (3)

N. **Molinia caerulea arundinacea 'Skyracer'.** Purple moor grass (3)

O. **Panicum virgatum 'Prairie Sky'.** Switch grass (1)

P. **Paeonia 'Festiva Maxima'.** Peony (1)

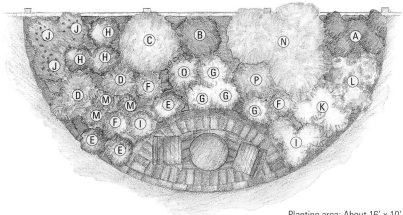

Planting area: About 16' x 10'

A SHADY GARDEN

PLANT LIST

A. **Aconitum carmichaelii (A. fischeri).** Monkshood (5)

B. **Anemone × hybrida 'Honorine Jobert'.** Japanese anemone (3)

C. **Astilbe chinensis 'Pumila'** (3)

D. **Bergenia 'Bressingham Ruby'** (8)

E. **Brunnera macrophylla** (4)

F. **Calamagrostis × acutiflora 'Overdam'.** Feather reed grass (3)

G. **Deschampsia caespitosa 'Goldschleier' ('Gold Veil').** Tufted hair grass (3)

H. **Digitalis × mertonensis.** Foxglove (6)

I. **Epimedium grandiflorum 'Lilafee'** (5)

J. **Helleborus orientalis.** Lenten rose (3)

K. **Hosta sieboldiana (H. glauca) 'Big Daddy'** (3)

L. **Pulmonaria saccharata 'Mrs. Moon'.** Bethlehem sage (5)

M. **Tricyrtis hirta 'Hatatogisa'.** Toad lily (1)

N. **Trollius chinensis 'Golden Queen'.** Globeflower (3)

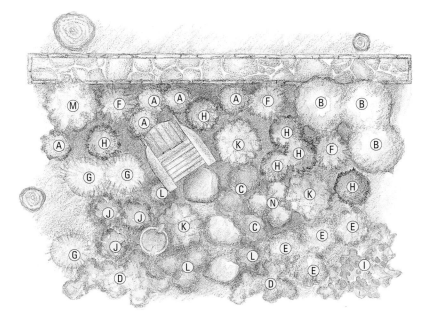

Planting area: About 16' x 10'

Plants for Shady Gardens

Thanks to trees, walls, or overhead structures, many gardens have shady spots. The plan on the facing page illustrates an artful arrangement of shade lovers set out beneath three trees. Numerous other perennials in addition to the dozen or so shown in this plan also prefer or accept some degree of shade; those described in our encyclopedia (pages 46–121) are listed below. Most ferns (pages 78–79) and a few ornamental grasses (pages 98–101) appreciate shade as well. And as noted in the encyclopedia, some other perennials need afternoon shade in hot-summer areas but grow well in sun in cooler regions.

Digitalis × mertonensis

Acanthus mollis. Zones 4–24, 28–32

Aconitum. Zones 1–9, 14–21, 34–45

Alchemilla mollis. Zones 2–9, 14–24, 31–43

Alstroemeria. Zones 5–9, 14–24, 26, 28, 31, 32, 34

Amsonia tabernaemontana. Zones 3–24, 28–33

Anemone × hybrida. Zones 3–24, 30–39, 41

Aquilegia. Zones vary

Aruncus. Zones 1–9, 14–17, 31–43

Astilbe. Zones 1–7, 14–17, 32–45

Astrantia major. Zones 3–9, 14–24, 31–41

Bergenia. Zones vary

✓ *Brunnera macrophylla.* Zones 1–24, 31–45

Centranthus ruber. Zones 1–9, 12–24, 28–43

Ceratostigma plumbaginoides. Zones 2–10, 14–24, 29–41

Chelone. Zones 3–9, 14–17, 28–43

Cimicifuga. Zones 1–7, 17, 32–45

Corydalis. Zones 3–9, 14–24, 32–35, 39–43

✓ *Dicentra.* Zones 1–9, 14–24, 31–45

Dictamnus albus. Zones 1–9, 31–45

Digitalis. Zones vary

Doronicum. Zones 1–7, 14–17, 31–43

Epimedium. Zones 1–9, 14–17, 31–43

Eupatorium. Zones vary

Filipendula. Zones vary

Geranium. Zones vary

✓ *Helleborus.* Zones vary

Heuchera. Zones vary

✓ *Hosta.* Zones 1–10, 12–21, 28, 31–45

Ligularia. Zones 3–9, 15–17, 32, 34, 36–41

Lobelia. Zones vary

Lychnis. Zones vary

Mertensia virginica. Zones 1–21, 31–45

✓ *Phlox* (some). Zones vary

Physostegia virginiana. Zones 1–24, 26–45

Platycodon grandiflorus. Zones 1–24, 26, 28–45

Polygonatum. Zones 1–7, 14–17, 28–43

Primula. Zones vary

Pulmonaria. Zones 1–9, 14–17, 32–42

Rheum palmatum. Zones 2–9, 14–24, 31–41

Sisyrinchium. Zones vary

Thalictrum. Zones vary

Tradescantia. Zones 1–24, 26, 28–43

Tricyrtis. Zones vary

Trollius. Zones 1–6, 32–43

Trollius chinensis 'Golden Queen'

An unthirsty garden

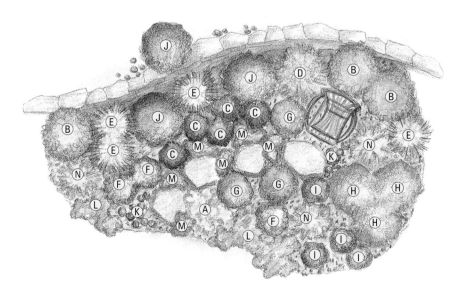

A. Achillea tomentosa. Woolly yarrow (1)

B. Artemisia 'Powis Castle' (3)

C. Euphorbia dulcis 'Chameleon' (5)

D. Gaura lindheimeri (1)

E. Helictotrichon sempervirens. Blue oat grass (4)

F. Lavandula × intermedia 'Fred Boutin'. Lavandin (3)

G. Nepeta × faassenii. Catmint (3)

H. Perovskia 'Blue Spire'. Russian sage (3)

I. Salvia × superba 'Blue Hill' (4)

J. Sedum spectabile 'Carmen'. Stonecrop (3)

K. Sempervivum tectorum. Hen and chicks (9)

L. Stachys byzantina 'Countess Helene von Stein' ('Big Ears'). Lamb's ears (6)

M. Thymus praecox arcticus 'Albus'. Creeping thyme (6)

N. Verbascum olympicum. Mullein (3)

Planting area: About 16' x 10'

Sempervivum tectorum

PLANTS FOR UNTHIRSTY GARDENS

If your region has a long dry season or experiences only scant rainfall or periodic drought years, consider planting perennials that thrive with only modest watering. The plan shown on the facing page combines a wide array of low-water-use choices; the list below includes these perennials as well as a number of other possibilities. Some ornamental grasses (pages 98–101) can also survive on moderate to little water.

Achillea. Zones 1–24, 26, 28–45

Armeria maritima. Zones 1–9, 14–24, 33–43

Artemisia. Zones vary

Asclepias tuberosa. All zones

Aurinia saxatilis. Zones 1–24, 32–43

Baptisia. Zones 1–24, 28–43

Catananche caerulea. All zones

Centaurea. Zones vary

Centranthus ruber. Zones 1–9, 12–24, 28–43

Ceratostigma plumbaginoides. Zones 2–10, 14–24, 29–41

Coreopsis. Zones vary

Echinacea purpurea. Zones 1–24, 26–45

Epilobium. Zones 2–11, 14–24

Erigeron. Zones vary

Eryngium. Zones vary

Euphorbia. Zones vary

Gaillardia × grandiflora. All zones

Gaura lindheimeri. Zones 3–35, 37, 38 (coastal), 39

Lavandula. Zones vary

Limonium. Zones vary

Linaria purpurea. Zones 2–24, 30–41

Lychnis coronaria. Zones 3–9, 14–24, 30–34

Nepeta. Zones 1–24, 30, 32–43

Oenothera. Zones vary

Origanum. Zones vary

Perovskia. Zones 3–24, 28–35, 37, 39

Phlomis. Zones vary

Salvia (some). Zones vary

Santolina. Zones vary

Sedum. Zones vary

Sempervivum tectorum. Zones 2–24, 29–41

Solidago and *Solidaster.* Zones vary

Stachys byzantina. Zones 1–24, 29–43

Thymus. Zones vary

Verbascum. Zones vary

Santolina chamaecyparissus

CREATING A PLANTING PLAN

Making a plan will help you decide just how to combine your perennials.

Some gardeners are able to create beautiful perennial gardens on the spot: they set out the plants (still in their containers) and move them around until they look "right," then plant. Others, however, feel the need for more consideration before putting the plants in the ground. Learning to draw a simple plan is a good way to clarify your thoughts, and it will help you avoid future digging and rearranging of plants to correct mistakes. Gather some basic tools—a tape measure, graph paper, ruler or T square, pencils, and colored pencils—and you're set to begin.

Start by measuring the proposed planting site, noting the location of existing trees and shrubs as well as any fences, paths, or other hardscape. Then draw an outline of the area on a sheet of graph paper, making each square equal to a foot or a fraction of a foot and marking in the trees, shrubs, and hardscape you noted. Make photocopies of this basic plan; you'll sketch a potential design on each copy.

Next, list the perennials you want to plant. Begin with a color scheme (see pages 15–17); then, for ideas on particular plants to suit your site, consult the charts noting flower color by season (pages 26–29) and the lists and sample designs suggesting perennials for sunny spots (pages 18–19), shady areas (pages 20–21), dry sites (pages 22–23), and moist soil (page 35). Also be sure to list any shrubs, trees, or vines you need.

Start sketching the plants into your plan, using circles to indicate each one. Begin with the largest plants—trees, shrubs, and any large perennials. See "Spacing Perennials" (page 14) for more on how much space to allot for each plant; "Grouping Perennials" (page 14) will help you arrange the plants. Color the circles to visualize color combinations. Keep trying out various combinations and arrangements until you find a satisfying design.

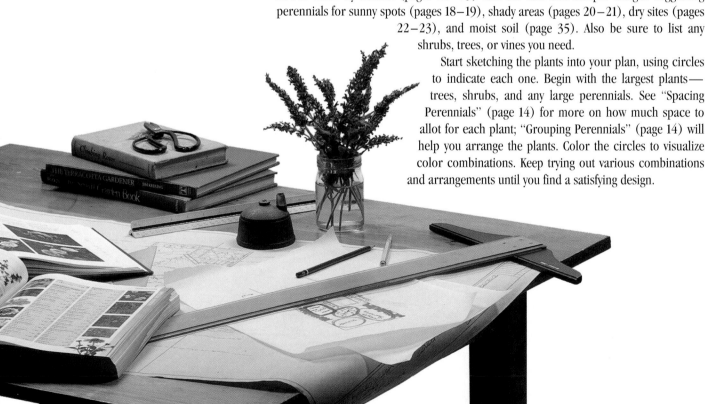

GROWING PERENNIALS IN CONTAINERS

Though gardeners often think of perennials as plants for beds and borders, many are also effective as container plants, returning to bloom year after year.

Portable containers for perennials come in a wide array of shapes, colors, and materials. You can choose pots in traditional terra-cotta, ceramic, or lightweight plastic, or opt for heftier wooden boxes and tubs. Raised beds constructed around a deck or patio are another type of container that's well suited to perennials.

The best perennials for containers are those that flower over a long period or have good-looking foliage throughout the growing season. Also focus on plants that won't get too large; a dwarf or smaller-growing variety of a species may be the most appropriate choice. The list below gives a number of suggestions. You may choose to feature just one kind of perennial per container, or group several sorts for a longer season of color; adding a few annuals brings extra interest to the arrangement. Perennials too tender for your normal winter temperatures may be grown outdoors in containers, then overwintered indoors or in a greenhouse.

SOIL MIXES. Plants in containers need fast-draining yet moisture-retentive soil that allows roots to grow easily. Quick drainage means roots won't run the risk of suffo-

cating in soggy soil; good moisture retention saves you from having to water constantly. Regular garden soil, even if it's good loam, is too dense for container use; it forms a solid mass that roots cannot penetrate easily, and it remains soggy for too long after watering. A better bet is one of the packaged potting mixes sold at nurseries and garden centers.

WATERING. Because they have only a limited amount of soil from which to draw moisture, container-grown plants require more frequent watering than those grown in the ground. During hot or windy spells, this can mean daily attention; in cool weather, it may be sufficient to water weekly or even less often. Check the soil in the containers and water when the top inch or two is dry.

FERTILIZING. Because the necessary frequent watering leaches nutrients from the potting mix, container plants need regular feeding. Liquid fertilizers are easy to use; start right after planting and repeat at least every 2 weeks, following label directions for amounts. You can also mix a controlled-release fertilizer into the potting mix before or after planting.

PERENNIALS FOR CONTAINERS

Acanthus mollis	*Diascia*	*Nepeta*
Achillea	*Erigeron*	*Origanum*
Agapanthus	*Ferns*	*Penstemon*
Agastache	*Geranium*	*Phormium*
Alstroemeria	*Ornamental grasses*	*Primula*
Aurinia saxatilis	(some)	*Salvia*
Campanula	*Hemerocallis*	*Scabiosa*
Canna (smaller	(smaller cultivars)	*Sedum*
cultivars)	*Hosta*	*Sempervivum*
Chrysanthemum	*Heuchera*	*tectorum*
Corydalis	*Iberis sempervirens*	*Stokesia laevis*
Coreopsis	*Limonium*	*Verbena*

These container-grown hosta and coral bells *(Heuchera)* cultivars offer cool, soothing color over a long season. Here, their green-and-white foliage complements the blue blossoms of *Corydalis flexuosa* 'Blue Panda'.

FLOWER COLOR BY SEASON

Though some perennials bloom longer than others, none flowers all season long. You may choose to have a glorious display of blossoms in June, then let the garden be quietly green for the rest of the growing season; or you may prefer to have some color throughout the year. The charts on the following pages will help you choose perennials by season of bloom and flower color.

What flowers when and how long the bloom season lasts does depend somewhat on your climate; in hot regions, for example, bloom usually starts earlier in the season and comes to an end more quickly. As an aid to future planning, many gardeners keep a calendar or notebook to record bloom seasons in their own and nearby gardens.

PERENNIAL NAME	SP	SU	F	W	ZONES
Acanthus mollis ❋ ❋ ❋		▩			4–24, 28–32
Achillea ❋ ❋ ❋ ❋		▩			1–24, 26, 28–45
Aconitum ❋ ❋ ❋ ❋		▩			1–9, 14–21, 34–45
Adenophora ❋ ❋		▩			1–10, 14–24, 30–43
Agapanthus ❋ ❋		▩			Zones vary
Agastache ❋ ❋ ❋ ❋ ❋		▩			Zones vary
Alchemilla mollis ❋		▩			2–9, 14–24, 31–43
Alstroemeria ❋ ❋ ❋ ❋ ❋ ❋	▩				5–9, 14–24, 26, 28, 31, warmer parts of 32, 34
Amsonia tabernaemontana ❋	▩				3–24, 28–33
Anchusa azurea ❋		▩			1–24, 29–45
Anemone × hybrida ❋ ❋		▩			3–24, 30–39, 41
Anthemis tinctoria ❋		▩			1–11, 14–24, 30–45
Aquilegia ❋ ❋ ❋ ❋ ❋	▩				Zones vary
Armeria maritima ❋ ❋ ❋	▩				1–9, 14–24, 33–43
Artemisia ❋		▩			Zones vary
Aruncus ❋		▩			1–9, 14–17, 31–43
Asclepias tuberosa ❋ ❋ ❋		▩			All zones
Aster ❋ ❋ ❋ ❋			▩		Zones vary
Astilbe ❋ ❋ ❋ ❋		▩			1–7, 14–17, 32–45
Astrantia major ❋ ❋ ❋		▩			3–9, 14–24, 31–41
Aurinia saxatilis ❋ ❋	▩				1–24, 32–43
Baptisia ❋ ❋ ❋		▩			1–24, 28–43
Bergenia ❋ ❋ ❋ ❋				▩	Zones vary
Boltonia asteroides ❋ ❋ ❋			▩		1–24, 28–45
Brunnera macrophylla ❋	▩				1–24, 31–45
Campanula ❋ ❋ ❋ ❋ ❋	▩				Zones vary
Canna ❋ ❋ ❋ ❋ ❋		▩			6–9, 12–31, warmer parts of 32
Catananche caerulea ❋ ❋		▩			All zones

TOP: *Aquilegia chrysantha*
BOTTOM: *Dicentra spectabilis*

Perennial Name	Bloom Season				Zones
	SP	SU	F	W	
Centaurea ✳ ✳ ✳		●			Zones vary
Centranthus ruber ✳ ✳ ✳	●	●			1–9, 12–24, 28–43
Ceratostigma plumbaginoides ✳		●	●		2–10, 14–24, 29–41
Chelone ✳ ✳ ✳		●	●		3–9, 14–17, 28–43
Chrysanthemum ✳ ✳ ✳ ✳ ✳ ✳	●	●	●		Zones vary
Cimicifuga ✳		●			1–7, 17, 32–45
Coreopsis ✳		●			Zones vary
Corydalis ✳ ✳	●	●			3–9, 14–24, 32–35, 39–43
Crambe cordifolia ✳		●			3–9, 14–17, 31–45, 37, 39–41
Delphinium ✳ ✳ ✳ ✳		●			Zones vary
Dianthus ✳ ✳ ✳ ✳	●	●			1–24, 30–45
Diascia ✳ ✳ ✳	●	●	●		7–9, 14–24, 31
Dicentra ✳ ✳ ✳	●	●			1–9, 14–24, 31–45
Dictamnus albus ✳ ✳ ✳		●			1–9, 31–45
Digitalis ✳ ✳ ✳		●			Zones vary
Doronicum ✳	●				1–7, 14–17, 31–43
Echinacea purpurea ✳ ✳ ✳ ✳		●			1–24, 26–45
Echinops ✳		●			1–24, 31–45
Epilobium ✳ ✳ ✳ ✳		●	●		2–11, 14–24
Epimedium ✳ ✳ ✳ ✳ ✳	●				1–9, 14–17, 31–43
Erigeron ✳ ✳ ✳ ✳		●			Zones vary
Eryngium ✳ ✳ ✳		●			Zones vary
Eupatorium ✳ ✳ ✳ ✳		●	●		Zones vary
Euphorbia ✳ ✳ ✳ ✳	●			●	Zones vary
Filipendula ✳ ✳		●			Zones vary
Gaillardia × grandiflora ✳ ✳ ✳		●			All zones
Gaura lindheimeri ✳ ✳		●	●		3–35, 37, 38 (coastal), 39
Geranium ✳ ✳ ✳ ✳ ✳	●	●			Zones vary
Geum ✳ ✳ ✳	●	●			1–24, 32–43

Echinacea purpurea

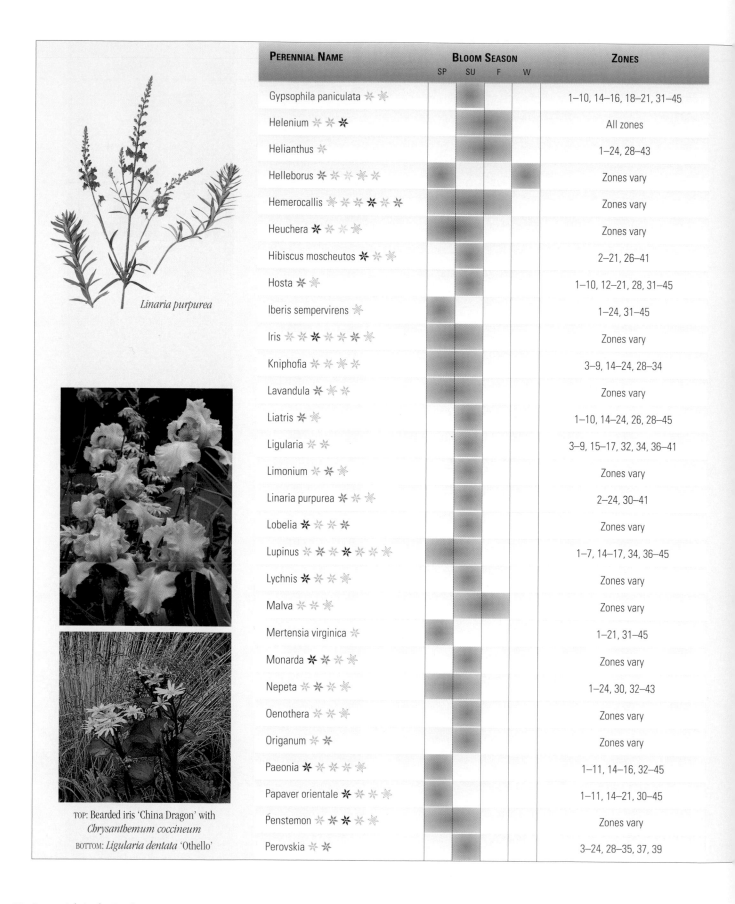

Perennial Name	Bloom Season				Zones
	SP	SU	F	W	
Gypsophila paniculata ❋ ❋		■			1–10, 14–16, 18–21, 31–45
Helenium ❋ ❋ ❋		■	■		All zones
Helianthus ❋		■	■		1–24, 28–43
Helleborus ❋ ❋ ❋ ❋ ❋	■			■	Zones vary
Hemerocallis ❋ ❋ ❋ ❋ ❋ ❋		■			Zones vary
Heuchera ❋ ❋ ❋ ❋	■				Zones vary
Hibiscus moscheutos ❋ ❋ ❋		■			2–21, 26–41
Hosta ❋ ❋		■			1–10, 12–21, 28, 31–45
Iberis sempervirens ❋	■				1–24, 31–45
Iris ❋ ❋ ❋ ❋ ❋ ❋ ❋	■				Zones vary
Kniphofia ❋ ❋ ❋ ❋		■			3–9, 14–24, 28–34
Lavandula ❋ ❋ ❋		■			Zones vary
Liatris ❋ ❋		■			1–10, 14–24, 26, 28–45
Ligularia ❋ ❋		■			3–9, 15–17, 32, 34, 36–41
Limonium ❋ ❋ ❋		■			Zones vary
Linaria purpurea ❋ ❋ ❋		■			2–24, 30–41
Lobelia ❋ ❋ ❋ ❋		■			Zones vary
Lupinus ❋ ❋ ❋ ❋ ❋ ❋ ❋	■				1–7, 14–17, 34, 36–45
Lychnis ❋ ❋ ❋ ❋		■			Zones vary
Malva ❋ ❋ ❋			■		Zones vary
Mertensia virginica ❋	■				1–21, 31–45
Monarda ❋ ❋ ❋ ❋		■			Zones vary
Nepeta ❋ ❋ ❋ ❋	■				1–24, 30, 32–43
Oenothera ❋ ❋ ❋		■			Zones vary
Origanum ❋ ❋		■			Zones vary
Paeonia ❋ ❋ ❋ ❋	■				1–11, 14–16, 32–45
Papaver orientale ❋ ❋ ❋ ❋	■				1–11, 14–21, 30–45
Penstemon ❋ ❋ ❋ ❋ ❋		■			Zones vary
Perovskia ❋ ❋		■			3–24, 28–35, 37, 39

Linaria purpurea

TOP: Bearded iris 'China Dragon' with *Chrysanthemum coccineum*

BOTTOM: *Ligularia dentata* 'Othello'

Perennial Name	Bloom Season				Zones
	SP	SU	F	W	
Phlomis		■			Zones vary
Phlox	■	■			Zones vary
Phormium		■			Zones vary
Physostegia virginiana		■			1–24, 26–45
Platycodon grandiflorus		■			1–24, 26, 28–45
Polygonatum	■				1–7, 14–17, 28–43
Primula	■			■	Zones vary
Pulmonaria	■				1–9, 14–17, 32–42
Ratibida		■			1–24, 26–43
Rheum palmatum	■				2–9, 14–24, 31–41
Rudbeckia		■			Zones vary
Salvia	■	■			Zones vary
Santolina		■			Zones vary
Scabiosa		■			Zones vary
Sedum		■			Zones vary
Sempervivum tectorum		■			2–24, 29–41
Sisyrinchium	■	■			Zones vary
Solidago and Solidaster		■			Zones vary
Stachys		■			Zones vary
Stokesia laevis		■			2–9, 12–24, 26, 28–43
Thalictrum		■			Zones vary
Thymus		■			Zones vary
Tradescantia	■	■			1–24, 26, 28–43
Tricyrtis			■		Zones vary
Trollius	■				1–6, 32–43
Verbascum		■			Zones vary
Verbena		■			Zones vary
Veronica		■			Zones vary
Yucca		■			Zones vary

TOP: *Platycodon grandiflorus*
BOTTOM: *Solidago sphacelata* 'Golden Fleece'

Tricyrtis formosana

PLANTING AND CARING FOR PERENNIALS

A flourishing perennial bed, brimming with dazzling flowers and healthy foliage, results from a combination of factors. The first step toward success is learning about your soil: its type and texture, how to work it, and how to improve it. Just as important are preparing the bed and setting out the plants (whether container-grown or bare-root) properly.

Of course, perennials still need attention after planting, with the particular care depending on the plant. We review watering, mulching, fertilizing, staking, and pruning. You'll also find a discussion of common-sense pest and disease control, including photographs of the culprits that most frequently mar perennial beds and borders. At the end of the chapter, we explain the art and science of propagation through sowing seeds, taking root or stem cuttings, layering, and division.

Finally, don't forget one other aspect of good care: simple observation. Throughout the year, tour the garden regularly to keep an eye on your plants' condition and catch any problems early.

Choosing healthy plants and planting them carefully helps ensure a beautiful perennial border.

For best results, give your perennials a well-prepared planting bed enriched with organic matter and fertilizer.

PREPARING YOUR SOIL

It's no secret that the healthiest, best-looking perennials grow in "good" soil. Here, we discuss the composition of garden soil and tell you how to make sure it's in top shape before planting.

LEARNING ABOUT YOUR GARDEN SOIL

All soils are based on mineral particles formed by the natural breakdown of rock; most also contain varying amounts of organic matter, air, and water, as well as numerous living creatures (earthworms, nematodes, bacteria, and many others). The size and shape of a soil's mineral particles determine its basic characteristics. As shown in the illustrations on the facing page, clay soils have the smallest particles, sand the largest; silt's particles are intermediate in size.

In clay (so-called "heavy") soils, the small particles pack together tightly, producing a compact mass with microscopic pore spaces (the area between soil particles). Air space is limited and drainage is usually slow, since water and nutrients percolate slowly through the tiny pores. Clay is difficult for roots to penetrate, and during prolonged rainy spells it remains airless and saturated, even to the point of causing root rot. Working it is a miserable job: it's sticky when wet and rock-hard when dry. On the plus side, its slower drainage does allow you to water and fertilize less frequently.

At the other end of the spectrum is sandy ("light") soil, with large, irregularly rounded particles and large pore spaces that allow water and nutrients to drain away freely. Plants growing in sandy soil are unlikely to suffer root rot, but you will need to water them more often to keep their roots moist. You'll be fertilizing more often, too, to replace nutrients leached away by the necessary frequent watering.

Most garden soils fall somewhere between the two extremes just described, containing a mixture of particle sizes—some clay, some sand, some silt. Loam, often con-

---

ACID OR ALKALINE SOIL: THE pH SCALE

Soil may be acid, neutral, or alkaline. A pH of 7 indicates a neutral soil; soils with a pH below 7 are acid, while those with a pH above 7 are alkaline. In general, alkaline soils are found in low-rainfall, dry-summer regions, while acid types are associated with high rainfall and humid summers.

Most perennials grow well in soils ranging from moderately acid to somewhat alkaline; a few, as noted in the encyclopedia on pages 46–121, *require* somewhat acid or alkaline soils. Extreme acidity or alkalinity, however, usually causes problems, since it makes certain nutrients chemically

unavailable to plant roots. If you suspect that your soil is strongly acid or alkaline, have it tested. The kits sold in nurseries and garden centers will give you a ballpark reading. For more precise information, have a professional test done (look in the Yellow Pages under "Soil Laboratories"); such tests can also uncover any nutrient deficiencies. Lime is typically added to make soil less acid, while sulfur is applied to neutralize alkalinity. If you use either of these materials to alter your soil's pH, follow the advice of the soil lab or your Cooperative Extension Office for amounts.

sidered the ideal soil, is about 20 percent clay and 40 percent each sand and silt; it also includes organic matter. It's fast draining, moisture retentive, and holds nutrients well.

Though you cannot change your soil's basic texture, you can make clay soil more porous and sand more retentive by adding organic matter (see below). In both cases, you'll be rewarded with healthier, longer-blooming perennials.

MAKING A PLANTING BED

Preparing a planting bed requires some time and effort, but your work will be repaid with robust, fast-growing perennials. Start by eliminating weeds from the area; then loosen the soil thoroughly and work in improvements.

CONTROLLING WEEDS. If you don't get rid of weeds before planting, they'll come back to haunt you, spoiling the bed's appearance and inhibiting your plants' growth. Tilling or hoeing will dispatch shallow-rooted annual weeds, but deep-rooted perennial sorts such as dandelions, bindweed, and Bermuda grass must be dug out by hand: they can regrow from root fragments, and deep hand digging is the best way to remove all the roots. Lawns earmarked for conversion to planting beds can be removed by hand as well; dig under the sod, then lift it out in sections.

Smothering is another way to kill weeds (or lawn), though it does take advance planning. Mow or cut off the top growth, then lay down a mulch of heavy cardboard, newspaper (in a layer at least three dozen sheets thick), or black plastic. Overlap these materials so weeds can't grow through the cracks. Anchor the covering in place with a layer of bark chips or other organic material. Leave this smothering mulch in place for at least a full growing season; for tough weeds, allow a year or more.

Herbicides offer yet another alternative for weed and sod removal. Spray with a product such as the systemic herbicide glyphosate, taking care not to contact plants you wish to keep. Before preparing the soil, wait 2 weeks to be sure the weeds won't sprout again. If they do reappear, a second application will be needed.

LOOSENING THE SOIL. Once weeds have been dispatched, use a spading fork or tiller to loosen the soil; the soil should be slightly damp when you work it, but not too wet or too dry. Dig down 10 to 12 inches if you can, breaking up clods of earth and removing stones as you go.

ADDING ORGANIC MATTER. As mentioned above, organic matter improves the structure of both clay and sand, and it helps plants grow better in loam, too. Organic materials include compost, peat moss, and nitrogen-fortified wood by-products (such as ground bark and sawdust); other choices may be available locally. Use generous quantities of organic matter—one-quarter to one-half the total volume of cultivated soil in the planting area. As a rule of thumb, spread a 3- to 4-inch-thick layer of organic matter over the soil surface.

ADDING FERTILIZER AND OTHER AMENDMENTS. As discussed in "A Fertilizer Primer" (page 37), the major nutrients phosphorus and potassium benefit plants most when placed near the roots. Thus, it's best to work a fertilizer high in these nutrients into the soil before planting rather than applying it to the surface afterwards. A 5-10-10 product is a good choice and also supplies some nitrogen. Spread the fertilizer over the soil, using the amount indicated on the label; also spread on any amendments needed to alter soil pH at this time.

INCORPORATING AMENDMENTS. With a spading fork or tiller, incorporate all the amendments evenly into the soil. Then level the bed with a rake. When you're finished, the soil will be soft and easy to work, and planting will be a pleasure.

SOIL TEXTURE AND TYPE

The size of a soil's mineral particles determines its texture and designates its type: clay, sand, or loam. Clay has the smallest particles, sand the largest; silt particles are intermediate in size. Loam, the ideal garden soil, contains a mix of all three particle sizes.

SOIL PARTICLES

Clay
Less than 1/12,500 in.

Silt
Up to 1/500 in.

Fine sand
Up to 1/250 in.

Medium sand
Up to 1/50 in.

Largest sand particles
1/12 in.

SOIL TYPES

Clay

Sand

Loam

1-gallon pot

4-inch pot

Six-pack with 1-inch cells

In addtion to the containers shown above, you may find perennials sold in jumbo packs with six 2½-inch cells.

Selecting and Planting Perennials

Select your perennials wisely and plant them carefully, and you'll soon have a flourishing garden. Turn to page 14 for advice on spacing and arranging perennials in your planting beds.

Nurseries and garden centers sell perennials in various containers, ranging from cell-packs to gallon-size (or occasionally larger) pots. Small plants are generally the best buy, and once in the ground they usually get established more quickly and put out new growth sooner than larger ones. When you shop, look for compact plants with good foliage color and a root ball that holds together well but is not tangled or matted. Once you bring the plants home, put them in a shaded location and keep the soil moist until planting time.

Mail-order nurseries ship perennials in small pots or bare-root; the latter, as the name implies, have most or all of the soil removed from around the roots, which are then surrounded with organic packing material and enclosed in plastic bags. When you receive any mail-order plants, unpack them as soon as possible. Water potted plants and keep them in a sheltered location until planting time. If you plan to plant bare-root perennials within a day or two, open the plastic bags a bit and add a little water; then set the plants in a cool place until you're ready to plant. If planting must be delayed for more than a few days, however, bare-root plants will need more attention. Pot them up in small containers, ready to plant out later; or heel them in—that is, plant them temporarily in a shallow trench in the garden. In either case, be sure to water as needed to keep the roots moist.

PLANTING BARE-ROOT PERENNIALS

1 Remove organic packing material and soak the roots in water for about 30 minutes.

2 Dig a hole about twice as wide as the root system. Then make a cone of soil in the center to support the roots.

3 Set the plant on the cone of soil and spread the roots evenly. Fill with soil so that the crown of the plant is level with or slightly above the soil, then water well.

WHEN TO PLANT

If you're planting an entire new bed, do so in early spring or early autumn. If you're adding just a few new plants, you may want to set out summer- or autumn-flowering sorts in early spring, so that they're well established by bloom time. For the same reason, plant spring bloomers in early fall. Try to avoid planting in the heat of summer— but if you must do so, be sure to shade the plants and give them extra water.

If possible, plant your perennials during cool, cloudy, calm weather; they'll get established more quickly and grow better if not stressed by heat, sun, and wind. Whenever you plant, spread a layer of mulch (see page 36) around the plants to keep the soil cool and conserve moisture.

PLANTING PERENNIALS FROM CONTAINERS

1   Soak the plant, still in its pot, in a bucket of water for about 30 minutes or until the soil is completely dampened.

2   Dig a hole for each plant, making it the same depth as the container and an inch or two wider.

3   With your fingers, lightly separate matted roots. If there's a pad of coiled white roots at the pot bottom, cut or pull it off so the new roots will form and grow into the soil.

4   Place each plant in its hole so that the top of the root ball is even with the soil surface. Firm soil around the roots; then water each plant with a gentle flow that won't disturb soil or roots.

Hibiscus moscheutos

PERENNIALS FOR MOIST SOIL

Listed below are a few perennials that are able to grow in constantly moist soil—that is, in conditions unfavorable to plants requiring good drainage. The listed plants will also succeed in well-watered garden beds.

Aconitum (Monkshood). Zones 1–9, 14–21, 34–45

Aruncus (Goatsbeard). Zones 1–9, 14–17, 31–43

Astilbe. Zones 1–7, 14–17, 32–45

Canna. Zones 6–9, 12–31, warmer parts of 32

Chelone (Turtlehead). Zones 3–9, 14–17, 28–43

Eupatorium. Zones vary

Filipendula (some). Zones vary

Hibiscus moscheutos. Zones 2–21, 26–41

Iris: Japanese, Siberian. Zones vary

Ligularia. Zones 3–9, 15–17, 32, 34, 36–41

Lobelia. Zones vary

Monarda (Bee balm). Zones vary

Primula (Primrose). Zones vary

Tradescantia (Spiderwort). Zones 1–24, 26, 28–43

Trollius (Globeflower). Zones 1–6, 32–43

CARING FOR PERENNIALS

Perennials, like other garden plants, need watering, fertilizing, and other basic care, such as pruning, staking, and, in some cases, winter protection. The key to successful maintenance is observation: check your plants frequently to see what they need. For information on rejuvenating and dividing perennials, see pages 43–44.

WATERING

All plants, even drought-tolerant sorts, must have water to grow and flower. Each perennial's general water requirements are noted in the encyclopedia (pages 46–121), but you'll also need to take climate, soil type, and the age of the plant into account.

If you garden where summers are long, hot, and dry, you will of course need to water more often than you would in a cool, moist climate. Likewise, if your soil is light and sandy, it will require more frequent irrigation than clay or a soil with a high percentage of organic matter. Young plants (including those that withstand dryness when mature) need more frequent watering than older ones with deeper, more extensive root systems.

APPLYING WATER. How you choose to water your perennials depends on how often they need watering and on how much water you have at your disposal. If watering is only necessary during the occasional dry spell, a simple hose-end sprinkler will suffice; this system also works well for small planting beds. If regular irrigation is needed all summer, plan to use soaker hoses laid among the plants, a rigid-pipe underground sprinkler system, or a drip irrigation setup. Drip irrigation is also a good choice where water is scarce or expensive: such systems allow

Mulch around your perennials to conserve water and suppress weeds. As the mulch breaks down, it will also improve the soil.

you to apply water only where it is needed, with no loss to runoff or wind, and they can be customized to fit narrow or irregularly shaped beds and borders.

Regardless of the watering system you choose, test the soil for moisture before turning on the faucet: dig down a few inches with your fingers or a trowel. For newly transplanted perennials and those that require regular to ample moisture, water when the top 1 to 2 inches of soil are dry; for established plants that require only moderate water, you can wait until the top 3 to 4 inches are dry.

Aim to soak the root zone when you water. Most perennials send their roots down a foot or so, though large-growing sorts have deeper roots. By watering the entire root zone rather than just the top few inches, you'll encourage the roots to grow deeply. Deeper roots have access to more moisture and can go longer between waterings; they're also less subject than shallow roots to the drying effects of heat and wind.

MULCHING

A layer of mulch around and between perennials serves several purposes. It helps conserve water, improves the soil as it decomposes, and aids in suppressing weed growth. Good mulches include compost (homemade or from a commercial source), bark (ground, shredded, or in chips), wood chips, pine needles, and various agricultural by-products such as aged manure, ground corncobs, and apple or grape pomace. Apply the mulch in a layer 1 to 2 inches thick, keeping it away from plants' main stems to avoid the possibility of rot.

A soaker hose lets water ooze slowly into the soil.

FERTILIZING

As noted in "A Fertilizer Primer" (at right), the three major nutrients plants need for healthy growth are nitrogen, phosphorus, and potassium. Various secondary and micronutrients are required as well—but while these are usually supplied in sufficient quantity by soil, the primary ones may not be, requiring you to make up any deficiencies. When you set out perennials (or any plants) in well-prepared soil fortified with organic matter and an initial application of complete fertilizer, you ensure that nutrient needs will be met for at least the first year of growth. After that, however, you may need to replenish the soil's nutrients to keep plants growing well. Many gardeners find that a yearly application of compost, spread over the soil as an inch-thick mulch, takes care of all or most nutrient needs; other gardeners also add fertilizer as insurance. If very poor growth leads you to suspect a chemical imbalance in your soil (or if you simply want a precise idea of which nutrients to add), have a professional soil test done before fertilizing (see page 32 for more on soil testing).

FERTILIZER CHOICES. Some fertilizers come from chemical sources; others, called organic fertilizers, are derived from the remains of living organisms.

Chemical (or *synthetic*) fertilizers are manufactured from the chemical sources listed on the product label. Because their nutrients are for the most part water soluble, they act faster than organic sorts. They're sold as dry granules to be applied to the soil and as soluble crystals or concentrated liquids to be diluted in water before use.

Chemical fertilizers used in liquid form can be applied to the soil, sprayed over plants, or both; check the product label. Such fertilizers provide nutrients especially quickly, making them a good choice for giving plants a quick boost.

To use granular types in established plantings, scatter them over the soil, then scratch them in (or dig them in, if you're preparing or reworking a bed). In standard dry fertilizers, moisture quickly dissolves the granules, releasing the nutrients they contain. Controlled-release sorts, on the other hand, deliver nutrients over a longer period: the fertilizer granules are covered in an inert permeable coating, and with each watering just a small amount of fertilizer diffuses through the coating and into the soil.

This bag of complete granular fertilizer contains 8 percent nitrogen (N), 4 percent phosphorus (P), and 4 percent potassium (K).

Organic fertilizers include blood meal, bone meal, cottonseed meal, fish emulsion, and a number of other choices. Rather than dissolving in water, they are broken down by bacteria in the soil, releasing their nutrients gradually as they decompose. Most are sold and applied in dry form, though a few (fish emulsion and seaweed extracts, for example) are available as concentrated liquids to be diluted before application. Organic amendments such as compost and manure, though not classified as fertilizers, also contain small amounts of nutrients.

WHEN TO FERTILIZE. After their first garden year, fertilize your perennials according to their seasonal growth patterns. The plants put on their greatest growth spurt in spring, so it's most useful to feed them at some point from late winter to midspring, with the exact timing depending on the climate and on when plants begin growing. Choose a fertilizer containing approximately 5 to 10 percent of each major nutrient, such as a 5-10-5 or 10-10-10 product; you can use a chemical fertilizer or a mix of organic ones. A second application in early to midsummer may be needed in sandy soils, since they allow nutrients to leach away from the root zone quickly.

A FERTILIZER PRIMER

The three major plant nutrients are nitrogen (N), phosphorus (P), and potassium (K). *Nitrogen* is needed in relatively large amounts for the synthesis of proteins, chlorophyll, and enzymes required for cell health and reproduction; it's the element most likely to be deficient in garden soil, since it's water soluble and easily leached away by rain and watering. *Phosphorus* promotes root growth and tissue maturation, while *potassium* encourages the manufacture of sugars and starches. Phosphorus and potassium become chemically "locked" into the soil at the point of application, so they must be placed near the root zone to do the most good. The best way to do this is to dig the fertilizer into the soil when you prepare it for planting.

Most commercial chemical fertilizers are *complete*, meaning that they contain all three major nutrients. *Incomplete* fertilizers contain just one or two of the three. The package label notes the percentage (by weight) of each nutrient the fertilizer contains, always presenting them in the N-P-K order. A 5-10-10 product, for example, contains 5 percent nitrogen, 10 percent phosphorus, and 10 percent potassium; a 0-10-10 fertilizer contains no nitrogen, while an 18-0-0 formulation contains nitrogen alone. Many organic fertilizers are high in just one of the three major nutrients and low or lacking in the other two. Blood meal and cottonseed meal, for example, are good sources of nitrogen; bone meal is high in phosphorus, while greensand is an organic source of potassium. Some manufacturers combine a variety of organic products in one package to make a complete fertilizer.

PRUNING

Perennials aren't woody plants, but some still need pruning—in the form of pinching, deadheading, thinning, and/or cutting back—to control growth and, often, to encourage more profuse bloom. To do most jobs, you can use small hand pruners (or even your thumb and forefinger), but you may prefer hedge or grass shears for large-scale cutting back.

Pinching off growing tips increases branching lower on the stem, making for a compact, bushy plant. Florists' chrysanthemum (*Chrysanthemum × morifolium*), for example, is pinched several times during the growing season to produce dense, leafy growth. Other perennials with a tendency toward ranginess benefit from a single pinching in late spring to early summer; these include the taller asters and artemisias, boltonia, *Eupatorium*, sneezeweed (*Helenium*), phlox, and false dragonhead (*Physostegia virginiana*). Since pinching reduces a plant's height, it can make staking unnecessary in some cases. It can also delay bloom; if you pinch back half of a clump of asters in early summer, for instance, that section will bloom a bit later than the unpinched section, prolonging the flowering season.

Deadheading is a rather macabre term for the removal of spent flowers. It's done partly for aesthetic reasons: the plant looks fresh and full of vigor without a drab and dreary load of dead blossoms. Beyond this, however, deadheading prevents plants from setting seed. It thus keeps prolific self-sowers from swamping you with volunteer seedings; and in many (though not all) cases, it induces longer bloom, since a deadheaded plant often continues to produce flowers in an attempt to form seed and complete its life cycle. Of course, in some cases you may choose not to deadhead. For example, certain perennials and most ornamental grasses have attractive seedheads that many gardeners leave in place until winter or early spring, both to decorate the garden and to provide food for seed-eating birds.

Thinning refers to cutting out stems at the base of the plant. It may be done to control the size of a plant that is impinging on its neighbors or to reduce the number of flowering stems. It's also a useful technique for improving air circulation around and within a plant, thus discouraging powdery mildew in susceptible perennials such as border phlox (*Phlox paniculata*) and bee balm (*Monarda*).

Cutting back, a more drastic form of pruning perennials, involves shearing or clipping off rangy growth and (often) spent flowering stems, all at once. It improves the plant's appearance and often promotes the growth of new bushy growth and flowering stems.

At some point after flowering and before the onset of growth the following spring, most perennials should be cut back to remove old growth. Besides making the garden look neater, this cleanup deprives pests (especially snails and slugs) of potential hiding places.

PRUNING TECHNIQUES

Pinching growing tips makes plants more compact and bushy.

Deadhead spent flowers to encourage more bloom and prevent seeding.

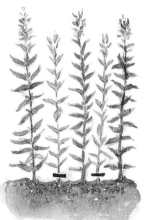

Thinning helps control the size of plants and improves air circulation.

Cutting back improves appearance and may promote more flowering.

WINTER PROTECTION

In colder climates, perennials sometimes need winter protection—not so much to shield them from cold (as is often thought) as to protect them from sharp fluctuations in temperature. Assuming you have chosen plants that are hardy to the low temperatures typical for your climate zone, winter damage generally occurs when the plants are subjected to alternate spells of freezing and thawing—a process that ruptures their cells, which then decay. Newly planted perennials without firmly established root systems may be heaved from the ground by freeze-thaw cycles; the exposed roots are then likely to be killed by cold and desiccation.

Snow provides excellent protection for garden plants, but if you can't count on a good snow cover for most of the winter, it's a good idea to lay down an insulating blanket of an organic material. Evergreen boughs, salt hay, marsh hay, and pine needles are all good choices; avoid materials such as leaves, which can pack down into an airtight mass. As soon as a hard frost has frozen the soil, put the protection in place. Use two layers of evergreen boughs (setting the top layer at right angles to the bottom one) or about 6 inches of hay or pine needles. When spring arrives, remove the material gradually, taking it off before the plants put on much growth but not so soon that emerging leaves and shoots will be killed by a late freeze.

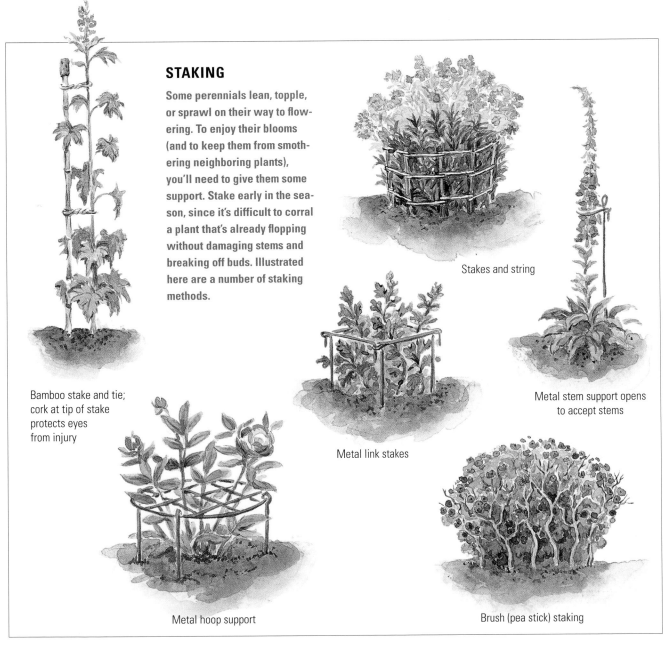

STAKING

Some perennials lean, topple, or sprawl on their way to flowering. To enjoy their blooms (and to keep them from smothering neighboring plants), you'll need to give them some support. Stake early in the season, since it's difficult to corral a plant that's already flopping without damaging stems and breaking off buds. Illustrated here are a number of staking methods.

Stakes and string

Bamboo stake and tie; cork at tip of stake protects eyes from injury

Metal link stakes

Metal stem support opens to accept stems

Metal hoop support

Brush (pea stick) staking

PESTS AND DISEASES

Pests and diseases are an inescapable part of garden life. Still, careful culture can prevent many infestations, and you can usually manage any problems that do occur without resorting to chemicals.

Prevention is the most important step in managing pests and diseases: you won't have to deal with problems if they don't crop up in the first place. To prevent infestations from plaguing your plants, do your best to keep them healthy and stress free. Set them out in well-prepared soil and give them the care they need throughout the growing season. Be sure they're adapted to their growing conditions; a plant that requires a cool, moist climate, for example, is quite likely to fall prey to diseases and pests if grown in a hot, dry region. Whenever possible, select varieties resistant to pests or diseases; many of these are described in the encyclopedia (pages 46–121). When you buy plants, look them over carefully to be sure you aren't importing problems to your garden. Finally, keep the garden free of debris and remove infected leaves—or whole plants, if necessary. A fall cleanup is especially helpful, since many pests and diseases overwinter on decaying foliage.

If you do spot trouble, take action only if the infestation is severe. A few aphids or chewed leaves are not cause for alarm, and problems often disappear quite quickly on their own as the

Beneficial insects help keep the garden healthy. Four beneficials are shown here. CLOCKWISE FROM TOP LEFT: *Assassin* bugs feed on aphids and mites. *Damsel bugs* and their nymphs consume aphids, leafhoppers, and small caterpillars. Small *ground beetles* eat caterpillars and soil-dwelling maggots and grubs; larger species eat snail and slug eggs as well as small snails and slugs. Adult *lacewings* feed only on nectar and honeydew, but their larvae consume aphids, leafhoppers, mealybugs, and whiteflies. NOT SHOWN: *Ladybugs* (ladybird beetles) and their larvae eat aphids, mites, and other soft-bodied insects.

pests die naturally or move on. In many cases, natural predators will take care of infestations for you; some of the most important beneficial insects are shown above. If you do decide that you must step in, identify the culprit before you act. The photos and descriptions given here will help; if you need more assistance, consult your Cooperative Extension Office or a local nursery. The controls suggested in the chart are listed in order of toxicity, beginning with the least toxic option (such as handpicking or water jets) and moving on to chemical remedies. If you opt for pesticides, read the product label carefully and follow all directions exactly—and be aware that most pesticides destroy helpful creatures as well as harmful ones.

DISEASE PROBLEMS

DISEASE	DESCRIPTION	CONTROLS
Powdery mildew	Fungal disease; shows up as a powdery white to gray coating on leaves, stems, and flower buds. Heavy infestations debilitate and disfigure plants. Favored by moist air, poor air circulation, and shade but needs dry leaves to become established.	Improve air circulation by thinning crowded plants. Spray with water to wash off fungus. Discard infected plant parts. Fungicides containing thiophanate-methyl or triforine may give partial control.
Root rot	Caused by fungal spores sometimes called water molds; active in warm, wet, or poorly drained soils. Young leaves turn yellow and wilt; plants may be stunted or may wilt and die, even in moist soil.	Keep soil moist, but do not overwater plants. Improve drainage. No chemical management; remove and discard diseased plants.
Rust	A great many rust fungi exist, each specific to a certain plant. Yellow, orange, red, or brown pustules appear on leaf undersides; the powdery spores are spread by wind and water.	Improve air circulation and try to avoid overhead watering; leaves must be wet for at least 4 to 5 hours for spores to germinate. Remove rust-infected leaves. Clean up plant debris. Fungicides containing propiconazole may be effective.

PEST PROBLEMS

PEST	DESCRIPTION	CONTROLS
Aphids	Soft-bodied, rounded insects, ranging from pinhead to matchhead size; green, gray, pink, reddish brown, or black. They cluster on new growth, sucking plant juices; heavy infestations distort growth and aid the spread of viruses.	Hose off with water or spray with insecticidal soap, neem, pyrethrum products, diazinon, malathion, or acephate.
Caterpillars	Caterpillars are moths and butterflies in the larval stage. Two of the many kinds harmful to perennials are armyworms (yellowish green to grayish green; feed at night) and cutworms (soil-dwelling caterpillars of various colors that often cut stems of young plants).	Handpick; look for cutworms at night, armyworms during the day. Spray armyworms with *Bacillus thuringiensis (Bt)* or neem. Carbaryl can be used for most kinds of caterpillars.
Japanese beetles	A ½-inch-long beetle with a distinctive metallic green sheen; attacks foliage of many perennials. A major pest in the eastern U.S., it has been gradually moving westward.	Handpick, use traps, or spray with rotenone, pyrethrum products, carbaryl, or acephate.
Leaf miners	A catchall term for certain moth, beetle, and fly larvae that tunnel within plant leaves, leaving a nearly transparent trail.	Pick off and destroy infected leaves. Insecticides are not effective, and they may harm beneficials.
Mites	Tiny spider relatives found on leaf undersides (webbing is often present); leaf surface is pale and stippled. Foliage eventually dries out, turns brown. To spot them, hold a piece of white paper under affected foliage and tap plant. Disturbed mites drop onto the paper; they look like specks of pepper. Infestations increase rapidly in hot weather.	Wash mites from plants with strong blasts of water. Buy and release native predatory mites. Spray with insecticidal soap or sulfur.
Slugs and snails	Both are night-feeding mollusks; snails have shells, slugs do not. They feast on leaves, stems, and flowers, leaving telltale trails of silvery slime.	Handpick and destroy. Containers filled with beer and set at ground level attract the pests, which then fall in and drown. Use barriers: surround plants or beds with rings of diatomaceous earth, or enclose containers and raised beds with copper strips. Use bait containing nontoxic iron phosphate. Apply metaldehyde bait (keep away from children, pets, birds).
Tarnished plant bugs	Fast-moving, shield-shaped insects about ¼ inch long; they suck plant juices from buds and stems, causing shoots to blacken and drop or become deformed.	Adults overwinter in plant debris; clean up garden in fall. Spray with insecticidal soap, carbaryl, or malathion.
Thrips	Almost microscopic pests that feed by rasping soft flower and leaf tissue; leaf surfaces take on a shiny silvery or tan cast.	Spray off with strong jets of water from hose. Trap with yellow sticky traps. Spray with insecticidal soap, rotenone, neem, or malathion.
Whiteflies	Tiny white pests that fly up in a cloud when disturbed; they suck plant juices from leaf undersides. Damaged foliage is sometimes stippled with yellow and may eventually curl, turn brown.	Hose off plants frequently with water jets; spray directly with insecticidal soap. Avoid insecticides: they are likely to kill natural predators, resulting in an increased whitefly population.

Aphids

Japanese beetle

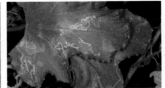
Leaf miners

Whiteflies

PROPAGATING PERENNIALS

Learning to propagate perennials gives you an ongoing supply of new plants to extend and expand your own beds and borders as well as those of your friends and neighbors. A number of techniques give good results, including sowing seeds, taking root or stem cuttings, layering, and division.

TRANSPLANTING SEEDLINGS

Transplant seedlings to the garden or to larger containers when they have at least their second set of true leaves.

SOWING SEEDS

Growing perennials from seed is an economical way to get lots of plants, and it's often an effective means of propagating those that are difficult to divide or start from cuttings. Growing from seed also allows you to experiment with new and unusual varieties (see "Resources," page 126, for mail-order seed sources). If you like, you can sow seeds collected from your own plants. And if your perennials self-sow, don't overlook the resulting "volunteers" as a source of free plants: carefully dig up young seedlings and transplant them to the desired location. (When growing plants from self-sown seed or from seeds you collect, keep in mind that most hybrids and cultivars do not come true from seed—that is, the seedlings may differ from their parents.)

While seed of some easy-to-grow perennials can be sown directly in the garden, most plants get off to a better start when started in containers and transplanted to garden beds later. Container-grown seedlings are more easily provided with the warm temperatures and bright light they need for quick growth, and they're also easier to protect from insects and birds. Sow seeds of most perennials in early to midspring. Some will be ready to transplant by early summer or fall; others may not be mature enough until the following spring.

Fill a plastic, wooden, or foam flat (with or without dividers) with moist seed-starting mix or potting soil. Firm the mix gently with your fingers or a block of wood. Check the seed packet for recommended planting depth. Sow seeds thinly over the mix. (For containers with individual cells, plant two seeds per cell.) Cover the seeds lightly with more mix and label the containers. Place the containers in a warm spot; after 3 days, check daily for germination. As soon as you spot green leaves, move the containers into bright light, as in a greenhouse or sunny south window or under fluorescent lights. Water gently when the soil surface feels dry. Once the seedlings have their first set of true leaves, fertilize weekly, using a product especially formulated for seedlings or a liquid type diluted to half strength.

When the seedlings have developed their second set of true leaves, you can thin or transplant them. If you need only a few plants, thin the seedlings to about 2 inches apart (or one per cell) and discard the thinnings. If you need more, transplant all the seedlings to larger (3- or 4-inch) containers filled with moist potting mix. When the seedlings are ready to transplant to the garden, set them out as shown on page 35.

THINNING SEEDLINGS

Thin seedlings to stand 1 to 2 inches apart by pinching them off with your fingers or snipping with scissors.

ROOT CUTTINGS

Root cuttings offer a less familiar but very useful method of propagating some perennials. In fact, if you've ever dug up part of a dandelion, then discovered a new weed growing and blooming from the roots left behind in the soil, you've seen how root cuttings work! For most perennials, plan to make these cuttings in late winter to early spring, when the plant is still dormant but about to begin growth. (Exceptions are bleeding heart, *Dicentra,* and Oriental poppy, *Papaver orientale;* these are dormant in late summer or fall, and you should take root cuttings then.)

To obtain roots for cuttings, you can dig up an entire plant or just a section of its roots. Using a sharp knife, remove vigorous, healthy pieces of root. Those growing closest to the plant's crown will form new plants most quickly. Being sure to note which end was closest to the crown, cut the pieces into 2- to 4-inch-long sections. If you have only a few cuttings, you can insert them upright in a container filled with damp potting mix, with the top cut ends (those that were closest to the crown on the parent plant) just at soil level. For larger numbers of cuttings (or very thin pieces of root), fill a flat to within an inch of the top with potting mix. Lay the cuttings flat on top of the mix (it doesn't matter which side is up), then cover them with ½ inch more mix. Note that rooting hormone is not needed and may actually delay rooting.

Water the planted containers well, then place them in a growing area such as a greenhouse or cold frame and provide protection from direct sun. Once stems and green leaves have formed, move the containers into full light and water them as needed. When the young shoots are several inches tall and new roots have formed (check by gently digging up a cutting), transplant them to individual pots and feed with liquid fertilizer. Once the cuttings have grown into sturdy plants, you can transplant them out to the garden.

LAYERING

Layering is a propagation technique that encourages new roots to form on branches still attached to the parent plant. Because the parent supplies the layer—the new plant—with water and nutrients during the rooting process, this method is an easy way to produce a few new plants. Perennials with trailing branches are best for layering; some of these even produce layers natu-

rally. Check around established plants of penstemon, tall, shrubby kinds of artemisia, and lavender cotton *(Santolina),* for example, for rooted sections you can dig up and transplant.

If you'd like to try layering, look in spring for a young, healthy, pliable shoot growing low on the perennial to be layered. Loosen the soil where the shoot will be buried and work in a shovelful of compost; then dig a shallow hole in the prepared area. Make a shallow cut at a leaf node that will be covered by soil. Some gardeners apply rooting hormone

to the cut. Lay the shoot (the layer) in the hole and fasten it down with a piece of wire or a forked stick. Tie the layer's tip to a stake to mark its position and help it grow upwards; then fill the hole, firming the soil around the layer. Put a small rock on top to help hold the layer in place.

During the growing season, keep the soil around the layer moist; covering it with 1 to 2 inches of mulch will help retain moisture. Cut the new plant free from the parent after you are sure that roots have formed; this usually takes a few months, but may take longer (gently dig into the soil to check). Dig the layer up, keeping plenty of soil around the roots, and move it to its new location.

DIVISION

To divide a perennial, you dig it up, separate it into sections, and replant the pieces. Gardeners turn to division for several reasons. Many perennials become overcrowded, forming a tight mass of roots and stems; flowering declines, and the plant may look shabby. In some cases, clumps become bare or woody in the center, with healthy new growth only around the perimeter; in these instances, division rejuvenates the plant, increasing bloom and improving overall appearance. Some fast-growing perennials require division to control their spread and keep them from overreaching their allotted space; examples include aster, bee balm *(Monarda),* and false dragonhead *(Physostegia virginiana).* You may also, of course, choose to divide perennials simply to obtain extra plants.

How often a particular perennial needs division depends on how fast it grows. We note the recommended frequency of division for each perennial in the encyclopedia (pages 46–121); as you'll learn, a few (also listed on page 14) grow best if left permanently undisturbed. Perennials that grow from taproots cannot be divided successfully and are best propagated from seeds or from root cuttings (see facing page).

1 Loosen the soil in a circle around the clump, cutting 6 to 12 inches beyond the plant's perimeter with a shovel or spading fork. Then dig under the roots to free them from the soil. Lift the whole clump out of the ground; or, if it's too heavy to lift, cut it into sections. Set the clump (or pieces) in a convenient working spot such as a path.

2 Gently tease some soil from the root ball so you can see what you are doing. For larger, fibrous-rooted perennials such as daylilies *(Hemerocallis),* hose off as much of the soil as possible.

3 Now make the divisions. Look at the plant, noting natural dividing points between stems or sections. You can easily divide some perennials by pulling the clumps apart by hand. Those with mats of small, fibrous roots can be cut with a knife, small pruning saw, or trowel; types with thick, tough roots may require a sharp-bladed shovel or an axe. Try to divide the clumps into good-sized sections, which will grow and bloom more quickly than small divisions. Trim any damaged roots, stems, or leaves from the divisions.

4 Replant the divisions as soon as possible, then keep them well watered while they get established. You can also plant divisions in containers (a good idea if they're very small) to set out later or share with other gardeners.

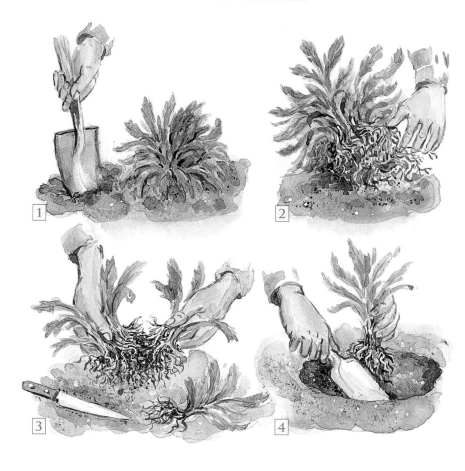

Most perennials can be divided in either fall or early spring, though for some plants a specific time of year is preferred (check the encyclopedia listings, pages 46–121). If you plan to divide in fall and you live in a cold-winter climate, do the job early enough in the season to let roots get established before freezing weather arrives; this usually means dividing 6 to 8 weeks before the first hard frost. In general, avoid dividing plants in the heat of summer.

A day or two before dividing, moisten the soil around the planting thoroughly. To make the plants easier to handle, cut back the stems of larger perennials, leaving about 6 inches of foliage (this isn't necessary for smaller plants). If you'll be planting in a new bed, prepare the soil (as described on page 33) before you divide, so the divisions won't have to spend too long out of the ground. If you're replanting in the same location as the parent clump, keep the divisions in a shady spot covered with damp newspapers while you replenish the soil.

It isn't always necessary to lift an entire clump to divide it. Many perennials can be divided by separating new plantlets from the clump's edges; look for rooted sections, then carefully dig them up and replant as soon as possible in well-prepared soil. Another option is to dig and transplant a wedge-shaped section—like a slice of pie—from the clump. Fill in the hole in the parent clump with compost or soil; the plant will soon grow to cover the gap.

ROOTING STEM AND BASAL CUTTINGS

Most perennials can be propagated from stem or basal cuttings. Like divisions, they reproduce the parent plant exactly. Stem cuttings, also called softwood cuttings, are taken from pieces of the stem or shoot. Basal cuttings, recommended for a few perennials, are quite similar; they consist of entire young shoots, cut from the parent plant so that each retains a piece of firm tissue at its base. They are rooted in the same way as stem cuttings (see below). Stem and basal cuttings are taken during the active growing season from spring until late summer; the encyclopedia notes the best time to take them for each perennial.

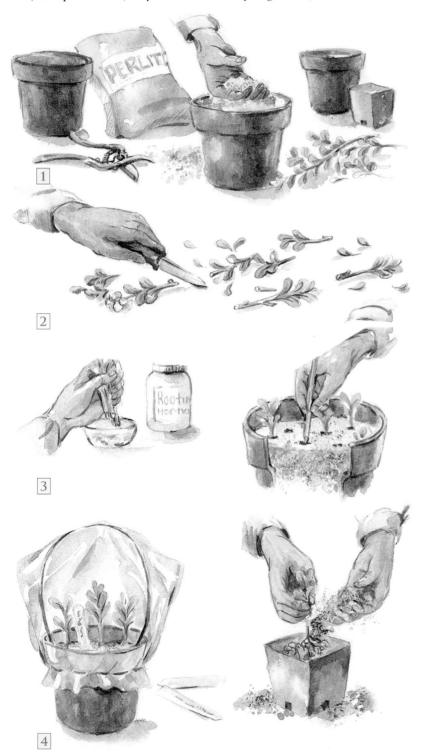

1 Prepare containers first. Use clean pots or flats with drainage holes. Fill them with a half-and-half mixture of perlite and peat moss, or with perlite or peat moss alone. Dampen the mixture.

2 Gather material for cuttings early in the day, when plants are full of moisture. The parent plant should be healthy and growing vigorously. With a sharp knife or bypass pruners, snip 5- to 6-inch-long pieces from the plant, choosing vigorous young tip or side shoots.

Remove and discard any flower buds, flowers, and small shoots growing laterally from the main stem. Then trim the stems into 3- to 4-inch lengths, each with at least two nodes (growing points). Make the lower cut just below a node, since new roots will form at this point. Remove leaves from the lower half of the cutting.

3 Dip the lower cut ends of the cuttings in liquid or powdered rooting hormone; shake off any excess. (Many gardeners omit this step and still get good results.)

Using the end of a pencil, make 1- to 1½-inch-deep holes in the rooting medium, spacing them 1 to 2 inches apart; then insert the cuttings. Firm the medium around the cuttings and water with a fine spray. Label each container (or group of plants within a container) with the name of the plant and the date.

Enclose each container in a plastic bag. Close the bag to maintain humidity, but open it for a few minutes every day to provide ventilation. Set the containers in a warm, shaded (but not dark) location.

4 The cuttings will usually take hold and begin growing roots in 1 to 5 weeks. To check, gently pull on a cutting; if you feel resistance, roots are forming. At this point, expose the cuttings to drier air by opening the bags; if the cuttings wilt, close the bags again for a few days (opening them briefly each day for ventilation).

When the plants seem acclimated to open air, transplant each to its own 3- to 4-inch pot of lightweight potting mix. When they're well rooted and growing new leaves, they're ready to go into the ground.

ENCYCLOPEDIA OF
PERENNIALS

Within the realm of perennials are enough plants to keep gardeners busy and happy for years—and each spring, nurseries introduce even more enticing choices. The following 74 pages present a diverse selection that includes long-time favorites as well as promising newer varieties.

You'll also find special features on ferns (pages 78–79) and ornamental grasses and grasslike plants (pages 98–101), all worthwhile additions to the perennial palette. While many of the plants we describe are widely available, you may need to obtain others from mail-order specialists. Twenty suppliers are listed on page 126.

As you peruse these descriptions, keep your own garden in mind, looking not only for appropriate flower color and plant size and form, but also for perennials well suited to your climate zone, soil type, and the amount of moisture available. To help you narrow down the possibilities, each entry begins with a list of at-a-glance information—a quick review of the plant's preferred climate zone, exposure (sun, or shade) and water needs, flower color, and bloom season. For a line-by-line explanation, turn to "Reading the Entries" on the next page.

This perennial border blends a wash of soft lavender catmint *(Nepeta × faassenii)* with deep indigo *Salvia × superba* 'May Night' and salmon pink twinspur *(Diascia* 'Ruby Field'). Spikes of red-hot poker *(Kniphofia uvaria)* provide vertical contrast.

PERENNIALS
READING THE ENTRIES

In the profiles that follow, you'll find a description of each plant, advice on its cultural needs, and a short list of other perennials that make attractive garden associates. Each entry begins with the plant's botanical name; any former botanical names (under which it may still be sold) appear in parentheses. Entries describing a number of species and hybrids are headed simply by the plant's genus—Achillea, for example. Other entries cover just one species and are headed by both genus and species, as in Acanthus mollis. The next line gives the perennial's common name or names and indicates whether it makes a good cut flower (✄) or attracts butterflies (🦋). The third line notes the plant's botanical family; the fourth, introduced with ✎, indicates the Sunset climate zones where the plant will succeed. For details on zones, see pages 122–125.

Recommended exposure is shown next. ☼ means the plant grows best with day-long bright, unshaded sun; ◑ describes plants that do equally well in partial shade (a spot that's sunny in the morning, shaded in the afternoon) or light shade (no direct sun but plenty of light). ● indicates that the plant prefers little or no direct sunlight.

Moisture needs are identified as well. ● indicates a need for regular water; the plant always requires moisture, but the soil shouldn't remain saturated. ◐ describes plants requiring moderate or little water: they need some moisture, but the soil can go somewhat to quite dry between waterings. ●● means the plant requires ample water and will grow happily even in soggy soil.

Finally, we indicate the range of flower colors and the main bloom season for each perennial. For comments on variation in bloom times, see page 26.

Acanthus mollis

ACANTHUS mollis
✄ ACANTHUS, BEAR'S BREECH
Acanthaceae

✎ ZONES 4–24, 28–32
☼ ◑ FULL SUN OR LIGHT SHADE
●◐ REGULAR TO MODERATE WATER
✻ ✻ ✻ FLOWERS IN LATE SPRING, EARLY SUMMER

A thriving clump of acanthus lends a sculptural effect to the garden. Borne on arching stems, the shiny dark green leaves are deeply lobed and can reach 2 feet long. Above the foliage, rigid spikes of tubular white, lilac, or rose flowers with spiny bracts rise to a height of 3 to 4 feet, providing a strong vertical contrast. **'Latifolius'** has larger leaves and does not always flower as freely; it reputedly tolerates more cold.

CULTURE. Where hardy, acanthus is almost too easy to grow. The roots spread rapidly underground, especially in loose, moist, well-enriched soil. To save yourself the task of constantly fighting the plants back, either give them plenty of space or confine them with an 8-inch-deep barrier around the roots. In areas with hot summers, locate acanthus in partial shade; hot sun causes the leaves to wilt. In dry-summer regions, plants go dormant if not regularly watered.

To propagate acanthus, divide the clumps in spring. Note that any roots left in the soil will sprout to form new clumps. You can also propagate these plants by taking root cuttings in early spring.

Effective with Anemone × hybrida, ferns, Polygonatum, Pulmonaria.

From foot-tall pastel front-of-the-border plants to bright yellow 5-footers, yarrows are carefree, generously blooming perennials. Most species have aromatic gray or green leaves that are narrow, fernlike, and finely dissected. The flowers are tiny daisies, tightly packed into flattened or somewhat rounded heads; they are useful both as cut flowers and dried for winter arrangements.

A. filipendulina 'Gold Plate' is one of the tallest yarrows, producing 6-inch-wide, deep yellow flower clusters on 5-foot stems that may require staking. A related hybrid, 'Coronation Gold', tolerates a wide range of soils and climates; its shiny golden flower heads are 3 to 4 inches across, carried on strong, 2- to 3-foot stems.

Common yarrow, *A. millefolium*, forms a spreading mat of green to gray-green leaves. Its basic form is a common roadside weed that sports off-white flowers on 1- to 2-foot stems. Selected forms and hybrids include 'Cerise Queen', a 1½-footer with bright cerise red flowers; 'Credo', growing 3 to 4 feet tall and bearing light yellow flowers that fade to creamy white; and 3-foot-tall 'Fireland', with flowers that open red, then fade to pink and gold. The **Summer Pastels** strain features 2-foot plants that flower the first year from seed in a range of colors.

Foliage of the **Galaxy** series of hybrids is similar to that of common yarrow, but the flower heads are borne on stronger stems. 'Great Expectations' produces primrose yellow flowers on 2-foot stems. 'The Beacon' ('Fanal') grows 2 to 3 feet tall and has rich red flowers with yellow centers, while 'Rodney's Choice', also 2 to 3 feet high, has burgundy red blooms.

'Moonshine', another popular hybrid, has deep lemon yellow flowers on 1- to 2-foot stems above filigreelike gray-green foliage. The related hybrid 'Anthea' bears light yellow blooms on plants that tend to be more erect in habit.

Woolly yarrow, *A. tomentosa*, forms a flat, spreading mat of deep green, fernlike leaves that have a woolly texture. The flat, golden yellow flower heads are borne on 6- to 10-inch stems.

A. ptarmica, which goes by the common name "sneezeweed" (but is not the same plant as another sneezeweed, *Helenium*), can be quite invasive. Selected forms such as 'Angel's Breath' and 'The Pearl' are less aggressive; they produce white flowers that are often used in bouquets as a substitute for baby's breath *(Gypsophila paniculata)*.

CULTURE. Yarrows grow best in reasonably good, well-drained soil. Once established, they are drought tolerant, but they look more attractive with moderate watering. Cut out the spent stems after flowering. Divide crowded clumps in spring.

Effective with Agastache, Anchusa azurea, Catananche caerulea, Centaurea, Crambe cordifolia, Gaillardia × grandiflora, Nepeta, Ratibida, Stachys byzantina, Stokesia laevis.

The curious helmet- or hood-shaped flowers of monkshood are closely set along tall, leafy spikes that rise above attractive clumps of dark green, deeply lobed foliage. These plants can substitute for delphiniums in shady locations and are effective in borders or near a bog garden. All parts of the plant are poisonous; be especially careful not to plant them in locations where the tuberous roots could be mistaken for edible roots.

Flowering in early summer, *A. septentrionale* 'Ivorine' is a compact 1½-foot-tall form bearing many clusters of creamy white flowers. Among the named selections of *A. cammarum (A. bicolor)* are two summer bloomers:

ACHILLEA
YARROW
Asteraceae (Compositae)
- ZONES 1–24, 26, 28–45
- FULL SUN
- MODERATE WATER
- FLOWERS IN SUMMER, EARLY AUTUMN

Achillea 'Moonshine'

ACONITUM
MONKSHOOD, ACONITE
Ranunculaceae
- ZONES 1–9, 14–21, 34–45
- FULL SUN OR LIGHT SHADE
- REGULAR WATER
- FLOWERS IN SUMMER, AUTUMN

Aconitum

Aconitum napellus

'Bressingham Blue', with violet blue flowers on strong 3-foot-tall stems that seldom need staking, and 4-foot **'Bicolor'**, with white flowers edged in blue. Flowering later (in late summer and early autumn) is ***A. carmichaelii (A. fischeri);*** it produces dense, branching clusters of deep purplish blue flowers on 2- to 4-foot stems. Common monkshood, ***A. napellus,*** grows 3 to 4 feet tall and bears blue, violet, pink, or white blossoms in late summer.

CULTURE. Plant monkshood in moist, fertile soil enriched with compost. Plants grow best in regions with cool summers and some winter chill; they are difficult to establish in warm, dry climates. It is best not to disturb established plants, but if you want to increase your plantings, carefully separate the tuberous roots in very early spring. Mulch new plants and transplanted roots the first winter.

Effective with Anemone × hybrida, Astilbe, Chelone, Cimicifuga, ferns, Hosta, Thalictrum.

ADENOPHORA

🌿 LADY BELLS

Campanulaceae (Lobeliaceae)

✎ ZONES 1–10, 14–24, 30–43

☼ ◑ FULL SUN OR LIGHT SHADE

🌢 ◔ REGULAR TO MODERATE WATER

✳ ✤ FLOWERS IN SUMMER

These are erect plants with narrow, leafy stems bearing rows of charming, fragrant blue bells along their upper portions. They look much like their campanula relatives, for which they may be substituted in the hot, humid climates where campanulas often fail. Group several of the slim, upright plants together for a showy display.

Common lady bells, **A. confusa,** has branching, leafy stems 2 to 2½ feet tall. The nodding flowers are deep blue. Lilyleaf lady bells, **A. liliifolia,** is similar but not as tall, reaching just 1½ feet; its blossoms are pale lavender blue or, in some forms, white.

CULTURE. Plant lady bells in rich, well-drained soil. Look for young plants to set out from containers; older plants have deep, fleshy roots that do not transplant readily. For the same reason, it is best to propagate lady bells by sowing the fine seeds in late winter; division harms the roots and is rarely successful. The plants may self-sow abundantly; pull out any seedlings you don't want.

Effective with Alchemilla mollis, Aquilegia, Gypsophila paniculata, Heuchera.

*Adenophora
confusa*

AGAPANTHUS

🌿 🌺 AGAPANTHUS,
LILY-OF-THE-NILE

Amaryllidaceae

✎ ZONES VARY

☼ ◑ FULL SUN OR LIGHT SHADE

🌢 ◔ REGULAR TO LITTLE WATER

✳ ✤ FLOWERS IN SUMMER

Agapanthus 'Peter Pan'

Elegant and stately, with fountainlike clumps of handsome strap-shaped foliage, agapanthus sends forth sturdy 1- to 5-foot-tall stems topped with rounded clusters containing dozens of tubular flowers. Colors include nearly every shade of blue, from the palest tints to deep midnight, as well as sparkling white.

A number of species and hybrids are available. ***A. africanus*** and ***A. orientalis*** (Zones 7–9, 12–21, 28–31) are usually evergreen. The former (which may be sold as *A. umbellatus)* has leaves that reach about a foot in length; its 1½- to 2-foot flower stalks carry rounded, 6-inch-wide clusters of 20 to 50 blue flowers. ***A. a.*** **'Albus'** is a white-flowered cultivar, especially showy on summer evenings. *A. orientalis* grows altogether larger, with 4- to 5-foot stems carrying 8- to 12-inch-wide heads of up to 100 blue or white flowers. Hybrid selections include **'Storm Cloud'**, with flowers of an exceptionally deep violet blue, and the outstanding dwarf **'Peter Pan'**, which grows only 8 to 12 inches tall and bears profuse blue flowers atop 1- to 1½-foot stems.

The more cold-hardy **Headbourne Hybrids** and *A. inapertus* (Zones 3–9, 12–21, 28–31, warmer parts of 32) are deciduous in winter. The Headbourne Hybrids produce 2- to 3-foot-tall stems bearing 6-inch-wide flower heads above fairly narrow, upright foliage; colors include many shades of blue as well as white. *A. inapertus* features deep blue blossoms in drooping clusters atop 4- to 5-foot stems.

CULTURE. Tough and durable, agapanthus thrives in loamy soil with regular water, but the plants will tolerate poor soils, and, once established, little or no irrigation. They flower most freely in sun but also grow and bloom fairly well in partial shade. Clumps can remain in place for many years before they require dividing; when division is needed, do the job in early spring.

In zones too cold for in-ground planting, grow agapanthus in containers placed in the garden, around a pool, or on the deck or patio. Keep the containers in a frost-free place over winter, allowing the crowns to dry out. As spring approaches, move into bright light and begin to water again.

Effective with Chrysanthemum × superbum, Coreopsis, Diascia, Erigeron, Kniphofia.

Agapanthus orientalis

Agastaches are showy mint-family members with aromatic foliage (often delightfully reminiscent of licorice) and spikes of small tubular flowers born in whorls. Though frequently planted in herb gardens, the agastaches described below are equally at home in borders and large containers.

A. barberi (Zones 8, 9, 14–24, 29, 30, warmer parts of 32) grows 2 feet tall and has reddish purple flowers on 6- to 12-inch spikes; its ovate green leaves are about 2 inches long. A related hybrid, **'Tutti Frutti'**, produces many spikes of raspberry red flowers that are nicely set off by gray-green foliage.

Anise hyssop, **A. foeniculum** (Zones 2–24, 28–41), forms an erect, bushy plant to 5 feet tall, clothed in lance-shaped, 2- to 3-inch leaves with downy undersides. Its dense clusters of lilac blue flowers are borne in 4-inch spikes. It blooms the first year from seed and reseeds freely. **'Snow Spike'** is a vigorous white-blossomed selection.

Giant Mexican lemon hyssop, **A. mexicana** (Zones 14–24, 29), grows 2 to 3 feet tall and has tooth-edged, 2½-inch, ovate to lance-shaped leaves and foot-long spikes of rosy red flowers. The selection **'Toronjil Morada'** has bright pink blossoms.

CULTURE. Plant agastaches in well-drained soil. Plants usually tolerate some drought, but they grow and bloom best with regular water. Full sun gives the most prolific show of flowers, but you'll get a good performance in light shade as well. Propagate by seed, division in spring, or stem cuttings.

Effective with Achillea, Echinops, Eryngium, Malva, Nepeta, Origanum, Perovskia.

AGASTACHE
AGASTACHE, HYSSOP
Lamiaceae (Labiatae).
- ZONES VARY
- FULL SUN OR LIGHT SHADE
- REGULAR TO MODERATE WATER
- FLOWERS IN SUMMER, AUTUMN

Agastache foeniculum

A soft-looking plant for the front of the border, lady's-mantle forms a mound of rounded, velvety gray-green leaves that glisten when beaded with droplets of dew or rain. The frothy sprays of yellow-green blossoms offer a soothing contrast to brighter flowers. Each plant grows to about 1½ feet high and spreads to 2 feet across. **'Thriller'** is a floriferous selection with larger, pleated-looking leaves.

CULTURE. Lady's-mantle requires good soil that is moist but well drained. In regions with mild summers, plant in sun or light shade. In warm-summer areas, a location in partial shade is important—but even if given a shady spot, plants tend to be short lived

ALCHEMILLA mollis
LADY'S-MANTLE
Rosaceae
- ZONES 2–9, 14–24, 31–43
- FULL SUN OR LIGHT SHADE
- REGULAR WATER
- FLOWERS IN LATE SPRING, SUMMER

Alchemilla mollis

where summers are long, hot, and dry. Lady's-mantle doesn't require division to stay healthy, but you can divide in early spring (before flowering) to increase your supply of plants. Self-sown seedlings often appear.

Effective with Adenophora, Corydalis, Digitalis, Geranium, Geum, Hosta, Lupinus, Paeonia, Polygonatum.

ALSTROEMERIA

🌿 ALSTROEMERIA, PERUVIAN LILY

Liliaceae

- ❄ ZONES 5–9, 14–24, 26, 28, 31, WARMER PARTS OF 32, 34
- ◐ LIGHT SHADE, EXCEPT AS NOTED
- ● REGULAR WATER
- ✳ ✳ ✳ ✳ ✳ ✳ FLOWERS IN LATE SPRING, SUMMER

Alstroemeria aurea

Growing from tuberous roots, alstroemerias form spreading clumps of wiry, upright, 1½- to 5-foot stems topped by long-lasting clusters of lilylike blossoms. Bright colors, bicolor combinations, and beautiful markings give the flowers an exotic appearance. Evergreen varieties bloom for a longer season if the spent flower stems are removed not by cutting back, but by gently pulling them away from the tuberous root; this technique encourages new growth from the roots, while cutting the stems slows new growth and bloom.

Cordu and **Meyer** are hybrid strains that are evergreen where temperatures remain above freezing. They form compact 1- to 3-foot-tall clumps and bloom over a long season, producing blossoms in colors including white to pink, red, lilac, and purple, usually bicolored and spotted. The older **Ligtu Hybrids** bear flowers in yellow, salmon, orange, and pink; they go dormant after flowering, leaving a gap in the garden.

A. aurea (A. aurantiaca) performs best in mild-winter areas of the West Coast. Plants grow 3 to 4 feet high and tend to spread widely; they can become invasive. Named selections include **'Lutea'**, with yellow flowers marked with carmine, and red-flowered **'Splendens'**. The parrot lily, ***A. psittacina (A. pulchella)***, grows 1 to 1½ feet tall and sports dark red flowers tipped with green and spotted with deep purple.

CULTURE. Alstroemerias require well-drained soil enriched with organic amendments. Plants do well everywhere in light shade (and must have afternoon shade where summers are hot); in cool-summer areas, they'll also take full sun. Handle the brittle roots carefully, setting them 6 to 8 inches deep and 1 foot apart. In warm regions, it's a good idea to mulch with ground bark, shredded leaves, or other organic material to help keep the soil cool. The plants tolerate some drought but grow best if given regular moisture. Mulch to protect the roots over winter.

Established clumps can be divided, but because plants reestablish slowly after transplanting, it's usually best to start new plants from seed. Sow in fall, winter, or earliest spring, either directly in the garden or in individual pots for later transplanting.

Note that contact with alstroemeria foliage may cause an allergic skin reaction in some people.

Effective with Artemisia, Digitalis, Heuchera, Verbena bonariensis.

AMSONIA

tabernaemontana

BLUE STAR

Apocynaceae

- ❄ ZONES 3–24, 28–33
- ☼ ◐ FULL SUN OR LIGHT SHADE
- ● ◐ REGULAR TO MODERATE WATER
- ✳ FLOWERS IN LATE SPRING, SUMMER

Blue star forms a handsome, bushy clump of 2- to 3-foot stems that are closely set with shiny, willow-shaped leaves and topped by nodding clusters of small (½- to ¾-inch) flowers. The foliage is as attractive as the flowers, remaining glossy throughout summer and turning bright golden yellow in fall. ***A. t. montana*** is more compact than the species and blooms earlier.

Amsonia tabernaemontana

CULTURE. Easy to grow and undemanding, blue star thrives in average, well-drained soil in full sun or light shade. In very shady sites, it becomes leggy and may need staking. It tolerates occasional lapses in watering. Clumps increase steadily in size but seldom require division to maintain top appearance; however, you can dig and divide in early spring to increase your planting. You can also propagate blue star by taking stem cuttings during summer.

Effective with Aquilegia, Brunnera macrophylla, Chrysanthemum × superbum, Geranium, Iris (bearded), Nepeta, Tradescantia.

Amsonia tabernaemontana

Sheaves of brilliant blue flowers reminiscent of oversized forget-me-nots characterize this rather short-lived perennial. The flower stems grow as tall as 4 feet in some selections, rising from clumps of hairy, lance-shaped leaves 4 to 16 inches long. **'Dropmore'** is a widely available cultivar with deep blue flowers; it grows 4 feet high. The bushier, sturdier **'Loddon Royalist'** is a 3-footer with lovely gentian blue flowers; **'Little John'** is a compact 1½-foot selection with dark blue blooms.

CULTURE. Plant in well-drained soil. Water frequently enough to keep soil moist but not saturated, since roots tend to rot in overly wet conditions. Taller varieties may need staking. Deadhead spent flowers to prevent excessive self-seeding and to encourage a second bloom flush. Italian bugloss declines after the second year and should be divided to rejuvenate the clump. You can also propagate by taking root cuttings in early spring.

Effective with Achillea, Artemisia, Coreopsis, Dianthus, Hemerocallis.

Anchusa azurea 'Loddon Royalist'

ANCHUSA azurea
ITALIAN BUGLOSS
Boraginaceae

- ✿ ZONES 1–24, 29–45
- ☼ FULL SUN
- ●● REGULAR TO MODERATE WATER
- ✳ FLOWERS IN LATE SPRING, SUMMER

Prized for its late-season bloom, this graceful perennial produces clumps of dark green, deeply veined, maplelike leaflets at the ends of long leafstalks. The wiry, somewhat leafy stems typically reach 3 to 5 feet tall and bear loose sprays of cupped, golden-centered flowers resembling wild roses. Japanese anemone is often slow to establish, but once settled in, it can spread to the point of invasiveness.

Classic varieties include **'Honorine Jobert'**, with single white flowers on 3- to 4-foot stems, and **'Queen Charlotte',** with semidouble pink blossoms on 3-foot stems. **'Alice,'** a shorter selection to about 2 feet tall, bears semidouble light pink flowers.

Other related and similar species may also be sold under the name "Japanese anemone." Among these are *A. hupehensis japonica*, with rose pink flowers; pale pink *A. tomentosa;* and white-flowered *A. vitifolia.*

CULTURE. Japanese anemone grows best in well-drained soil enriched with organic matter. Plant in light or partial shade or in filtered sun; where summers are cool, plants will also do well in full sun. Clumps don't need dividing for rejuvenation, but you can dig up and transplant rooted shoots in spring to increase your supply. Or propagate by root cuttings taken in late winter.

Effective with Acanthus mollis, Aconitum, Bergenia, Chelone, ferns, Hosta, Physostegia virginiana, Tricyrtis.

ANEMONE × hybrida
JAPANESE ANEMONE
Ranunculaceae

- ✿ ZONES 3–24, 30–39, 41
- ◐ LIGHT SHADE, EXCEPT AS NOTED
- ● REGULAR WATER
- ✳ ✳ FLOWERS IN LATE SUMMER, AUTUMN

Anemone × hybrida 'Honorine Jobert'

ANTHEMIS tinctoria
GOLDEN MARGUERITE
Asteraceae (Compositae)

- ZONES 1–11, 14–24, 30–45
- FULL SUN
- MODERATE WATER
- FLOWERS IN SUMMER, EARLY AUTUMN

Anthemis tinctoria

Cheery yellow daisies to 2 inches across brighten mounding, shrubby plants 2 to 3 feet high and wide. The finely cut light green leaves are somewhat downy on the underside. The species bears bright yellow blooms, as do selections such as **'Kelway's Variety'**. Other selections—among them pale yellow **'Moonlight'** and creamy **'Sauce Hollandaise'**—offer softer yellows that mix well with many other flower colors.

CULTURE. Given well-drained soil, golden marguerite is easy to grow, requiring only a sunny location and a moderate amount of water. After the first flush of bloom, cut back lightly to encourage new flowering growth. Plants tend to be short lived. To rejuvenate them, divide the clumps in early spring. Or propagate from stem cuttings taken in spring.

Effective with Aster, Catananche caerulea, Hemerocallis, Penstemon, Solidago.

AQUILEGIA
COLUMBINE
Ranunculaceae

- ZONES VARY
- LIGHT SHADE, EXCEPT AS NOTED
- REGULAR WATER
- FLOWERS IN SPRING, EARLY SUMMER

Aquilegia chrysantha

Graceful and full of charm, columbines bring lacy foliage and intricate, delicate flowers to the garden. Heights vary from only a few inches to 4 feet (depending on the species or hybrid); leaves are typically lobed and gray green, reminiscent of maidenhair fern foliage. Flowers are erect or nodding, carried on slender, branching stems. Many sorts have sepals and petals in contrasting colors, and most have backward-projecting spurs. There are also short-spurred and spurless sorts, as well as some kinds with double flowers.

Three North American species are especially noted for their stately form. Rocky Mountain columbine, **A. caerulea** (Zones 1–11, 14–24, 32–45), has classic, long-spurred, blue-and-white flowers on 2- to 3-foot stems; the blooms are held erect and reach about 2 inches wide. Canadian columbine, **A. canadensis** (Zones 1–10, 14–24, 30–45), is a 1- to 2-footer with nodding red-and-yellow flowers about 1½ inches wide. A selected form, **A. canadensis 'Corbett'**, blooms in creamy yellow. Four-foot-tall golden columbine, **A. chrysantha** (Zones 1–11, 14–24, 32–45), forms a many-branched plant with clear yellow flowers 1½ to 3 inches across.

European columbine, **A. vulgaris** (Zones 1–10, 14–24, 32–45), grows 1 to 2½ feet high and has nodding, very short-spurred, 2-inch flowers in blue, violet, or white; there are selected forms without spurs. The Japanese native **A. flabellata** (Zones 1–9, 14–24, 32–45) forms a compact foot-high mound, well suited to the front of a border. Its leaves are thicker and darker than those of other columbines. The nodding flowers are lilac blue or creamy white.

Many hybrid columbine strains are available. Among these are the graceful, long-spurred **McKana Giants** and double-blossomed **Spring Song.** Both of these bloom in a range of colors, reach 3 feet tall, and grow in Zones 2–10, 14–24, 32–43.

CULTURE. Columbines are not fussy about soil as long as it is well drained. Plant in light shade or filtered sun; where summers are cool, plants also grow well in sun. Cut back old stems for a second crop of flowers. Most columbines are not long lived; plan on replacing them every 3 to 4 years. If you let the spent flowers form seed capsules, you'll get a crop of volunteer seedlings—but if you're growing hybrids, the seedlings may differ from the parents. Seedlings from species (if grown isolated from other columbines) should closely resemble the parents, however.

Leaf miners are a potential pest, especially on hybrids. Cut off affected foliage; new leaves will soon appear.

Effective with Adenophora, Amsonia tabernaemontana, Corydalis, ferns, Geum, Papaver orientale, Polygonatum, Primula.

Aquilegia, McKana Giants strain

Clustered in tight pompoms at the ends of 6- to 10-inch stems, thrift's bright little flowers appear above compact, grassy mounds of linear, 4- to 8-inch-long leaves. Tolerant of seaside conditions, this perennial is also at home in inland gardens between stepping-stones and as a low edging for borders. Selected forms include rosy red **'Bloodstone'**, deep salmon pink **'Vindictive'**, and **'Alba'**, a useful white-flowered sort that fits well in many planting schemes.

CULTURE. Like other plants adapted to the seashore, thrift must have excellent drainage. If this requirement is met, it will tolerate regular watering—but the safest tactic is to water moderately in dry climates, sparingly in moister regions. The clumps spread slowly; divide in spring when they start to show bare centers, or replace with new plants. Deadheading prolongs bloom.

Armeria maritima

Effective with Geranium, Iberis sempervirens, Lychnis coronaria, Sedum, Sempervivum tectorum, Stachys.

ARMERIA martima

🌺 THRIFT, SEA PINK
Plumbaginaceae

- 🌿 ZONES 1–9, 14–24, 33–43
- ☼ FULL SUN
- ●● REGULAR TO LITTLE WATER
- ✳ ✳ ✳ FLOWERS IN SPRING; YEAR-ROUND IN MILD CLIMATES

Armeria maritima

Artemisias are valued for their interesting leaf texture and for the aromatic, silvery gray or white foliage that always enhances its surroundings—providing an admirable foil for vivid flower colors, blending subtly with soft blues, lavenders, and pinks. In height, the plants vary from a foot or so to over 4 feet tall; some are woody based, while others die back in winter.

Among the taller shrubby species, southernwood **(A. abrotanum,** Zones 3–24, 27–41) features finely cut gray-green foliage on a spreading, bushy plant 3 to 5 feet high. Common wormwood, **A. absinthium,** grows 2 to 4 feet tall, with silvery gray, finely divided leaves. **'Lambrook Silver'** is a 2-foot form with especially finely cut foliage. A related hybrid, **'Powis Castle'** (Zones 4–24, 29–34), forms a splendid lacy mound of soft, silvery gray green; it reaches 3 feet tall and 6 feet wide.

Two other shrubby species are shorter, useful for soft gray foreground accents. **A. stellerana 'Silver Brocade'** (one of several plants called dusty miller) is a dense, low-growing plant (to 1 foot tall and 2 feet wide) with beautifully felted, lobed leaves. **A. schmidtiana 'Silver Mound'** (**'Nana'**) forms a dense mound of shimmering silvery gray to 1 foot tall and wide. Its foliage tends to rot in summer in hot, humid climates.

Unlike the plants described above, **A. ludoviciana albula 'Silver King'** is deciduous, with stems that die down at the onset of frost. During the growing season, it reaches 2 to 3½ feet, with many slender, spreading branches covered in silvery white, 2-inch leaves. **'Silver Queen'** is a somewhat shorter selection with slightly larger leaves. Both spread widely by underground roots and can be seriously invasive in a border or small garden. Plant where they can colonize freely; or confine them with an 8-inch-deep barrier around the roots.

Listing continues >

ARTEMISIA

ARTEMISIA, SOUTHERNWOOD, WORMWOOD, MUGWORT
Asteraceae (Compositae)

- 🌿 ZONES 1–24, 29–45, EXCEPT AS NOTED
- ☼ FULL SUN
- ● MODERATE WATER
- ✳ FLOWERS IN LATE SUMMER

Artemisia schmidtiana 'Silver Mound'

Artemisia 'Powis Castle' and A. absinthium

The stems of white mugwort, **A. lactiflora,** also die down in winter. This is the only artemisia grown primarily for its attractive flowers rather than its foliage. Elegantly plumed spikes of small, creamy white blossoms appear in late summer atop upright, 4- to 6-foot stems clad in lobed, dark green leaves. The cultivar **'Guizho'** features handsome purple-red stems.

CULTURE. All artemisias require well-drained soil, and all but white mugwort (*A. lactiflora*) tolerate drought (white mugwort needs regular moisture during the growing season). Cut back stems of shrubby kinds fairly heavily in late winter or early spring to keep growth compact. For the two deciduous species, cut spent stems down to the basal rosette of leaves in autumn or early spring.

Propagate clump-forming artemisias by division in early spring. The tall shrubby kinds may form layers, which can be separated from the parent plant in spring. All types can be propagated by stem cuttings in spring or summer.

Effective with Alstroemeria, Anchusa azurea, Centaurea, Crambe cordifolia, Eryngium, Lychnis, Malva, Origanum, Verbascum.

ARUNCUS
GOATSBEARD
Rosaceae

- 🌿 ZONES 1–9, 14–17, 31–43
- ☀ ◑ ● FULL SUN, LIGHT SHADE, OR FULL SHADE
- ◗ ◗◗ REGULAR TO AMPLE WATER
- ✳ FLOWERS IN SUMMER

Aruncus dioicus

Well suited to woodland gardens, the goatsbeards have the look of an airy form of astilbe; their elegant, feathery plumes of tiny white or creamy flowers rise above slowly spreading clumps of finely divided leaves.

At just 8 to 12 inches tall and wide, **A. aethusifolius** is an excellent choice for the front of the border. The deep green, finely divided foliage gives the plant a delicate appearance; white flower plumes add a graceful note in summer.

A much larger species is **A. dioicus;** it forms a 4-foot-tall, shrublike mound of broad, fernlike foliage topped with a foam of white flowers in many-branched clusters to 20 inches long. The cultivar **'Kneiffii'** is only half as tall as the species, with leaves finely divided into threadlike segments. **'Child of Two Worlds'** (**'Zweiweltenkind'**, often sold as *A. sinensis)* reaches 5 feet; its branched flower clusters droop gracefully.

CULTURE. Plant goatsbeards in moist soil. Where summers are cool or mild, you can grow them in sun or shade; in hot-summer regions, they require shade throughout the day. They do not thrive in regions where summers are both hot and dry.

A. dioicus has large, deep roots that make it difficult to move once established. For the same reason, division, while possible, is difficult. The smaller *A. aethusifolius* is easier to divide (do the job in spring). Both species can be propagated by seed.

Effective with Astrantia major, Bergenia, Epimedium, Hibiscus moscheutos, Iris (Siberian), Ligularia, Lobelia.

ASCLEPIAS tuberosa
🦋 BUTTERFLY WEED
Asclepiadaceae

- 🌿 ALL ZONES
- ☀ FULL SUN
- ◗ MODERATE TO LITTLE WATER
- ✳ ✳ ✳ FLOWERS IN SUMMER

Common name notwithstanding, gardeners (and butterflies too!) count butterfly weed a desirable plant. Rugged and easy to to grow, it sends up many stems from the dormant root each spring; these are clothed in lance-shaped leaves to 4 inches long and reach 2 to 3 feet tall by the time bloom begins in summer. The many small, starlike flowers are carried in broad, flattened clusters at the stem tips. Vivid orange is the usual color, but other bright colors also occur naturally. The aptly named **Gay Butterflies** strain is a mix containing yellow, orange, and red flowers. **'Hello Yellow'** bears vibrant yellow blossoms.

CULTURE. Plant butterfly weed where you want it to grow permanently; the plants are slow to establish but long lived. Plant in well-drained soil, since too much moisture

Asclepias tuberosa, Gay Butterflies strain

around the roots, especially in winter, can lead to rot. Plants are drought tolerant but perform best with moderate watering. Because the stems emerge later in spring than those of many other plants, mark the location of your plantings or leave the old stems in place as markers.

The easiest way to increase a planting is to raise new plants from seed, but you can also take root cuttings or divide clumps in spring. For best results when dividing, dig deeply, removing as much of the root system as possible.

Effective with Gaillardia × grandiflora, Rudbeckia, Salvia, Yucca.

ASTER

ASTER, MICHAELMAS DAISY
Asteraceae (Compositae)

ZONES 1–24, 31–43, EXCEPT AS NOTED

FULL SUN, EXCEPT AS NOTED

REGULAR WATER

FLOWERS IN LATE SUMMER AND AUTUMN, EXCEPT AS NOTED

A sters bear cheerful daisy flowers in a wide variety of cool colors, on plants that range from low front-of-the-border mounds to imposing 6-footers. White wood aster, **A. divaricatus,** is a spreading plant up to 2 feet high, with nearly black stems and a generous show of small flowers in pure white aging to pink. Unlike most asters, it grows well in shade. Heath aster, **A. ericoides,** reaches 3 feet high; it has narrow leaves and a strong horizontal branching pattern. Its flower heads are small but profuse, in colors including white, pink, and blue. **A. e. 'Monte Cassino' (A. pringlei)** produces tall stems—up to 5 feet—set with short branches bearing clouds of starry white, ¾-inch blossoms. It's an especially good cut flower.

The hybrid **A. × frikartii** has produced excellent selections with exceptionally long flowering seasons. **'Mönch'** and **'Wonder of Stafa'** are bushy plants in the 3-foot range, both bearing clear lavender blue blossoms; bloom time runs from early summer to fall in most areas, almost all year in mild-winter areas (with regular deadheading). These plants may be short lived.

Smooth aster, **A. laevis** (Zones 1–24, 31–45), grows 3½ feet tall; its smooth foliage is mildew free. The selection **'Bluebird'** bears charming clusters of 1-inch violet blue flowers on arching stems.

Cultivars of calico aster, **A. lateriflorus** (Zones 1–24, 31–45), are also attractive and easy to grow. **'Horizontalis'** is a bushy, mounding 2½-footer with spreading branches bearing small white flowers with reddish centers; the bloom colors are echoed by the reddish fall tint of the tiny leaves. **'Prince'** is even darker in foliage, with flowers centered in a deeper red.

An old-fashioned classic fall bloomer is New England aster, **A. novae-angliae.** It rises to 6 feet or more in its basic form, bearing great, airy sprays of violet blue flowers and stems clothed in grayish green, hairy leaves. Several pink and nearly red selections are available, including 3- to 4-foot-tall **'Alma Potschke'** (bright rose) and 3-foot **'Honeysong Pink'** (pink). A compact form, **'Purple Dome',** forms a 1½- to 2-foot mound covered in deep blue flowers.

Another old favorite is **A. novi-belgii**—New York aster, also known as Michaelmas daisy. Like New England aster, it blooms primarily in violet blue, but it grows only 3 to 4 feet high and has smooth foliage. Its hundreds of cultivars range in height from about 1 foot to over 4 feet. A few choice selections are foot-tall **'Professor Anton Kippenburg',** with semidouble lavender blue blossoms; 2- to 3-foot **'Winston Churchill',** sporting handsome red flowers; and **'Climax',** a 5- to 6-foot giant bearing outstanding medium blue flowers that measure 2 to 3 inches across.

CULTURE. Asters are undemanding plants, needing only a sunny location (except for white wood aster, **A. divaricatus,** which prefers shade) and reasonably good, well-drained soil. New York aster (**A. novi-belgii**) is particularly susceptible to powdery mildew; keeping it well watered helps minimize this problem. Most of the taller asters flop over by flowering time. To deal with this problem, either stake them early in the

TOP: *Aster × frikartii* 'Wonder of Stafa'
BOTTOM: *Aster novae-angliae* 'Purple Dome'

season or cut back the stems by about a third in early summer (early to mid-June) to make them more compact (plants cut back in this way may bloom a bit later than unpruned plants). While most asters don't need winter protection, the cultivars of A. × frikartii may benefit from a blanket of evergreen boughs when growing in the colder zones.

Especially vigorous asters, notably New England and New York asters (*A. novae-angliae* and *A. novi-belgii*), spread rapidly and can become invasive. Dig and divide the roots at least every other year in spring, replanting only the strong divisions from the clump's perimeter. Other kinds of asters need dividing only when vigor diminishes and the center of the clump becomes bare and woody. Asters can also be propagated by stem cuttings taken in summer.

Effective with Anthemis tinctoria, Centranthus ruber, Chrysanthemum parthenium, Cimicifuga, Eupatorium, Helenium, Helianthus, Physostegia virginiana.

Aster lateriflorus 'Prince'

ASTILBE
🌿 🦌 ASTILBE, FALSE SPIRAEA, MEADOWSWEET
Saxifragaceae

- 🌱 ZONES 1–7, 14–17, 32–45 (SEE BELOW)
- ☼ LIGHT SHADE, EXCEPT AS NOTED
- 💧 REGULAR WATER
- ✳ ✳ ✳ ✳ FLOWERS IN LATE SPRING, SUMMER

Astilbe's airy, plumelike flower clusters are an invaluable addition to summer borders and woodland gardens. Either upright or gracefully arching, the floral plumes range from 6 inches to 3 feet or taller; they are carried above clumps of handsome, fernlike green to bronze leaves. By selecting varieties with staggered bloom times, you can enjoy flowers from late spring or early summer right through to summer's end.

Most astilbes sold in nurseries are listed as **A. × *arendsii*,** though some have been reclassified into other species. **'Deutschland'** flowers early in the season, bearing dense 1½-foot plumes of white flowers; bronzy-foliaged **'Fanal'** also blooms quite early, carrying its blood red flowers on 1½- to 2½-foot stems. Blooming in mid- to late summer is **A. × *thunbergii* 'Ostrich Plume'**, with drooping pink flower clusters on 3- to 3½-foot stems.

Astilbe × arendsii 'Fanal'

A. chinensis is a late-summer bloomer that tolerates somewhat drier soils than other astilbes. One of its well-known cultivars is **'Pumila'**, with foot-tall, rosy lilac flower spikes held stiffly upright over spreading mats of foliage. Pink-flowered **'Finale'**, to 20 inches tall, is one of the latest to bloom. Another late-blooming selection is **A. c. taquetii 'Superba' (A. taquetii 'Superba')**, which grows 4 to 5 feet tall and has bright pinkish purple flowers.

A. simplicifolia 'Sprite', an excellent front-of-the-border plant, has bronze-tinted foliage and abundant shell pink, drooping, 1-foot spires. These summer blooms are followed by long-lasting, attractive rust-colored seed heads.

CULTURE. Grow astilbes in moist but not saturated soil enriched with plenty of organic matter. They thrive in light shade, though they can withstand full sun in cool-summer climates if given plenty of moisture. Tall kinds are self-supporting and require no staking. When bloom production noticeably declines (usually after 3 to 5 years), it's time to divide the clumps; do the job in early spring. Survival in the coldest zones (41, 43, 45) depends on good snow cover.

Effective with Aconitum, Astrantia major, Chelone, Filipendula, Hibiscus moscheutos, Hosta, Ligularia, Trollius.

Astilbe × thunbergii 'Ostrich Plume'

A charming plant for a woodland garden or moist shaded border, astrantia bears intricately formed flowers that somewhat resemble pincushions only an inch or so wide: each consists of a dome of tightly packed florets within a collar of papery bracts (modified leaves). These delicate flowers appear on branching, 2- to 3-foot stems above attractive deeply divided foliage. **'Alba'** bears white flowers; **'Rose Symphony'** (**'Rosensymphonie'**) has rosy pink flowers with a silvery collar of bracts. Belonging to the subspecies ***A. m. involucrata,*** **'Shaggy'** (also known as **'Margery Fish'**) features extra-long white bracts tipped with green.

CULTURE. Astrantia requires evenly moist soil and, in most climates, grows best in partial shade. In cool-summer regions, it will take full sun if given adequate moisture. To keep the flowers coming through summer, deadhead plants consistently, removing spent blossoms to lateral buds. Astrantia often reseeds; keep some seedlings to increase your planting. If growing happily, the plants also spread to form clumps that can be divided in spring or fall.

Effective with Aruncus, Astilbe, Campanula, Cimicifuga, Geranium.

P roviding a welcome splash of bright color in spring, basket-of-gold forms a spreading mound (9 to 12 inches high and 1½ feet wide) of narrow, lance-shaped gray-green leaves 2 to 5 inches long. Individual flowers are small, but they're grouped in many rounded 1-inch clusters that cover the plant with color. Basket-of-gold is a traditional component of large-scale rock gardens; it also looks good planted at the front of a sunny border or spilling over a wall.

In addition to the basic bright yellow form, you can choose **'Citrina'** (**'Lutea'**), with pale yellow flowers; **'Compacta'**, which forms a smaller, tighter-growing clump; **'Silver Queen'**, a compact grower with pale yellow blooms; and **'Dudley Neville Variegated'**, an apricot-flowered form with leaves handsomely edged in creamy white.

CULTURE. Plant in a sunny location, in average well-drained soil. If soil is too rich, basket-of-gold tends to become sprawling and untidy. After the flowers finish, shear plants back by about a third; this diverts energy from seed production (preventing excess seedlings) and helps keep the plant more compact. In hot, humid areas, basket-of-gold is short-lived. Gardeners in these areas often treat it as a biennial, setting out new plants in fall for springtime bloom, then removing them once the show is over.

You can propagate basket-of-gold by division in fall or by stem cuttings taken in spring or summer.

Effective with Euphorbia, Geum, Iberis sempervirens, Iris (bearded), Papaver orientale, Phlox subulata.

R eliable, long-lived, large-scale perennials native to the eastern and midwestern United States, the false indigos provide spires of sweet pea–shaped flowers held above clumps of bluish green, cloverlike foliage. Inflated, dark brown to black seedpods add interest in summer and fall. Plants emerge early in spring and grow quickly to their full size.

Baptisia australis

Listing continues >

ASTRANTIA major
🌿 ASTRANTIA, MASTERWORT
Apiaceae (Umbelliferae)
- 🌿 ZONES 3–9, 14–24, 31–41
- ◐ LIGHT SHADE, EXCEPT AS NOTED
- ● REGULAR WATER
- ✳ ✳ ✳ FLOWERS IN SUMMER

Astrantia major 'Rose Symphony'

AURINIA saxatilis
(Alyssum saxatile)
BASKET-OF-GOLD
Brassicaceae (Cruciferae)
- 🌿 ZONES 1–24, 32–43
- ☼ FULL SUN
- ◒ MODERATE WATER
- ✳ ✳ FLOWERS IN SPRING

Aurinia saxatilis 'Dudley Neville Variegated'

BAPTISIA ✓
🌿 FALSE INDIGO
Fabaceae (Leguminosae)
- 🌿 ZONES 1–24, 28–43
- ☼ FULL SUN
- ◒ MODERATE WATER
- ✳ ✳ ✳ FLOWERS IN LATE SPRING, EARLY SUMMER

Baptisia alba

White false indigo, **B. alba,** grows 2 to 3 feet tall and spreads to about 3 feet wide. Borne in foot-long spikes, its white blossoms (sometimes blotched with purple) contrast well with the charcoal gray stems. The more widely grown blue false indigo, **B. australis,** is a larger plant, reaching 3 to 6 feet tall and 4 feet wide. The flowers are deep indigo blue. **'Purple Smoke'**, a hybrid between *B. alba* and *B. australis,* grows 4½ feet tall and has violet flowers with dark purple centers.

CULTURE. False indigos are easy to grow, needing only moderately fertile, nonalkaline soil. Their deep taproots make them drought tolerant once established. Clumps gradually increase in size but do not require division, and established plants resent transplanting. To start more plants, sow seed or transplant young volunteer seedlings.

Effective with Centranthus ruber, Coreopsis, Digitalis, Oenothera, Paeonia.

BERGENIA ✓
BERGENIA
Saxifragaceae

- ✄ ZONES 1–9, 12–24, 30–45, EXCEPT AS NOTED
- ☽● LIGHT TO FULL SHADE, EXCEPT AS NOTED
- ●◐ REGULAR TO MODERATE WATER
- ❋ ❋ ❋ ❋ FLOWERS IN WINTER, EARLY SPRING

Even if bergenias never flowered, they'd be worth planting for their handsome foliage alone. Growing in informal rosettes 1 to 1½ feet high, the substantial, oval to nearly round leaves are leathery and deeply veined; they grow up to a foot long and are carried on equally long leafstalks. They often take on purple tints in cold weather. Graceful clusters of small flowers appear on thick, leafless, 1- to 1½-foot stalks.

B. ciliata is the most elegant species, though it's less hardy than the rest (Zones 4–9, 14–24, 29–34, 39). Its lustrous light green leaves are covered with short, silky hairs; they are damaged by frosts and die down completely in the colder parts of the range. The spring flowers are light pink or white.

Heartleaf bergenia, **B. cordifolia,** has glossy, wavy-edged leaves; its rose or lilac springtime flowers are partially hidden by the foliage. Winter-blooming bergenia, **B. crassifolia,** bears its dense clusters of rose, lilac, or purple flowers any time from midwinter to early spring, depending on climate. The blossoms rise above clumps of glossy, rubbery leaves.

Named hybrid bergenias are increasingly available from specialty nurseries. Choices include **'Abendglut' ('Evening Glow')**, a slighter shorter selection with dark red blooms and leaves that turn dark red in cold weather; **'Baby Doll'**, which reaches about 1 foot tall and has soft pink flowers; **'Bressingham White'**; **'Bressingham Ruby'**; and **'Bressingham Salmon'**.

CULTURE. Though bergenias tolerate dry shade and poor soil, their foliage and flowers are much more attractive when the plants are given good soil and regular watering. In mild- and warm-summer areas, they prefer filtered sun to full shade; where summers are cool, they can also take full sun. Divide crowded clumps and replant vigorous divisions in late winter or early spring.

Effective with Anemone × hybrida, Aruncus, Brunnera macrophylla, Dicentra, ferns, Epimedium, Filipendula, Polygonatum.

Bergenia 'Bressingham Salmon'

BOLTONIA
BOLTONIA
Asteraceae (Compositae)

- ✄ ZONES 1-24, 28-45
- ☼ FULL SUN
- ●◐ REGULAR TO MODERATE WATER
- ❋ ❋ ❋ FLOWERS IN LATE SUMMER, AUTUMN

Forming a big, billowy mass of daisylike flowers with golden centers, boltonia is a showy background plant for the late-season garden. The wild species grows up to 7 feet high; at bloom time, its abundance of ¾-inch white, lilac, or pink daisies makes it top-heavy. The selection **'Snowbank'** is more compact (to 5 feet tall and 4 feet wide), forming an upright mound of narrow, bluish green leaves; blooming plants are nearly hidden by white, 1-inch flowers. **'Pink Beauty'** is similar in size, but it has a more fine-textured appearance and bears lilac pink flowers. Both of these selected forms are usually self-supporting if grown in full sun, but they may require staking in shade. A dwarf boltonia, **B. latisquama** 'Nana', grows only 2 feet tall; it has greener, broader leaves than *B. asteroides* and bears pale lilac flowers.

CULTURE. Boltonia grows best in full sun and reasonably good, moist soil, but it will tolerate drier conditions. Clumps spread, but they aren't invasive; divide them in early spring every 3 to 4 years.

Effective with Crambe cordifolia, Eupatorium, ornamental grasses, Helianthus, Papaver orientale, Perovskia, Solidago.

Boltonia asteroides 'Pink Beauty'

I n early spring, airy sprays of ¼-inch, azure blue flowers— like little forget-me-nots— rise above clumps of lush, dark green, heart-shaped leaves to 4 inches wide and 6 inches long. As the season progresses, the leaves become larger and the stems grow taller, reaching 1½ to 2 feet by the time flowering is over. The foliage maintains its good looks for the rest of the growing season, making brunnera a good choice for a small-scale ground cover near a shady pool or stream, under high-branching shrubs, or naturalized in a woodland. Several selections offer variegated foliage; among these is **'Variegata'**, with elegant creamy white bands along the leaf margins.

CULTURE. Brunnera looks best when grown in well-drained, moisture-retentive soil. It is at home anywhere in partial shade; where summers are cool, you can also plant it in sun. Keep in mind, however, that variegated forms always require shade to keep their leaves from scorching. Brunnera self-sows freely once established; it can also be propagated by root cuttings taken in late winter.

Brunnera macrophylla 'Variegata'

Effective with Amsonia tabernaemontana, Bergenia, Corydalis, Doronicum, Epimedium, ferns, Pulmonaria, Thalictrum.

BRUNNERA macrophylla
BRUNNERA, SIBERIAN BUGLOSS, PERENNIAL FORGET-ME-NOT
Boraginaceae

- ZONES 1–24, 31–45
- LIGHT SHADE, EXCEPT AS NOTED
- REGULAR WATER
- FLOWERS IN SPRING

Brunnera macrophylla

A vast and varied group, campanulas range in form from stately back-of-border plants to low, spreading or compact mounds suitable for rock gardens, small-scale ground covers, or the front of the border. The five-petaled flowers are typically bell shaped, but some kinds have upward-facing cup-shaped blossoms, while others bear star-shaped blooms. Canterbury bells *(C. medium)*, the popular campanula of cottage gardens, is a biennial: it flowers the second year from seed, then dies. The perennial campanulas discussed here are divided into two groups— those with upright flowering stems and those that grow as spreading mounds. In the descriptions that follow, the second category is represented only by Dalmatian and Serbian bellflowers, *C. portenschlagiana* and *C. poscharskyana.*

At about 1 foot tall, tussock bellflower, **C. carpatica**, is the shortest of the upright campanulas. Wiry, branching stems rise from low clumps of narrow bright green leaves in late spring, bearing cup-shaped flowers in white and various blue shades; bloom continues into summer if the spent flowers are removed. **'White Clips'** and **'Blue Clips'** are reliable selections. Somewhat taller (to 1 to 2 feet or more) is summer-blooming clustered bellflower, **C. glomerata.** Its dense clusters of flaring bell-shaped blooms are carried on erect stems above clumps of broadly lance-shaped leaves. Blue violet is the typical blossom color, but named selections vary in color (and in plant

CAMPANULA
CAMPANULA, BELLFLOWER
Campanulaceae (Lobeliaceae)

- ZONES 1–9, 14–24, 31–45, EXCEPT AS NOTED
- FULL SUN, EXCEPT AS NOTED
- REGULAR TO MODERATE WATER
- FLOWERS IN SPRING, SUMMER

Campanula portenschlagiana

Campanula punctata

height as well). **'Crown of Snow'** is a 1½- to 2-foot plant with white flowers; **'Superba'** glows with intense violet flowers on stems that may reach 2½ feet; violet purple **'Joan Elliott'** grows 1½ feet tall.

Graceful peach-leafed bluebell, **_C. persicifolia_,** has leafy, 2- to 3-foot stems above low clumps of narrow, 4- to 8-inch-long leaves. In summer, each stem bears loose spires of outward-facing, cupped bells in blue, pink, or white. Named selections include **'Telham Beauty',** with 3-inch blue blossoms; double-flowered **'White Pearl';** and **'Blue Gardenia',** also with double blooms.

Spotted bellflower, **_C. punctata_,** is a mounding plant with arching stems to 2 feet high and heart-shaped, 3- to 5-inch basal leaves. It blooms in summer, producing nodding, elongated bells in white, lilac, or pink. Its cultivar **'Cherry Bells'** has reddish flowers edged in white; **'Elizabeth Rose'** features rosy purple flowers with throats spotted in white and purple.

Tallest of the widely grown bellflowers is **_C. lactiflora_** (Zones 3–9, 14–24, 31–34, 39). Its upright stems, clothed with 3-inch, pointed leaves, top out in the 3- to 5-foot range. Large conical clusters of open, starry bells bloom in summer. Named selections include pale pink, 3- to 4-foot-high **'Loddon Anna';** 3-foot-tall, blue-violet **'Prichard's Variety';** and the dwarf **'Pouffe',** which forms a mound of pale blue flowers just over 1 foot tall.

Forming a low, leafy mound just 6 inches tall, easy-to-grow Dalmatian bellflower, **_C. portenschlagiana_** (Zones 2–9, 14–24, 31–41), produces bell- to cup-shaped, purplish blue flowers from late spring through summer. The more aggressive Serbian bellflower, **_C. poscharskyana_,** has clumps of heart-shaped leaves and spreads by rooting runners to form a solid foliage carpet. Starlike blooms in soft blue or white appear along semiupright, foot-tall stems in spring to early summer.

CULTURE. Plant campanulas in well-drained soil enriched with compost. Most need regular watering for good performance, though Dalmatian and Serbian bellflowers (_C. portenschlagiana_ and _C. poscharskyana_) are somewhat drought tolerant. In cool- and mild-summer regions, campanulas grow well in full sun; in warmer areas, give them partial shade. Tall kinds require staking. To encourage repeat bloom, remove spent flowers. Slugs and snails can be serious pests.

Dig and divide crowded clumps in early spring. Plants can also be propagated by stem cuttings or, for species and some cultivars, by seed.

Effective with Astrantia major, Diascia, Dictamnus albus, Geum, Linaria purpurea, Platycodon grandiflorus, Veronica.

CANNA
CANNA LILY, INDIAN SHOT
Cannaceae

- ZONES 6–9, 12–31, WARMER PARTS OF 32; OR DIG AND STORE OVER WINTER
- ☼ FULL SUN
- ◖ AMPLE WATER
- ✳ ✳ ✳ ✳ ✳ FLOWERS IN SUMMER, AUTUMN

Bringing a bold, tropical accent to garden borders and containers, cannas grow 2 to 7 feet tall, flaunting spikes of big, showy, irregularly shaped flowers and large leaves that may be rich green, bronzy red, or variegated. Numerous varieties (most are hybrids between several species) are available. Just three of the many choices are **'Pretoria' ('Bengal Tiger')**, a 6-footer with dramatic green-and-yellow striped leaves and bright orange flowers; and the lower-growing **'Pfitzer Chinese Coral'** and **'Pfitzer Crimson Beauty'**, both just 2½ to 3 feet tall.

CULTURE. Cannas require moist soil enriched with compost or manure. They thrive in hot, bright locations. Cut stems to the ground as they finish flowering; new stems will continue to appear throughout summer and early fall. Every 3 or 4 years, divide crowded clumps in early spring. Dig the rhizomes and cut them apart; let the cuts heal (this takes about 24 hours), then replant, covering with 2 to 4 inches of soil.

In the colder parts of their range, protect cannas with a 6-inch layer of mulch over winter. In zones beyond their hardiness limit, cut off the stalks and dig the rhizomes after the first frosts have killed the leaves. Let rhizomes dry in a warm place for a few days; then place in a box, cover with dry vermiculite or peat moss, and store in a frost-free location over winter. In spring, plant the rhizomes indoors in pots about 4 weeks before the expected last-frost date; transplant to the garden after the weather has warmed.

Effective with ornamental grasses, Helianthus, Hemerocallis, Verbena bonariensis.

Canna

Catananche caerulea

Rising above gray-green, grassy foliage, the thin, 2-foot stems of cupid's dart carry 2-inch daisies clasped in strawlike, shining bracts (modified leaves). The blossoms are beautiful in fresh and dried arragements; they're typically blue with a darker center, but named selections include deep blue-violet **'Major'** and white **'Alba'.** Because cupid's dart is rather wispy, it looks best set out in groups of five or more.

CULTURE. Give cupid's dart well-drained soil of average fertility. It's quite drought tolerant and performs well with moderate water; it will not survive if the soil is kept too moist. It's easy to grow from seed and will bloom the first year from seed sown in March or April.

Cupid's dart is rather short lived; you can divide clumps to rejuvenate them or propagate from root cuttings taken in late winter. Volunteer seedlings usually provide plenty of replacement plants.

Effective with Achillea, Anthemis tinctoria, Oenothera, Veronica.

CATANANCHE caerulea
🌿 ✕ CUPID'S DART
Asteraceae (Compositae)
- ✂ ALL ZONES
- ☼ FULL SUN
- ◖ MODERATE WATER
- ✴ ✴ FLOWERS IN SUMMER, EARLY AUTUMN

The knapweeds are hardy, easy-to-grow plants for the border or wild garden. The best-known species are annuals such as bachelor's button *(C. cyanus)* and sweet sultan *(C. moschata)*; perennial members of the genus include kinds grown primarily for flowers as well as sorts valued for their downy gray foliage.

The showy-flowered perennials include two species hardy in Zones 1–9, 14–24, 29–43. Persian cornflower **(C. dealbata,** usually offered in the cultivar **'Steenbergii')** bears thistlelike, white-centered purple flower heads on slender, 2-foot stems. Foliage grows in spreading clumps of lobed, 8- to 12-inch-long leaves that are soft green on the upper surfaces, gray green beneath. **C. hypoleuca 'John Coutts'** (sometimes listed as a variety of *C. dealbata*) is more compact, with deep rose pink flowers.

C. cineraria, one of a number of plants called dusty miller, is grown for its clumps of lobed, velvety white leaves. Perennial only in Zones 8–30, it is popular as an annual in regions beyond its hardiness range. Though its foliage is the main attraction, it also bears yellow blooms in summer.

CULTURE. Plants grow vigorously in moderately fertile, well-drained soil. For best performance, add lime to acid soils. Clumps spread easily and may need dividing every 3 to 4 years to renew growth and keep plantings in bounds. Persian cornflower *(C. dealbata)* usually requires staking.

Effective with Achillea, Artemisia, Coreopsis verticillata, Salvia.

CENTAUREA
🌿 ✕ KNAPWEED, PERSIAN CORNFLOWER
Asteraceae (Compositae)
- ✂ ZONES VARY
- ☼ FULL SUN
- ◖ MODERATE WATER
- ✴ ✴ ✴ FLOWERS IN SUMMER

Centaurea hypoleuca 'John Coutts'

CENTRANTHUS ruber
🌿 🐝 JUPITER'S BEARD,
RED VALERIAN
Valerianaceae

- 🌡 ZONES 1–9, 12–24, 28–43
- ☀ ◑ FULL SUN OR LIGHT SHADE
- 💧 MODERATE TO LITTLE WATER
- ❄ ✳ ❅ FLOWERS IN SPRING, SUMMER

Centranthus ruber 'Albus'

Trouble-free Jupiter's beard has naturalized in the far western states and in parts of England and Europe. Its upright stems, clothed in 4-inch-long, bluish green leaves, form bushy clumps to about 3 feet high; tiny carmine to rosy pink flowers appear in elongated, fluffy clusters at the stem ends. **'Albus'** produces clean white flowers that combine well with many other perennials.

CULTURE. Though Jupiter's beard will grow in poor, dry soils, it looks best if given reasonably good, well-drained soil and moderate watering. Cut off spent flower stems to shape plants, encourage repeat flowering, and prevent excessive self-seeding. You can start Jupiter's beard from seed; it will bloom the first year, with the seedlings usually producing flowers in reddish hues as well as white. To propagate a selected color, take basal cuttings during spring and summer; or divide plants in spring.

Effective with Aster, Baptisia, Chrysanthemum × superbum, C. parthenium, Iris (bearded), Malva.

CERATOSTIGMA plumbaginoides
🐝 DWARF PLUMBAGO,
LEADWORT
Plumbaginaceae

- 🌡 ZONES 2–10, 14–24, 29–41
- ☀ ◑ FULL SUN OR LIGHT SHADE
- 💧 MODERATE WATER
- ✳ FLOWERS IN SUMMER, EARLY AUTUMN

Ceratostigma plumbaginoides

Dwarf plumbago adorns the garden with phloxlike flowers of an intense blue. Bloom is heaviest and longest lasting where the growing season is long. The oval, 3-inch leaves are arrayed along wiry, 6- to 12-inch stems; they turn from bronzy green to reddish with the first frost. Clumps spread by underground stems to make an effective small-scale ground cover, and the plants are also attractive at the front of the border and in beds beneath shrubs and trees.

Dwarf plumbago is semievergreen in the mildest-winter areas; where winters are colder, it dies back. It leafs out later in spring than most deciduous perennials, making it a good choice for overplanting spring-blooming bulbs such as crocus and daffodil.

CULTURE. Though dwarf plumbago grows well in a range of soils (from clay to sandy types), it spreads fastest in light soils. Cut old stems to the ground each year before new growth begins in spring. To keep clumps in bounds or rejuvenate sparse growth, dig and replant rooted divisions at the start of the growing season.

Effective with Chrysanthemum × morifolium, Epilobium, ornamental grasses, Oenothera, Penstemon, Sedum, Stachys byzantina.

CHELONE
🌿 🐝 TURTLEHEAD
Scrophulariaceae

- 🌡 ZONES 3–9, 14–17, 28–43
- ☀ ◑ FULL SUN OR LIGHT SHADE
- 💧 💧💧 REGULAR TO AMPLE WATER
- ❄ ✳ ❅ FLOWERS IN LATE SUMMER, AUTUMN

These natives of the southeastern United States bear inch-long, puffy, two-lipped flowers of a vaguely reptilian appearance—hence the common name "turtlehead." From spring into summer, plants are clumps of good-looking, glossy foliage; then, as bloom time approaches, leafy, branching stems rise 2 to 3½ feet, bearing the blossoms in branching spikes. *C. lyonii,* the most widely available species, produces bright pink flowers; it needs partial shade in hot-summer regions. More tolerant of heat and sun is rosy purple *C. obliqua.* Its cultivar **'Alba'** has white flowers; **'Bethelli'** is more floriferous than the species, with blooms of a deeper rose. *C. glabra* has white flowers tinged with rose.

Chelone obliqua

CULTURE. Grow turtleheads in naturally damp places, such as bog gardens or stream banks. They also succeed in borders if given soil enriched with organic matter and watered frequently. When clumps become crowded, divide them in spring; or increase your supply of plants by stem cuttings taken in spring or summer.

Effective with Aconitum, Anemone × hybrida, Astilbe, Cimicifuga, Monarda, Tradescantia, Tricyrtis.

While the name "chrysanthemum" is often associated with fall-blooming mums, the genus also includes favorite spring- and summer-flowering daisies, among them the brightly colored painted daisy, tender marguerite, feverfew, and the perennially popular Shasta daisy. Taxonomists have split *Chrysanthemum* into a number of new genera—and, in certain cases, changed their minds and returned some species to the original genus. In the following descriptions, the former, often more familiar names are given first, followed by the new names in parentheses.

Painted daisy, **C. coccineum (Tanacetum coccineum,** once known as **Pyrethrum roseum),** grows in Zones 2–24, 33–41. It forms a bushy, 2- to 3-foot plant with very finely divided, bright green leaves. The long-stemmed blooms are single or double, in shades of pink as well as red and white. Flowering starts in midspring where winters are mild, in late spring in colder regions. If you cut the stems to ground level after flowering, plants will sometimes bloom again in late summer. Cultivars include dark red **'James Kelway'** and the double-flowered **Robinson's Hybrids,** available in mixed colors.

CULTURE. Painted daisy grows best where summers are warm to hot, but it does not tolerate high humidity. Divide clumps or sow seeds in spring (seedlings flower in their second year).

Effective with Chrysanthemum × superbum, Coreopsis verticillata, Delphinium, Nepeta.

Marguerite, **C. frutescens (Argyranthemum frutescens),** is a short-lived shrubby perennial in Zones 14–24, 26, 28; elsewhere, it's grown as an annual. It is an excellent container plant in any region. Marguerite is a fast grower; a young plant can form a dense, 4- by 4-foot mound of coarsely cut green leaves in just a few months. In summer, plants are thickly dotted with 2½-inch flowers. The typical form has single white blossoms with yellow centers, but named selections offer variations; among these are **'Snow White',** with double flowers, and **'White Lady'** and **'Pink Lady',** both with buttonlike flower heads.

CULTURE. Plant marguerite in loose-textured, well-drained soil in full sun. Water regularly. Cut plants back lightly and frequently to maintain bushiness, encourage rebloom, and limit size. Since individual plants last just a few years, start replacements from stem cuttings taken in spring or summer.

Effective with Digitalis, Hemerocallis, Stachys byzantina.

Shasta daisy, **C. × superbum (C. maximum, Leucanthemum maximum)** succeeds in Zones 1–24, 26 (northern portion), 28–43. A charming and versatile summer-flowering perennial for the border, it forms robust clumps of linear, toothed leaves from which rise leafy flower stalks, each bearing one to several showy white

CHRYSANTHEMUM

CHRYSANTHEMUM, PAINTED DAISY, MARGUERITE, SHASTA DAISY, FEVERFEW
Asteraceae (Compositae)

- ZONES VARY
- FULL SUN, EXCEPT AS NOTED
- REGULAR WATER, EXCEPT AS NOTED
- FLOWERS IN SPRING, SUMMER, AUTUMN

TOP: *Chrysanthemum coccineum*
BOTTOM: *Chrysanthemum × superbum*

daisies. The original forms featured 3- to 4-inch flowers with big yellow centers on 2- to 4-foot stems; **'Alaska', 'Polaris',** and **'Tinkerbell'** are good examples, as is the more recently introduced **'Becky',** which grows exceptionally well in hot, humid regions. **'Esther Read'** is a widely grown long-blooming cultivar with double white flowers on 2-foot stems. Dwarf forms include 8- to 12-inch **'Little Miss Muffet'** and 15- to 18-inch **'Snowcap'.**

CULTURE. Shasta daisies thrive in fairly rich, moist soil. They prefer sun but do well in partial shade in hot-summer climates; the double-flowered kinds hold up better in very light shade. Deadhead to keep the flowers coming. In the coldest zones, mulch around the plants for winter, taking care not to smother the foliage. Clumps increase quickly and usually need division every other year or so. Divide in early spring (or in fall, in mild-winter areas). Shasta daisies are easy to grow from seed; catalogs offer many strains, including some that bloom the first year.

Effective with Agapanthus, Amsonia tabernaemontana, Centranthus ruber, Chrysanthemum coccineum, Delphinium, Monarda, Paeonia, Veronica.

Chrysanthemum × morifolium 'Debonair'

The florists' chrysanthemum, ***C. × morifolium* (Dendranthema × grandiflorum)**, suitable for Zones 2–24, 26 (northern portion), 28–41, is the mainstay of the autumn perennial flower show—both in the garden and in containers. Also known simply as "garden mums," these plants are available in an incredible array of flower forms, flower colors, and growth habits. Popular among home gardeners are types with single, semi-double, and double flowers, in a basic daisy shape or a pompom, shaggy, or quilled form. For general garden display, the lower-growing kinds (usually under 1½ feet tall) with smaller flowers and a bushy, compact habit are best. Large-flowered exhibition types are often rangy and require staking, even with frequent pinching to control growth. It's also important to consider your climate when choosing mums. The shorter the growing season (within the overall hardiness range), the more important it is to select early-flowering types, since fall frosts will destroy late bloomers before the flowers have a chance to open.

CULTURE. Plant mums in good, well-drained garden soil improved with organic matter and a complete fertilizer. In hot climates, provide shade from afternoon sun. Set out young plants in early spring. Water deeply as needed to keep soil moist but not saturated: too little water leads to woody stems and loss of lower leaves, while overwatering causes leaves to yellow, then blacken and drop. All but the lowest-growing mums (the "cushion" type) should be pinched back several times during the growing season. As soon as a stem reaches 5 inches long, nip out the tip to force branching and create a dense, leafy plant. In cold-winter regions, stop pinching in early summer; in less severe climates (where lows seldom dip below 0°F/–18°C), continue pinching into August. After flowering has finished, cut down stems to about 8 inches; in cold regions, use the cut stems as a mulch over the plants. When growth begins the next year, cut the remainder of the stems to the ground. Clumps will need dividing about every other year. Do the job in early spring, replanting small, single-stem divisions taken from the outside of the clump and discarding the woody center.

Effective with Ceratostigma plumbaginoides, ornamental grasses, Sedum.

Chrysanthemum × morifolium, mixed

Feverfew, ***C. parthenium* (Tanacetum parthenium,** Zones 1–24, 28–45), is an old-fashioned favorite that makes a useful filler in the perennial border and provides excellent cut flowers. Clumps of bright green, somewhat feathery leaves with a pungent, peppery scent send up 2- to 3-foot stems in summer; these produce clusters of single white daisies less than an inch across. **'Aureum'** grows 8 to 12 inches tall and has chartreuse foliage; **'Snowball'** reaches 1 to 2 feet and bears double flowers.

CULTURE. Plant this adaptable perennial in full sun in well-drained, average soil. It isn't long lived, but an ample supply of volunteer seedlings usually appears. You can also propagate feverfew by dividing the clumps in spring or by sowing seeds in spring for bloom by midsummer.

Effective with Aster, Centranthus ruber, Delphinium, Eryngium.

Listed in catalogs as cultivars of **C. × rubellum** or **Dendranthema × zawadskii** are two other pretty chrysanthemum relatives with finely cut leaves on spreading, 2-foot-tall plants; they succeed in Zones 1–24, 28–43. Their single, 2- to 3-inch-wide daisy flowers appear over a long season, beginning earlier than garden mums and continuing into fall. **'Clara Curtis'** has bright pink flowers; **'Mary Stoker'** blooms in an unusual soft yellow touched with apricot.

CULTURE. Give plants full sun and moderate water. When clumps become crowded (usually every other year), divide them in spring.

Effective with Dianthus, Hemerocallis, Veronica.

Chrysanthemum parthenium 'Snowball'

The various bugbanes are slender, tall plants that bring an airy, delicate texture to woodland gardens or borders. Clumps of coarsely fernlike, dark green leaves may reach 2½ feet; slim, branching stems that terminate in spikes of small bristly flowers rise from the foliage mounds. One of the tallest is North American black snakeroot, **C. racemosa,** which easily reaches 6 feet when in bloom—in midsummer in southern regions, in late summer or early fall farther north. Its white flower spikes are erect. The floral plumes of Kamchatka bugbane, **C. simplex,** in contrast, are arching; they appear in autumn on 4-foot stems. **C. s. 'White Pearl'** has especially large, dense spikes of flowers.

Another fall bloomer is **C. ramosa 'Atropurpurea'**, which bears its blooms on 4- to 6-foot stems held above dark reddish purple foliage. **'Brunette'** grows 3 to 4 feet tall with even more richly colored foliage.

CULTURE. Where summers are cool or mild, bugbanes can be planted in full sun or in partial shade; in hot areas, they require some shade (as at the edge of a woodland, for example). Plant in organically enriched soil; provide regular water. Plants seldom need division, but if you want to divide to increase your planting, do so in early spring.

Effective with Aconitum, Aster, Astrantia major, Chelone, ferns, Ligularia, Monarda, Phlox paniculata, Thalictrum.

CIMICIFUGA ✓
BUGBANE, SNAKEROOT
Ranunculaceae
- ✎ ZONES 1–7, 17, 32–45
- ☀ ◑ FULL SUN OR LIGHT SHADE
- ● REGULAR WATER
- ✳ FLOWERS IN SUMMER, AUTUMN

Cimicifuga racemosa

Coreopsis brightens the garden with sunny yellow daisies over a long season, on plants ranging from a few inches to several feet in height. The choices described here are native to the southern and eastern United States.

At only 6 inches tall, **C. auriculata 'Nana'** (Zones 1–24, 26–45) is the shortest of the group, useful as an edging at the front of a border. Rising above a mat of 2- to 5-inch-long leaves, its flower stems bear vivid orange-yellow flower heads from spring to early fall. **C. grandiflora** (Zones 1–24, 26, 28–43) includes several excellent selections that bloom from late spring through summer. **'Early Sunrise'** is a 1½- to 2-footer bearing semidouble bright yellow, 2-inch-wide flowers; **'Sunray'** is similar in height but has double blooms. **C. lanceolata 'Goldfink'** (Zones 1–24, 26, 28–45) produces 8- to 10-inch-tall clumps of linear foliage topped by bright yellow single daisies; **'Summer**

COREOPSIS
⚘ ❀ COREOPSIS, TICKSEED
Asteraceae (Compositae)
- ✎ ZONES VARY
- ☀ FULL SUN
- ◒ MODERATE TO LITTLE WATER
- ✳ FLOWERS IN SPRING, SUMMER, AUTUMN

Coreopsis lanceolata

'Sprite' is a bit taller (10 to 12 inches) and has yellow flowers with a mahogany red ring around the center. Both bloom from late spring to midsummer.

As the common name indicates, threadleaf coreopsis, *C. verticillata* (Zones 1–24, 26, 28–45), has finely divided, very narrow leaves. The plant is bushy and mounding, ranging from 1 to about 2½ feet high. The 2-inch, bright yellow daisies are borne freely over a long summer-to-autumn season. The selection '**Moonbeam**' features blossoms of a soft pale yellow on a 1½- to 2-foot plant; '**Golden Showers**' grows 2 to 2½ feet tall.

CULTURE. Coreopsis are trouble-free plants, thriving even in relatively poor soil (as long as it is well drained). Once established, they grow well with relatively little water. Remove spent blossoms to prolong flowering. Most kinds spread rapidly and may need frequent division—as often as every 2 to 3 years—to stay in bounds. They can also be propagated from seed.

Effective with Agapanthus, Anchusa azurea, Baptisia, Centaurea, Chrysanthemum coccineum, Gaillardia × grandiflora, Nepeta, Ratibida, Stokesia laevis, Verbena.

CORYDALIS
CORYDALIS
Fumariaceae

- ✎ ZONES 3–9, 14–24, 32–35, 39–43
- ☼ LIGHT SHADE
- ● REGULAR WATER
- ❋ ❋ ❋ FLOWERS IN SPRING, SUMMER

Corydalis lutea

These shade lovers feature charming little spurred flowers and handsome clumps of dainty, divided, fernlike leaves much like those of bleeding heart (*Dicentra*, to which they are closely related) or maidenhair fern (*Adiantum*, to which they are not).

C. cheilanthifolia grows 8 to 10 inches high, with green foliage and clusters of deep yellow, ½-inch-long flowers in spring.

C. flexuosa (sometimes called blue corydalis), a recent introduction from Western China, forms a 9- to 12-inch mound of blue-green foliage; narrow, erect clusters of beautiful sky blue, long-spurred flowers bloom in early spring, often continuing into summer. It may go dormant in summer, especially in hot climates, but will reappear the following spring. Selected forms include '**Blue Panda**', with brilliant gentian blue flowers, and '**Père David**', with lavender to light blue flowers.

C. lutea, a many-stemmed plant to 15 inches tall with masses of gray-green foliage, bears golden yellow, ¾-inch-long, short-spurred flowers throughout summer. It often self-sows, popping up in shady places throughout the garden.

CULTURE. Give corydalis rich soil that is moist but well drained. Plants grow well and look good in shady areas among rocks, in open woodland, or near a pool or stream. Divide clumps or sow seed in spring or fall (seed germinates best if freshly collected).

Effective with Alchemilla mollis, Aquilegia, Brunnera macrophylla, Dicentra, ferns, Primula.

CRAMBE cordifolia
COLEWORT
Brassicaceae (Cruciferae)

- ✎ ZONES 3–9, 14–17, 31–45, 37, 39–41
- ☼ FULL SUN
- ● REGULAR WATER
- ❋ FLOWERS IN SUMMER

This impressive perennial produces a handsome 2- to 3-foot mound of long-stemmed, heart-shaped, crisp green leaves to 1 foot long and wide. A single intricately branched and rebranched stem rises 6 feet above the foliage, bearing small, starlike flowers in a billowing cloud that can reach up to 5 feet wide. Give colewort plenty of room in your garden: when in bloom, it may occupy a space 4 to 6 feet across.

Crambe cordifolia with *Achillea*

CULTURE. Plant colewort in rich, well-drained soil. It's one of those "permanent perennials" that should be planted where you'll enjoy it year after year, since it reestablishes only very slowly if divided. Propagate from root cuttings or seed.

Effective with Achillea, Artemisia, Boltonia asteroides, ornamental grasses, Hemerocallis.

Stately and aristocratic, delphiniums epitomize both the classic English border and the cottage garden. Though most gardeners associate these old-fashioned favorites with the color blue, they're available in a range of colors. Some of the hybrids have bi- or even tricolored blooms, with the center petals (sometimes called a "bee") offering a white, black, or gold contrast to white, blue, lilac, or pink outer petals. Ranging in height from 15-inch dwarfs to 8-foot giants, delphiniums bear their rounded blossoms on spikes; the lobed or fanlike leaves are variously cut and divided. All require considerable effort to grow to perfection.

The familiar tall delphiniums, known as **D. × elatum** (Zones 1–10, 14–24, 32, 34, 36–41), are complex hybrids of several species. Selection and further hybridization have resulted in groups of plants referred to as strains or series. Within each strain or series are plants similar in habit and cultural needs but differing in flower color. An important *D. × elatum* strain is the **Pacific** strain (also known as **Pacific Hybrids, Pacific Giants,** and **Pacific Coast Hybrids**). Reaching 5 to 8 feet under optimal conditions, Pacific strain delphiniums are available as seed-raised mixed-color plants and in named series that produce specific colors, including light blue **'Summer Skies'**, medium blue **'Blue Bird'**, dark violet **'Black Knight'**, white **'Galahad'**, and **'Percival'**, which has white flowers with a black center. Many other purple, lavender, and pink named varieties are sold. The *D. × elatum* group also includes shorter-growing strains, among them **Blue Fountains, Blue Springs,** and **Magic Fountains,** all in the 2- to 2½-foot range. Even shorter is the 15- to 20-inch **Stand Up** strain.

Another hybrid group, **D. × belladonna** (Zones 1–9, 14–24, 32, 34, 36–43), includes plants that reach 3 to 4 feet high when in bloom. Unlike the *D. × elatum* hybrids, which have a central flower stem followed by smaller branches, these delphiniums produce many flower stems at the same time with airier, more loosely arranged flower clusters; in addition, the plants are somewhat longer lived. Selections include light blue **'Belladonna'**, dark blue **'Volkerfrieden'** (**'People of Peace'**), white **'Casa Blanca'**, and deep turquoise blue **'Cliveden Beauty'**.

CULTURE. Delphiniums grow best in a classic "English" climate with cool to warm (not hot), humid summers. They are much less successful where summers are hot, dry, or both. In marginal locations, shelter plants by placing them in dappled sunlight, and take care to provide sufficient moisture. These plants require soil that is cool, moist but well drained, and slightly acid to slightly alkaline. Add lime to strongly acid soils. Incorporate plenty of organic matter and a balanced fertilizer into the soil a few weeks before planting time. To prevent rot, take care not to cover the crown of the plant. Taller varieties require staking. Slugs and snails can ruin young plants; bait or handpick and destroy these pests.

During the bloom season, cut off spent blossom spikes just below the lowest flower, leaving part of the stalk and its foliage. Then, when new basal shoots reach about 6 inches tall, cut the old spikes to the ground and apply a complete fertilizer around the plant. The new stems should flower in late summer or early autumn.

Even with the best care, hybrid delphiniums tend to be short lived. You can take basal cuttings in spring or divide clumps and set out individual plants in well-prepared

DELPHINIUM
DELPHINIUM
Ranunculaceae

- ZONES VARY
- ☼ FULL SUN
- REGULAR WATER
- ✳ ✳ ✳ ✳ FLOWERS IN SUMMER

Delphinium × elatum 'Summer Skies'

soil—but most gardeners find it easier to start fresh with young seedlings or cutting-grown plants from a nursery. You can also treat delphiniums as annuals by planting them in autumn (in mild-winter regions) or early spring (in all regions) to flower in summer. This is the best tactic in areas with hot summers and/or mild winters.

Effective with Chrysanthemum coccineum, C. × superbum, Gypsophila paniculata, Iris (Siberian), Lupinus, Monarda, Phlox.

DIANTHUS
🌸 🌿 PINK
Caryophyllaceae

💧 ZONES 1–24, 30–45

☼ FULL SUN, EXCEPT AS NOTED

💧💧 REGULAR TO MODERATE WATER

❋ ❋ ❋ ❋ FLOWERS IN SPRING, SUMMER

TOP: *Dianthus gratianopolitanus* 'Tiny Rubies'
BOTTOM: *Dianthus × allwoodii* 'Horatio'

For centuries, gardeners have planted pinks for the pleasure of their cheerful flowers and delightful clove fragrance. The many perennial species and hybrids are quite similar, differing chiefly in size. The plants form dense mats or mounds of very narrow (almost grasslike), gray-green to blue-green leaves; narrow stems rise above the foliage, each bearing one to several circular flowers up to an inch across. There are single, semi-double, and double kinds, often with fringed petal margins and eyes or edges in contrasting colors. All are delightful in low borders, in rock gardens, and as edgings.

The Allwood pinks, ***D. × allwoodii***, are hybrids developed in the early part of the 20th century; they vary somewhat, but most have gray-green foliage and two blossoms per stem. Among the many varieties are **'Aqua'**, with double blooms in clear white, and **'Doris'**, with salmon pink flowers accented by a deep pink eye; both grow 10 to 12 inches tall. **'Horatio'** is smaller—just 6 inches tall—and has double pink flowers.

Maiden pink, ***D. deltoides***, grows well in light shade. The plants spread to form broad, loose mats of green leaves about 6 inches high, making a good small-scale ground cover. Branched stems bear ¾-inch-wide flowers at their tips in summer. The species has purple to rose-colored flowers; **'Albus'** is pure white, **'Vampire'** has deep red flowers, and **'Zing Rose'** produces rose red blossoms with a darker ring around the eye.

Cheddar pink, ***D. gratianopolitanus***, forms a ground-hugging mat of blue-green leaves, with single pink flowers appearing on 6- to 10-inch stems. This species and its varieties grow well in hot, humid areas. Selected forms vary in size and flower color. **'Bath's Pink'** has fringed soft pink blooms about an inch across, carried on 12- to 15-inch stems. Smaller-growing cultivars include 6-inch-tall, red-and-white **'Spotty'** and 4-inch **'Tiny Rubies'**, with small double blooms in ruby red.

Cottage or grass pink, ***D. plumarius***, grows in a loose mat of gray-green foliage and has 10- to 18-inch-tall flowering stems. Some of the oldest members of *Dianthus* are classified here, including the legendary 17th-century **'Dad's Favorite'**, with ruby-edged double white flowers centered in maroon, and **'Musgrave's White'**, a classic at least two centuries old that bears intensely fragrant single flowers with a green eye.

CULTURE. Pinks need light (even gritty) soil that drains well. Good drainage is especially important in winter, since soggy soil then can be fatal. They prefer neutral to slightly alkaline soil; add lime to acidic soils. In hot-summer regions, plant pinks where they will receive a little afternoon shade. To encourage summer-long bloom, remove faded blossoms, breaking or cutting the stems at the nodes where new growth is starting. In colder regions (where winter lows reach −10°F/ −23°C), protect plants with a loose cover of evergreen boughs.

After several years, individual plants begin to decline. Replace them with plants grown from seed (many kinds bloom the first year from seed) or cuttings. Take stem cuttings in spring from new growth that has not flowered; the cuttings should be about six nodes in length. You can also layer stems that spread along the ground.

Effective with Anchusa azurea, Iberis sempervirens, Linaria purpurea, Lychnis coronaria, Papaver orientale, Phlox subulata, Stachys byzantina, Thymus.

Planted to edge a border, weave through other low plants, or spill over the edges of a container, twinspurs form a 6- to 18-inch-tall mat that spreads about 2 feet wide. Clothed with small green or gray leaves, the many slender stems terminate in elongated clusters of tubular flowers, each with two spurs on the back. Individual blossoms are small—just ½ to 1 inch long—but they're borne profusely enough to make a showy splash of color. **D. fetcaniensis** is particularly floriferous, producing salmon rose flowers on 10-inch stems. **D. integerrima** is reputed to be more drought tolerant than other species; it's also more upright growing, with wiry stems reaching 1½ feet tall. It has narrow gray leaves and showy salmon pink flowers. Robust **D. rigescens** has spreading stems that turn up at the ends to display 6- to 8-inch spikes of rich pink blooms. **D. vigilis** features small pale pink flowers on long, wiry stems; it spreads by stolons.

Among the many available hybrids are **'Blackthorn Apricot'**, forming a 6- to 12-inch mat with airy sprays of apricot flowers; **'Langthorn's Lavender'**, with upright 8- to 12-inch stems; and **'Ruby Field'**, reaching 10 to 12 inches tall and bearing salmon pink blossoms.

CULTURE. Plant twinspurs in average, well-drained soil. They are intolerant of wet soil, especially in winter. Trim off old flower spikes to encourage new bloom. Often short lived, these perennials can be propagated by stem cuttings taken in spring or summer. In cold-winter regions, grow twinspurs as annuals.

Effective with Agapanthus, Campanula, Erigeron, Iris (bearded), Kniphofia, Nepeta, Phormium, Scabiosa, Stachys byzantina.

Delicate wands of heart-shaped flowers and finely dissected, almost feathery foliage make bleeding heart a springtime favorite. Eastern and western North America are home to two similar low-growing species. The Eastern species, fringed bleeding heart **(D. eximia)**, forms tidy, nonspreading clumps of blue-gray foliage 1 to 1½ feet high. The bare stems rise just above the leaves, carrying dangling deep pink flowers from midspring into summer. **'Alba'** is a white-flowered selection. Foot-tall Western bleeding heart, **D. formosa**, has blue-green foliage; pale to deep rose flowers are clustered on slim stems that rise 6 to 8 inches above the leaves. Under favorable conditions, this species spreads widely (but not invasively). **D. f. oregana** is shorter than the species, with pink-tipped cream blossoms.

Nurseries offer a number of superior 12- to 15-inch-tall selections of uncertain ancestry; they may be hybrids of D. eximia and D. formosa or selected forms of one species. **'Bacchanal'**, bearing deep red flowers, is nearly everblooming during the growing season, as is pink-flowered **'Bountiful'** (**'Zestful'**). **'Luxuriant'** can endure drier soil and stronger light than most; its flowers are deep pink. **'Margery Fish'** is a vigorous selection with masses of white flowers and exceptionally blue foliage.

Common bleeding heart **(D. spectabilis)**, native to Japan, is the showiest and largest leafed of the bleeding hearts. Clothed in soft green leaves, the plants grow 2 to 3 feet high; in late spring, branched stems carry nearly horizontal sprays of pendulous, heart-shaped rose pink flowers with protruding white inner petals. **'Alba'** and **'Pantaloons'** are pure white selections. After flowering, the plants begin to die down and are generally dormant by midsummer, though they tend to last longer in cool-summer climates if given adequate moisture. Plant summer-maturing perennials such as hostas or ferns nearby to fill the gap.

CULTURE. Plant bleeding hearts in light, well-drained soil enriched with organic matter. The roots must be kept cool and moist, but not soggy. Most prefer filtered sunlight to partial shade, but in cool regions, common bleeding heart *(D. spectabilis)* and the

DIASCIA
TWINSPUR
Scrophulariaceae

⚥ ZONES 7–9, 14–24, 31
☼ FULL SUN
💧 REGULAR WATER
✳ ✳ ✳ FLOWERS IN SPRING, SUMMER

Diascia 'Ruby Field'

DICENTRA
BLEEDING HEART
Fumariaceae

⚥ ZONES 1–9, 14–24, 31–45
◐ LIGHT SHADE, EXCEPT AS NOTED
💧 REGULAR WATER
✳ ✳ ✳ FLOWERS IN SPRING, SUMMER

Dicentra spectabilis

hybrid 'Luxuriant' will tolerate full sun. All but common bleeding heart may need dividing after several years. Do this in earliest spring, before growth is really underway. All can be propagated by root cuttings taken in summer or fall.

Effective with Bergenia, Corydalis, Doronicum, Epimedium, ferns, Helleborus, Iberis sempervirens, Mertensia virginica, Pulmonaria.

DICTAMNUS albus
GAS PLANT, BURNING BUSH, FRAXINELLA
Rutaceae

- ☀ ZONES 1–9, 31–45
- ☀ ◑ FULL SUN OR LIGHT SHADE
- ● ◐ REGULAR TO MODERATE WATER
- ✳ ✳ ✳ FLOWERS IN LATE SPRING, SUMMER

Dictamnus albus

Sturdy and long lived, this handsome perennial forms bushy, 2½- to 4-foot-tall clumps of glossy, citrus-scented, 3-inch pointed leaflets on sturdy stems. Loose spires of blossoms appear at the branch tips. The narrow-petaled flowers with prominent stamens resemble wild azaleas; pink is the basic color, but nurseries also offer lilac **'Purpureus'** and white **'Albiflorus'**. The seedpods that follow are also attractive. In warm, humid weather, volatile oils from the immature seed capsules may briefly ignite if you hold a lighted match immediately beneath a flower cluster—hence the common names "gas plant" and "burning bush." (This "ignition test" does not harm the plant.)

Some people have an allergic skin reaction to the foliage and flowers of gas plant.

Dictamnus albus

CULTURE. Give gas plant well-drained, moderately fertile soil. It grows best in regions with cool nights. Plants may take 2 to 3 years to get well settled in, but they can remain in place indefinitely (and should, in fact, be left in one place; they reestablish slowly if divided). Start new plants from seed or from root cuttings taken in late winter.

Effective with Campanula, Geranium, Iris (bearded, Siberian), Paeonia.

DIGITALIS
FOXGLOVE
Scrophulariaceae

- ☀ ZONES VARY
- ◑ LIGHT SHADE, EXCEPT AS NOTED
- ● REGULAR WATER
- ✳ ✳ ✳ FLOWERS IN LATE SPRING, SUMMER

Digitalis grandiflora

Among the foxgloves, the classic cottage garden sort *(D. purpurea)* is a biennial: it develops a foliage clump during its first year, sends up stately 4- to 6-foot bloom spires the second year, and then usually dies. Other species are perennial, with the typical foxglove clumps of bold gray-green leaves but somewhat shorter flower spikes. Yellow foxglove, **D. grandiflora (D. ambigua),** succeeds in Zones 1–24, 31–43. It grows 2 to 3 feet tall and has 2-inch-long, pale yellow flowers lightly spotted brown on the inside. Its cultivar **'Carillon'** grows only 12 to 15 inches high. Grecian foxglove, **D. lanata** (Zones 2–24, 31–41), has dark green leaves and narrow, 3-foot spikes of small cream-colored flowers with purplish veining and a small near-white lip. **D. × mertonensis** (Zones 2–24, 31–41) bears 2- to 3-foot spikes of flowers in a deep pink shade often described as strawberry. Though it is a hybrid, it comes true from seed.

CULTURE. Foxgloves are at their best in filtered sun to light or partial shade; where summers are cool, however, you can plant them in sun. Give them good soil enriched with organic matter, and keep it moist but not saturated. Set out plants in early spring; divide established clumps in the same season. Remove spent spikes to encourage a second flower display in late summer or autumn. If you want seeds to start new plants, leave a few spikes.

Effective with Alchemilla mollis, Alstroemeria, Baptisia australis, Chrysanthemum frutescens, ferns, Thalictrum, Tradescantia.

The 2- to 3-inch daisies of leopard's bane add a bright touch of glossy yellow to the early spring garden. The blossoms are carried on long, slender, branching stems that rise from low, dense clumps of toothed, rounded to heart-shaped green leaves. Foliage of most kinds dies back by midsummer, so it's best to combine these plants with annuals or perennials (such as hostas or ferns) that will expand in summer to cover the bare space. The most widely sold species is **D. cordatum** (also listed as **D. caucasicum, D. columnae,** or **D. orientale**). Its flowering stems reach 1½ feet, each holding a single flower. The variety '**Magnificum**' is taller (2 to 2½ feet high) and has somewhat larger flowers. '**Miss Mason**' is a choice hybrid featuring large daisies on 1½- to 2½-foot plants; its foliage is less likely to die back in summer than that of the others.

CULTURE. Set out plants in good, organically enriched soil. In all regions, a spot in partial shade (at the edge of a woodland, for example) is ideal, but you can also grow leopard's bane in sun where summers are cool. Plants need regular water when in leaf and at least moderate moisture during dormancy. Divide clumps every 2 to 3 years in spring; young plants bloom best.

Effective with Brunnera macrophylla, Dicentra, ferns, Helleborus, Mertensia virginica.

DORONICUM
🌿 LEOPARD'S BANE
Asteraceae (Compositae)

- 🌡 ZONES 1–7, 14–17, 31–43
- ☼ LIGHT SHADE, EXCEPT AS NOTED
- 💧 REGULAR WATER
- ✳ FLOWERS IN EARLY SPRING

Doronicum cordatum

Purple coneflower bears showy, 4-inch-wide daisies with dark, beehivelike centers and rosy purple petals (ray flowers) that are typically slightly drooping. Bristly, oblong, 3- to 4-inch long leaves form dense foliage clumps; from these, sparsely leafed flowering stems rise 2 to 4 feet and bear flowers over a long summer bloom period. Where winters are mild, flowering may even start in mid- to late spring. '**Bright Star**' is a free-flowering, 2½-foot-tall cultivar with rose-colored flowers; '**Crimson Star**' reaches 2 feet high. The rose pink ray flowers of 3-foot-tall '**Magnus**' do not droop, but are held horizontally. '**White Swan**' and '**White Lustre**' feature white blooms with an orange-yellow cone.

CULTURE. Purple coneflowers are productive, trouble-free plants that need only a sunny spot in average, well-drained soil. In hot-summer regions, they'll also do well in light shade. The plants are drought tolerant but perform better with moderate watering. Deadheading encourages repeat flowering and keeps plants looking neat, but many gardeners leave some of the seedpods in place for birds to enjoy during winter. Purple coneflower grows from a rhizomatous taproot and is better left undivided; because it grows slowly, individual plants can be left in place for a long period. To increase your supply of plants, take root cuttings in fall. The plant self-sows readily; remove seedlings if you don't want them of ir they don't bloom true to the parent.

Effective with Gaura lindheimeri, ornamental grasses, Gypsophila paniculata, Liatris, Rudbeckia, Sedum 'Autumn Joy', Solidago.

ECHINACEA purpurea
🌿 🌼 PURPLE CONEFLOWER
Asteraceae (Compositae)

- 🌡 ZONES 1–24, 26–45
- ☼ FULL SUN, EXCEPT AS NOTED
- 💧 MODERATE WATER
- ✳ ✳ ✳ ✳ FLOWERS IN SUMMER, EXCEPT AS NOTED

Echinacea purpurea

As the common name implies, globe thistle is indeed a thistle relative. The rugged-looking, erect, branching plants reach 2 to 4 feet tall, with somewhat prickly, deeply cut, foot-long leaves that are typically green on the surface, gray and woolly beneath. Handsome, globular blue flower heads offer a striking contrast to other blossom shapes in the border. The named varieties described here are generally offered as **E. ritro,** but may also be encountered under the names **E. exaltatus** and **E. humilis.** '**Taplow Blue**' is the most popular cultivar, featuring 2-inch-wide, bright

ECHINOPS
🌿 🌼 GLOBE THISTLE
Asteraceae (Compositae)

- 🌡 ZONES 1–24, 31–45
- ☼ FULL SUN
- 💧💧 REGULAR TO MODERATE WATER
- ✳ FLOWERS IN SUMMER

Echinops ritro

metallic blue flowers on plants 3 to 4 feet high. **'Veitch's Blue'** sports darker blue flowers and grows 2½ to 3 feet tall.

CULTURE. Plant globe thistles in full sun, in well-drained soil of average fertility; provide moderate water. (If given plenty of moisture and good soil enriched with organic matter, they may grow a bit too robustly and require staking.) Once planted, they can remain in place for years without requiring division, but if you want more plants you can divide established clumps in spring, or sow seeds or take root cuttings in early spring. The flowers are excellent for dried arrangements; cut them before they open and dry them upside down.

Effective with Agastache, Gypsophila paniculata, Helenium, Lavandula, Malva, Rudbeckia.

EPILOBIUM
(Zauschneria)
CALIFORNIA FUCHSIA,
HUMMINGBIRD FLOWER
Onagraceae

🌢 ZONES 2–11, 14–24

☀ FULL SUN

🌢 🌢 REGULAR TO LITTLE WATER

✳ ✳ ✳ ✳ FLOWERS IN SUMMER, AUTUMN

Epilobium canum latifolium

Thriving in hot, sunny locations, these natives of western North America grow best in areas with little summer rain and low humidity. At bloom time, they offer a lavish display of bright, tubular, 1- to 2-inch-long blossoms on shrubby plants 1 to 2 feet high. They spread by underground stems and can be somewhat invasive in manicured gardens, but they're good choices for naturalistic plantings, banks, and the fringes of cultivated areas.

Though many nurseries still sell these plants under their former name *Zauschneria,* botanists now classify them as *Epilobium* (and have reduced the number of species as well).

E. canum canum (Z. californica) has upright or somewhat arching stems and narrow green to gray-green leaves. The species bears bright red-orange flowers; cultivars include white-blossomed **'Alba'**, soft pink **'Solidarity Pink'**, and heavy-blooming **'Dublin'** (**'Glasnevin'**), a shorter plant (to 1 foot) with scarlet blooms. The most widely grown form of **E. c. latifolium (Z. latifolia)** is **'Arizonica'**, a 2-foot plant with broader light green leaves and bright orange blossoms.

CULTURE. California fuchsias survive in poor, even rocky soil, but they also do well in better soil, as long as it is well drained. They require little water but will accept regular garden watering (again, as long as drainage is good). To curb the plants' spread, you may need to remove sections from the clump's outer edges. Start new plants from rooted segments of established clumps or from stem cuttings taken in spring.

Effective with Ceratostigma plumbaginoides, Eryngium, Gaura lindheimeri, Oenothera, Perovskia, Santolina.

EPIMEDIUM
EPIMEDIUM, BARRENWORT,
BISHOP'S HAT
Berberidaceae

🌢 ZONES 1–9, 14–17, 31–43

◐ ● LIGHT TO FULL SHADE

🌢 MODERATE WATER

✳ ✳ ✳ ✳ ✳ FLOWERS IN SPRING

Elegant, low-growing plants for a shaded border, rock garden, or ground cover, epimediums grow from a creeping network of underground stems. Their heart-shaped, 3-inch-long leaves, carried on wiry leafstalks, overlap to form handsome foliage clumps. New growth emerges bronzy pink in spring, turns green by summer, and changes to reddish bronze in fall; foliage is deciduous or evergreen, depending on the species or hybrid. Airy spikes of small spurred or hooded flowers appear in very early spring.

Deciduous **E. grandiflorum** is a vigorous, easy-to-grow species bearing relatively large (1½- to 2-inch) rose or violet flowers with prominent white spurs. The plants have spiny-edged leaves and grow 1 foot high. Named selections include **'Rose Queen'**, **'White Queen'**, and lavender-and-violet **'Lilafee'**. Another deciduous epimedium, the hybrid **E. × youngianum,** is a smaller plant, forming clumps to

8 inches high and bearing pinkish white flowers just ¾ inch across. Its most common cultivars are pure white **'Niveum'** and mauve pink **'Roseum'**.

Among evergreen or semievergreen epimediums, the 1½-foot-tall hybrid **E. × perralchicum 'Frohnleiten'** is noted for its vigorous growth and bright yellow flowers, while **E. pinnatum colchicum** forms foot-high clumps of broad, glossy leaflets and bears dark yellow flowers with prominent spurs. **E. × rubrum,** another hybrid, produces showy clusters of bright crimson-and-white flowers on plants reaching 1 foot tall. Hybrid **E. × versicolor** is best known through its vigorous, 12- to 20-inch-tall selection **'Sulphureum'**, which produces clusters of light yellow flowers and has leaves marked with brownish red.

CULTURE. Epimediums need a shady location and slightly acid soil amended with plenty of organic matter. Though they will tolerate dry conditions, they look best with moderate watering. To keep plants neat and allow a better view of the new foliage and flowers, cut off old leaves in early spring, just as new growth begins. Though plants don't require division for good growth, you can divide in early spring if you need more plants. Cut through the clump with a sharp spade and transplant sections with some soil attached.

Effective with Aruncus, Bergenia, Brunnera macrophylla, Dicentra, ferns, Helleborus, Polygonatum, Primula, Pulmonaria, Tricyrtis.

Epimedium grandiflorum 'Lilafee'

Free blooming and easy to grow, these daisy-family perennials look much like their *Aster* relatives, but their petals (ray flowers) are threadlike rather than flattened. Santa Barbara daisy, **E. karvinskianus** (Zones 8, 9, 12–28), is a graceful, trailing plant 10 to 20 inches high. Its small white or pinkish flowers are only ¾ inch across but bloom in great profusion over a long season. It is useful in borders, containers, and as a small-scale ground cover (especially in dry areas). Keep in mind that it self-sows prolifically and can be invasive. **'Moerheimii'** is a somewhat smaller selection with lavender-tinted flowers.

Many garden-worthy hybrids are listed as **E. speciosus** (Zones 1–9, 14–24, 31–43). These form erect, leafy-stemmed plants 1½ to 2½ feet tall, with flowers about 2 inches wide. **'Azure Fairy'** (**'Azurfee'**) bears semidouble lavender blue blooms on a 2½-foot-tall plant; **'Darkest of All'** is a popular 2-foot-high cultivar with double violet blue flowers. The semidouble carmine pink blossoms of **'Förster's Liebling'** bloom on a shorter plant—just 1½ feet high. **'Quakeress'** reaches a height of 1½ to 2 feet and has double blooms in light mauve pink; **'White Quakeress'** is similar but bears off-white blossoms.

Erigeron 'Azure Fairy'

CULTURE. Plant fleabanes in light, well-drained soil. Give them full sun except in hot-summer areas, where they do best in light shade. Cut plants back after the first flush of bloom to encourage reblooming. Divide crowded clumps in early spring. Fleabanes are easily propagated from seed.

Effective with Agapanthus, Diascia, Gaura lindheimeri, Gypsophila paniculata, Helenium, Helianthus, Malva, Physostegia virginiana.

ERIGERON

🌿 FLEABANE,
SANTA BARBARA DAISY
Asteraceae (Compositae)

- ✎ ZONES VARY
- ☼ FULL SUN, EXCEPT AS NOTED
- ◗ MODERATE WATER
- ✳ ✳ ✳ ✳ FLOWERS IN SPRING, SUMMER

Erigeron karvinskianus

ERYNGIUM

🌱 🦌 SEA HOLLY

Apiaceae (Umbelliferae)

- 🌿 ZONES 1–24, 29–43, EXCEPT AS NOTED
- ☀ FULL SUN
- 💧 MODERATE WATER
- ❋ ❋ ❋ FLOWERS IN SUMMER

Eryngium alpinum

Handsome plants valued for the strong texture of their foliage and flowers, the sea hollies produce a rosette of foliage that sends up leafy, branched stems carrying oval flower heads surrounded by spiny bracts (modified leaves) arranged in an unusual starburst pattern. In most sea hollies, the blossoms, bracts, and stems are a steely blue.

The favorite sea holly *E. giganteum* (also known as Miss Willmott's ghost) is not a perennial, but a hardy biennial. It produces only foliage the first year; in its second summer, 3-foot stems bearing 3- to 6-inch-wide, metallic silver bracts topped by 2-inch, pale blue flower heads appear and last for many weeks.

Among perennial sea hollies is 2-foot-tall alpine sea holly, *E. alpinum*; despite its spiny appearance, it's actually rather soft to the touch. It features 2-inch blue flower heads and prominent, finely divided blue bracts. **'Blue Star'** and the larger-flowered **'Superbum'** are choice varieties. One of the most cold-hardy sea hollies, *E. amethystinum* (Zones 1–24, 26, 28–45), grows 2½ feet tall and has blue to violet flower heads. Flat sea holly, *E. planum*, grows 3 feet high, producing many small rounded blue flower heads on branching plants. Selected forms include 2-foot **'Blue Cap'** and dwarf **'Blue Diamond'**, which reaches just 1½ feet; both feature deep blue flowers. The taller **'Silver Stone'** grows 3 to 4 feet tall and bears creamy white blossoms, offering a variation on the usual theme.

CULTURE. Plant sea hollies in light, sandy or even gravelly soil. They are permanent plants that never need dividing; in fact, division of the long taproots is difficult. Propagate by seed (which germinates best when fresh) or by root cuttings taken in late winter. Plants often self-seed.

Effective with Agastache, Artemisia, Chrysanthemum parthenium, Epilobium, Lavandula, Limonium latifolium.

EUPATORIUM

🦌 HARDY AGERATUM, JOE PYE WEED, WHITE SNAKEROOT

Asteraceae (Compositae)

- 🌿 ZONES VARY
- ☀ ◑ SUN OR LIGHT SHADE
- 💧 REGULAR WATER
- ❋ ❋ ❋ ❋ FLOWERS IN SUMMER, EARLY AUTUMN

Eupatorium maculatum 'Gateway'

Bearing huge, loosely formed clusters of tiny blossoms atop robust, shrublike foliage clumps, these imposing yet graceful plants give substance to the garden. The species described here are native to the eastern and central United States; they're popular components of wild gardens, restored meadows, and large-scale borders.

E. coelestinum (Conoclinium coelestinum, Zones 1–9, 14–17, 25–43) produces broad clusters of fluffy blue flowers that much resemble those of annual ageratum—hence its common name, hardy ageratum. Reaching 3 feet tall, this vigorously spreading plant has freely branching set with dark green, toothed leaves. Its selection **'Wayside Variety'** is more compact than the species, growing only 15 inches high; **'Album'** has white flowers. Spotted Joe Pye weed, *E. maculatum* (Zones 1–9, 14–17, 28–43), grows 6 to 7 feet high, with green stems streaked with purple. Its eye-catching form **'Atropurpureum'** features purple leaf veins and stems as well as purple flowers; **'Gateway'** (sometimes listed as a form of *E. fistulosum)*, with dusky rose blooms, is a more manageable 4 to 5 feet tall. The dark green leaves and 3- to 9-foot stems of Joe Pye weed, *E. purpureum* (Zones 1–9, 14–17, 28–45), make a good backdrop for its rosy pink to lilac purple flowers. White snakeroot, *E. rugosum* (Zones 1–9, 14–17, 28–45), features puffy clusters of white flowers on 3- to 5-foot plants; the cultivar **'Chocolate'** has striking dark maroon to bronze foliage.

CULTURE. These perennials thrive in moist soil well enriched with organic matter. They can remain in place for many years, but if you want to increase your supply of plants, you can dig and divide them in early spring.

Effective with Aster, Boltonia asteroides, ornamental grasses, Helianthus, Hibiscus moscheutos, Ligularia, Rudbeckia, Solidago.

Besides the perennial euphorbias, there are hundreds of other sorts, ranging from the familiar holiday poinsettia, *E. pulcherrima* (a large shrub in its native Mexico), to desert-dwelling cactus lookalikes and annuals such as snow-on-the-mountain (*E. marginata*). In many, what appear to be petals actually are bracts (modified leaves) that surround the insignificant true flowers. The spurges described here have narrowly oval leaves that encircle the stems like a bottlebrush, leading up to clusters of showy bracts. Note that all spurges have a milky sap that irritates the eyes (and the skin of some people, as well).

E. amygdaloides (Zones 3–24, 31–34) grows nearly 3 feet high and blooms in late winter and early spring. The stems die down in winter. Variety '**Rubra**' has handsome deep red stems and bronze foliage, brilliantly accented by its bright yellow-green bracts. Evergreen *E. characias* (Zones 4–24, 31, 32, warmer parts of 32) forms an impressive, upright-growing shrubby clump to 4 feet high, with narrow blue-green leaves crowded along its stems. Large, cylindrical clusters of lime green bracts, each with a dark central eye, appear in late winter and early spring. The most common form is *E. c. wulfenii* (*E. veneta*), with broader, yellower clusters of bracts that lack dark centers. Also blooming in late winter and early spring are compact, 2- to 3-foot '**Portuguese Velvet**', with velvety blue-gray foliage and coppery gold bracts; and evergreen *E.* × *martinii* (a hybrid between *E. amygdaloides* and *E. characias*), a 2½-footer with yellow-green clusters of bracts and bronze-tinted leaves and stems.

E. dulcis (Zones 1–10, 14–24, 28–43) is best known by its cultivar '**Chameleon**'. This colorful plant's purple foliage emerges in spring, forming a foot-high mound that's soon covered with bright yellow bracts tinted purple and green. Summer-blooming *E. griffithii* (Zones 1–10, 14–24, 28–43) is distinguished by clumps that spread by creeping rhizomes. It grows erect to 3 feet high and dies back in winter. The species has orange-red bracts held above narrow, medium green leaves with pale pink midribs. Selections include '**Fireglow**', with brick red bracts, and '**Dixter**', distinguished by its red-flushed foliage and deep orange bracts.

An excellent choice for the rock garden or the front of the border is evergreen *E. myrsinites* (Zones 1–24, 31–43), with prostrate, trailing stems closely set with broadly oval blue-gray leaves; flattish clusters of greenish yellow bracts appear at the stem ends in late winter and early spring. Another excellent front-of-the-border plant is cushion spurge, *E. epithymoides* (often sold as *E. polychroma*), successful in Zones 1–24, 26, 28–45. It forms dense, rounded clumps 1 to 1½ feet high and wide. Flattened clusters of greenish yellow bracts appear at the stem tips in spring and last into summer. Foliage turns red in autumn before the plants go dormant.

Euphorbia griffithii
'Fireglow'

CULTURE. Plant spurges in well-drained soil and give moderate water. Most do best in full sun, but *E. amygdaloides* and *E. griffithii* accept light shade. Flowering stems are long lasting but should be cut out when the bracts fade and new replacement stems have grown in. Propagate by terminal cuttings taken in midsummer or by seed; many self-sow to provide replacement plants.

Effective with Aurinia saxatilis, ornamental grasses, Helleborus, Lavandula, Limonium, Papaver orientale, Phormium, Yucca.

EUPHORBIA
EUPHORBIA, SPURGE
Euphorbiaceae

✿ ZONES VARY

☼ FULL SUN, EXCEPT AS NOTED

🌢 MODERATE WATER

❋ ❋ ❋ ❋ FLOWERS IN LATE
WINTER, SPRING, SUMMER

Euphorbia characias wulfenii

Euphorbia × *martinii*

FERNS

Thanks to their airy, delicate texture, ferns provide a wonderful counterpoint to many shade-loving perennials. The following choice, easy-to-grow ferns all prefer moist and shaded sites, though the degree of shade and water they need varies (as noted).

Maidenhair or five-finger fern, **Adiantum pedatum (A. p. aleuticum),** is a North American native suited to Zones 1–9, 14–21, 36–40. A graceful plant with slender, shiny black stems and fronds that fork to make a fingerlike pattern, it grows 12 to 20 inches tall and spreads rapidly if given partial to full shade and rich, moist soil. The leaves die back in hard frosts.

Athyrium nipponicum 'Pictum'

Two ferns in the genus **Athyrium** (Zones 1–9, 14–24, 31–43) are valuable additions to the garden. Evergreen in the mildest zones, their fronds turn brown after repeated frosts. Leave the dead fronds on the plants to shelter emerging fronds in early spring; then cut them back. Lady fern **(A. filix-femina)** is narrow at the bottom and spreading at the top, providing a vertical accent in the garden. Its thin, finely divided fronds reach 4 feet or higher. If grown in constantly moist soil, it will tolerate full sun, but it's better adapted to partial shade. It can be invasive, spreading beyond the area you have allotted for it; dig out excess clumps. The colorful fronds of Japanese painted fern **(A. nipponicum 'Pictum')** are purplish at the base, changing to lavender and then silvery green toward the tips. Slowly spreading to form a tight clump, this fern prefers well-enriched, moist soil and partial shade.

The genus **Dryopteris** includes over 100 species of ferns. They are found over most of the world, but only a few are generally offered by nurseries. They prefer moderate water and rich soil with adequate organic matter. Autumn fern **(D. erythrosora,** Zones 4–9, 14–28, 31, 32) is one of the few ferns with seasonal color variation. In spring, the expanding new fronds are a blend of copper, pink, and yellow. They turn green in summer; in fall and winter, they're highlighted by bright red spore cases produced on the leaf undersides. Autumn fern is deciduous in colder regions, as is male fern **(D. filix-mas,** Zones 1–9, 14–17,

TOP: *Adiantum pedatum*
BOTTOM: *Athyrium felix-femina*

Dryopteris erythrosora

31–45), a 2- to 5-foot plant with finely cut, fresh green fronds that reach 1 foot wide.

Ostrich fern **(Matteuccia struthiopteris,** Zones 1–10, 14–17, 32–45), native to northern regions of North America, forms a gracefully arching plant with plumy dark green fronds. When grown in areas with long, moderate summers, it reaches 4 to 6 feet; in mountain regions with a shorter growing season, it tops out at 1½ to 2 feet. The spreading clumps have a bold appearance, with a shape like a shuttlecock—narrow at the base, spreading at the top. In cool, moist areas, ostrich fern will take full sun; elsewhere, it prefers partial to full shade. Give it rich soil and regular water. It's deciduous in winter.

Ferns in the genus **Osmunda** grow robustly in temperate climates. Given moisture and rich soil, they survive in hot-summer areas, but they grow shorter there than in cooler regions. They are deciduous in winter. Native to the eastern United States is cinnamon fern, **O. cinnamomea** (Zones 1–6, 32–45). Its fertile spore-bearing fronds emerge in early spring—bright green at first, turning to cinnamon brown as the spores ripen. The sterile fronds unfold later from handsome fiddleheads. Plants are erect, arching outward toward the top, and up to 5 feet tall; tufts of woolly, cinnamon-colored fibers grow at the base of each frond, giving the fern its common name. The fronds turn a showy yellow to orange in fall. Royal fern **(O. regalis,** Zones 1–9, 14–17, 26–45) is another large plant (up to 6 feet high), with twice-cut, bright green fronds. It is coarser in texture than most ferns. The fronds turn yellow to brown in fall. This fern does well in light shade but also thrives in sun if grown in wet soil, even in mud. It is especially attractive beside streams or ponds.

Ferns in the genus **Polystichum** form symmetrical, medium-size evergreen plants. They combine well in shady beds with many perennials and are easy to grow if given rich, organic, well-drained soil. Christmas fern **(P. acrostichoides,** Zones 1–9, 14–24, 28–43), a native of eastern North America, reaches 1 to 1½ feet tall. Its fronds are still dark green at Christmas, providing a beautiful contrast to the white of a light snowfall. Mulch with leaves in the coldest climates. Western sword fern **(P. munitum,** Zones 2–9, 14–24, 36–38), native to western North America, produces large clumps of leathery, shiny dark green, 2- to 4-foot-long fronds. Once established, it needs little water.

FILIPENDULA

MEADOWSWEET,
QUEEN OF THE PRAIRIE,
QUEEN OF THE MEADOW,
DROPWORT

Rosaceae

- 🌿 ZONES 1–9, 14–17, 31–45, EXCEPT AS NOTED
- ☼ LIGHT SHADE, EXCEPT AS NOTED
- ● REGULAR WATER
- ✳ ✳ FLOWERS IN SUMMER

Filipendula ulmaria 'Flore Pleno'

Attractive planted beside ponds, in borders, and in naturalistic landscapes, the meadowsweets are impressive perennials with dense plumes of tiny flowers floating over handsome clumps of large compound leaves.

Siberian meadowsweet, *F. palmata,* is a strong-textured plant with coarse, palmately lobed, 4- to 8-inch-wide leaves and 3- to 4-foot stems topped with pale pink flowers. The selection 'Nana' grows only 8 to 10 inches tall. Somewhat less hardy than the other species is Japanese meadowsweet, *F. purpurea,* successful in Zones 3–9, 14–17, 31–34, 39. From broad clumps of large, maplelike leaves, its reddish flower stems rise to 4 feet, carrying plumes of dark pink blossoms. 'Alba' is a white-flowered form. More imposing is 6- to 8-foot queen of the prairie, *F. rubra,* native to the central and eastern United States. Its flowers are pink; the selection 'Venusta' bears purplish pink plumes and is a bit shorter, reaching 4 to 6 feet.

Similar to *F. rubra* is queen of the meadow, *F. ulmaria,* a European native with creamy white flowers on stems to 6 feet tall. Its form 'Flore Pleno' grows just half that high and bears double blooms. Two selections with decorative foliage are more widely grown than the species: 'Variegata', with leaves margined in light yellow, and 'Aurea', with bright golden foliage (plant this one in shade to protect its leaves from sunburn).

Dropwort, *F. vulgaris,* differs somewhat from the other meadowsweets in cultural needs (see below) and appearance. Its foliage is fernlike, growing in low, spreading mounds. Slender stems rise to 3 feet, bearing branched sprays of white blossoms.

CULTURE. With the exception of dropwort (*F. vulgaris),* the meadowsweets need good soil liberally enriched with organic matter and do best with regular watering to keep the soil evenly moist. Give them light shade in areas with warm to hot summers; where summers are cool and in northern latitudes, plants also do well in full sun. Dropwort prefers full sun in all but the warmest regions and will tolerate fairly dry soils, though it looks better with moderate watering. Propagate by division (in spring) or by seed.

Effective with Astilbe, Bergenia, Hosta, Lobelia cardinalis, Monarda.

GAILLARDIA × grandiflora

🌿 🌸 GAILLARDIA,
BLANKET FLOWER

Asteraceae (Compositae)

- 🌿 ALL ZONES
- ☼ FULL SUN
- ◐ MODERATE WATER
- ✳ ✳ ✳ FLOWERS IN SUMMER, AUTUMN

The showy daisylike flowers of gaillardia bloom all summer and into fall, enlivening the garden with their warm, bright colors. Developed from two species native to the central and western United States, this hybrid forms a clump of rough-textured gray-green foliage; slender flower stems in a range of heights rise above the foliage mound, bearing 3- to 4-inch, single or semidouble blooms. Among the taller (2- to 3-foot) selections are 'Dazzler', which produces

Gaillardia × grandiflora 'Burgundy'

yellow blooms with crimson-tipped petals (ray flowers); 'Mandarin', featuring yellow-orange ray flowers surrounding a maroon center; 'Burgundy', with flowers of solid wine red; and entirely yellow 'Yellow Queen'. The seed-grown Monarch Strain produces a full range of solid and bicolor combinations. For front-of-the-border plants, look for yellow, foot-tall 'Golden Goblin' or red-and-yellow 'Goblin'. Even shorter, to about 8 inches, is 'Baby Cole', with bicolored blooms of bright red and yellow.

CULTURE. Gaillardia requires well-drained sandy to loam soil; in heavy clay, it tends to rot over winter. When clumps become crowded or develop bare centers, divide in early spring. Seed-raised plants bloom the first year.

Effective with Achillea, Asclepias tuberosa, Coreopsis, Salvia, Solidago.

Gaura lindheimeri

L ong, wispy reddish stems bearing spikes of starry flowers provide a delicate, airy accent for a border or sunny wild garden. Graceful and long blooming, this native of the Southwest forms a vase-shaped, shrubby plant 2 to 4 feet high, its numerous slender stems clothed in narrow leaves. In the basic species, pink buds open to inch-wide white flowers. Selected forms include 2- to 2½-foot **'Corrie's Gold'**, featuring gold-edged foliage; **'Siskiyou Pink'**, a 2-footer with maroon-mottled leaves and deep maroon buds opening to pink flowers; and **'Whirling Butterflies'**, with slightly larger white flowers on a 3-foot plant.

CULTURE. Plant gaura in deep, well-drained sandy to loam soil. It tolerates heat and drought and also performs well in humid regions. To prevent overly enthusiastic self-seeding, deadhead plants, removing spent stems. Division is not necessary—and is difficult in any case, since gaura grows from a deep taproot. For additional plants, let a few volunteer seedlings grow; if you want to transplant them, do so while they are young.

Effective with Echinacea purpurea, Epilobium, Erigeron, ornamental grasses, Limonium, Oenothera, Perovskia, Salvia, Verbena.

T he cranesbills are a diverse and rewarding group. All have round, five-petaled flowers 1 to 1½ inches across and lobed, maplelike to finely cut leaves carried on long leafstalks—but beyond these similarities, the variety is tremendous. The plants vary from ground-hugging sorts to vigorous 4-footers; they may be mounding or trailing, with flower colors ranging from subtle to vibrant. The blooms are followed by beaklike fruits that give the plants their common name. Though cranesbills do belong to the genus *Geranium*, don't confuse them with the indoor/outdoor plants commonly called "geranium"—the latter are members of a different genus, *Pelargonium*.

One popular hybrid is **G. × cantabrigiense** (Zones 1–24, 31–43), best known for its selection **'Biokovo'**, with pink-tinged white flowers; it grows only 6 to 8 inches tall but spreads to make a small-scale ground cover. **G. cinereum** (Zones 1–24, 31–43) is another low, spreading cranesbill (to 6 inches high), with deeply cut leaves and inch-wide blossoms. Its cultivar **'Ballerina'** has lilac pink flowers with purple veining. A beautiful selection of **G. clarkei** (Zones 3–9, 14–24, 31–39) is **'Kashmir White'**, a 2-foot plant with finely cut leaves and a profuse show of 2-inch-wide, clear white blossoms veined in pink.

Bushy and vigorous, **G. endressii 'Wargrave Pink'** (Zones 1–9, 14–24, 31–43) reaches 1 to 1½ feet high and bears salmon pink flowers from late spring into fall. Related long-blooming hybrids (often sold as **G. × riversleaianum)** include **'Mavis Simpson'**, with satiny light pink blossoms, and **'Russell Prichard'**, with blooms of bright magenta; both are spreading, 8-inch-tall plants suited to Zones 6–9, 14–24, 30, 31.

G. himalayense (Zones 1–24, 31–43), growing just over a foot tall, has deeply lobed leaves that turn a rich bright red in autumn. It blooms all summer long, bearing 2-inch-wide flowers of bright violet blue with pinkish centers. Its double-flowered form **'Birch Double' ('Plenum')** has somewhat paler flowers, while the vigorous and popular related hybrid **'Johnson's Blue'** (Zones 3–9, 14–24, 30–39) offers blue-violet, 2-inch-wide flowers from spring to fall.

Listing continues >

GAURA lindheimeri

GAURA
Onagraceae

- ✿ ZONES 3–35, 37, 38 (COASTAL), 39
- ☼ FULL SUN
- ● ◌ REGULAR TO LITTLE WATER
- ✳ ✳ FLOWERS IN LATE SPRING, SUMMER, AUTUMN

Gaura lindheimeri 'Siskiyou Pink'

GERANIUM

CRANESBILL, HARDY GERANIUM
Geraniaceae

- ✿ ZONES VARY
- ☼ ◑ FULL SUN OR LIGHT SHADE
- ● REGULAR WATER
- ✳ ✳ ✳ ✳ ✳ FLOWERS IN LATE SPRING AND EARLY SUMMER, EXCEPT AS NOTED

Geranium × cantabrigiense 'Biokovo'

TOP: *Geranium psilostemon*
CENTER: *Geranium 'Johnson's Blue'*
BOTTOM: *Geranium sanguineum striatum*

Magenta red **G. macrorrhizum** (Zones 1–24, 30–43) reaches 12 to 14 inches high and spreads by rhizomes into sizable patches, making it a useful ground cover; it tolerates more heat and dryness than other cranesbills. The lobed, aromatic leaves turn yellow and red in autumn. Selections include white **'Album'**; 8- to 10-inch-tall **'Bevan's Variety'**, with deep reddish purple flowers; and pale pink **'Ingwersen's Variety'**.

Mourning widow geranium, **G. phaeum** (Zones 2–9, 24–27, 32–41), is a 2-foot plant bearing blossoms of a purple so deep it is nearly black. It tolerates heavy shade. **G. pratense** (Zones 1–7, 32–43) is a widely grown border perennial also suited to naturalizing in meadows and at woodland edges. Forming a bushy clump 2 to 3 feet high, it produces violet blue blossoms veined in red; selections include white **'Galactic'** and light blue **'Mrs. Kendall Clark'**.

G. psilostemon (Zones 2–9, 14–24, 30–41) is a large plant—to 4 feet tall—with 6- to 8-inch-wide, deeply cut basal foliage and bright magenta flowers centered with a black spot. A related hybrid, **'Ann Folkard'**, bears similar blooms but has yellowish green foliage; it trails through neighboring plants, making a memorable display.

Adaptable and easy to grow, **G. sanguineum** (Zones 1–9, 14–24, 30–43) reaches 1½ feet high, with purple to crimson flowers and trailing stems spreading to 2 feet. Its deeply lobed leaves turn bright red in autumn. Selections include white **'Album'**; **'John Elsley'**, bearing pink blossoms with deeper pink veins; deep purple **'New Hampshire'**; and the dwarf **G. s. striatum** (sometimes sold as **G. lancastriense)**, a lovely form for the rock garden with light pink flowers veined in red.

CULTURE. Cranesbills grow best in cool- and mild-summer regions, where you can plant them in full sun or light shade. In the hottest areas, give them afternoon shade. Soil should be moist but well drained. You can leave clumps of most kinds in place for many years before they decline due to crowding. When division is needed, do the job in early spring. If you just want to increase a planting, dig and transplant rooted portions from the edge of the clump.

Effective with Alchemilla mollis, Amsonia tabernaemontana, Armeria maritima, Astrantia major, Dictamnus albus, Geum, Lupinus, Paeonia, Scabiosa.

GEUM

🌿 GEUM, AVENS
Rosaceae

🌡 ZONES 1–24, 32–43
☼ FULL SUN, EXCEPT AS NOTED
💧 REGULAR WATER
✳ ❋ ❋ FLOWERS IN SPRING, SUMMER

Geum 'Borisii'

Geum's cheerful single to double, roselike blossoms are carried in airy, branched clusters that stand sturdily above the foliage clumps. The handsome strap-shaped leaves are divided into many leaflets; established clumps form attractive mounds up to 15 inches high.

The largest and showiest geums are selections of **G. chiloense** (also sold as **G. quellyon)**, with 15-inch foliage clumps, flowering stems to 2 feet tall, and blossoms 1 to 1½ inches across. Selections include semidouble bright orange **'Dolly North'**; semidouble **'Mrs. Bradshaw'**, with scarlet flowers; **'Princess Juliana'**, featuring double copper blossoms; **'Coppertone'**, a foot-tall plant with apricot-colored flowers; and 16- to 24-inch **'Lady Stratheden'**, with double yellow blossoms.

Pretty, 12- to 15-inch-high **G. × heldreichii 'Georgenburg'** has soft apricot blossoms. The cultivar **'Starker's Magnificum'**, of uncertain parentage, bears clear tangerine flowers on a plant to 15 inches high. An especially low geum, effective planted at the front of a border or in a rock garden, is **G. 'Borisii'**. Its foliage clumps are just 6 inches high; foot-tall stalks rise above these, carrying single 1- to 2-inch blooms in bright orange red.

CULTURE. Plant geums in good, well-drained soil; water regularly throughout the growing season. Give full sun except in hot-summer areas, where plants need dappled sunlight or light shade during the hottest months. Deadhead to prolong the flowering season. When clumps become crowded and bloom lessens, divide in early spring. Plants can also be grown from seed sown in early spring.

Effective with Alchemilla mollis, Aquilegia, Aurinia saxatilis, Campanula, Geranium, Rheum palmatum.

GYPSOPHILA paniculata
🌸 BABY'S BREATH
Caryophyllaceae

- 🌱 ZONES 1–10, 14–16, 18–21, 31–45
- ☼ FULL SUN
- 💧 REGULAR WATER
- ❄ ❋ FLOWERS IN SUMMER

Gypsophila paniculata 'Bristol Fairy'

B illowy, mounded plants bearing a froth of small blossoms have an airy, softening effect in gardens—and the cut blooms play the same role in bouquets. The much-branched plants have small or sparse leaves and grow from 1 to 4 feet high, depending on the cultivar. **'Bristol Fairy'** is the classic 3-foot-tall, a double-flowered white variety; **'Pink Fairy'** grows about half as high. Both of these have individual blossoms about ¼ inch across. White-flowered **'Perfecta'**, a favorite among florists, has larger blossoms (about ½ inch wide) on 4-foot plants. **'Compacta Plena'** is a double white dwarf 1½ feet tall; other dwarfs are the double pink cultivars **'Pink Star'** (to 1½ feet) and **'Viette's Dwarf'** (12 to 15 inches). **Festival** is a seed-propagated series that produces white- and pink-flowered plants 1 to 1½ feet high.

CULTURE. Baby's breath requires deep, well-drained soil to accommodate its long taproot. Add lime to strongly acid soils. Provide support for the taller varieties; if left unsupported, they may break apart in wind or heavy rain or with overhead watering. For repeat bloom, cut back the flowering stems before seeds form. This a permanent plant that should not be divided; propagate from seed.

One note of caution: Its demure looks notwithstanding, baby's breath has naturalized and become invasive in the coastal zones of the Great Lakes area, where it threatens to crowd out native plants. If you live in this region, check with a local nursery or cooperative extension agent before you plant.

Effective with Adenophora, Delphinium, Echinacea purpurea, Echinops, Erigeron, ornamental grasses, Papaver orientale.

HELENIUM
🌸 SNEEZEWEED
Asteraceae (Compositae)

- 🌱 ALL ZONES
- ☼ FULL SUN
- 💧 REGULAR WATER
- ❄ ❋ ❋ FLOWERS IN SUMMER, AUTUMN

Helenium 'Moerheim Beauty'

S neezeweed's bright daisies appear over a long period from midsummer into autumn. Each 1- to 2-inch blossom features broadly fan-shaped petals (ray flowers) around a velvety, dome-shaped central disc. A number of named hybrids of **H. autumnale** are available, ranging in height from 2 to 5 feet. All are branching plants characterized by linear leaves.

At just 2 to 3 feet tall, **'Crimson Beauty'** is a good choice for smaller gardens; despite the name, its flowers are bronzy red. **'Moerheim Beauty'** offers another shade of red, bearing mahogany-colored blossoms on a 3- to 4-foot plant. **'Riverton Beauty'**, 3½ to 4 feet high, produces tawny golden yellow blooms with a bronze center, while 4-foot-high **'Waldtraut'** has extra-large flowers in burnt orange.

CULTURE. Plant sneezeweeds in average soil. Don't fertilize them generously; they'll bloom better with only scant feeding. Topnotch performance comes where summers are hot, but plants do need regular water to look their best. Taller varieties require staking. Clumps become crowded quickly and should be divided every 2 or 3 years in spring.

Effective with Aster, Echinops, Erigeron, Liatris, Solidago.

HELIANTHUS

🌿 SUNFLOWER

Asteraceae (Compositae)

- 🌿 ZONES 1–24, 28–43
- ☼ FULL SUN
- 💧 REGULAR WATER
- ✳ FLOWERS IN SUMMER, AUTUMN

Helianthus × multiflorus 'Capenoch Star'

Perennial relatives of the common annual *H. annuus*, these sunflowers are upright, 3- to 8-foot plants with rough-textured, oval leaves and numerous 3-inch-wide flower heads. They're attractive in tall borders and wild gardens. Best known are the hybrid varieties sold as *H. × multiflorus* (sometimes as *H. decapetalus)*. Reaching 3 to 4 feet, 'Capenoch Star' has single lemon yellow flowers with a large central brown disc. A taller choice (to 4 to 5 feet) is 'Flore-pleno', with fully double bright yellow blossoms; the equally tall 'Morning Sun' has lovely single yellow flowers. Willowleaf sunflower, *H. salicifolius,* features narrow, willowy, gracefully drooping leaves on stout 6- to 8-foot stems. The stems are topped by many 2-inch-wide yellow blooms with purplish brown centers.

CULTURE. These are tough plants by nature, but they perform best with good soil and regular water. Plant in full sun; in shade, they grow tall and leggy, and the stems are apt to break. Even in sun, they often need staking to remain upright. Plants increase rapidly and should be divided about every 3 years in early spring, both to control spreading and to revitalize the plant.

Effective with Aster, Boltonia asteroides, Canna, Erigeron, Eupatorium, ornamental grasses, Rudbeckia, Salvia, Solidago.

HELLEBORUS

🌿 HELLEBORE, CHRISTMAS ROSE, LENTEN ROSE

Ranunculaceae

- 🌿 ZONES VARY
- ☼ ● LIGHT TO FULL SHADE
- 💧 ◌ REGULAR TO MODERATE WATER
- ✳ ✳ ✳ ✳ ✳ FLOWERS IN WINTER, EARLY SPRING, EXCEPT AS NOTED

Helleborus argutifolius

Hellebores are distinctive, elegant plants that bear lovely blossoms for several months in winter and spring. Long-lived evergreen perennials, they form basal clumps of handsome, substantial, long-stalked leaves, usually divided fanwise into leaflets. The blossoms comprise five petal-like sepals surrounding a large cluster of stamens; they look a bit like single roses, hence the common names of some species. All parts of these plants are poisonous if ingested.

The largest species is Corsican hellebore, *H. argutifolius (H. lividus corsicus),* successful in Zones 4–24, 31, 32. It is almost shrubby in appearance, with leafy stems to 3 feet high and pale blue-green leaves divided into three leaflets with sharply toothed edges. Clusters of large light chartreuse flowers are borne among the upper leaves. In mild-winter areas, these may appear from late fall to late spring; in the colder parts of the range, bloom time comes in early spring. Corsican hellebore can take some sun and is fairly drought tolerant once established.

H. foetidus (Zones 3–9, 14–23, 30–34, 39) has exceptionally graceful foliage, with seven to nine narrow, leathery, blackish green leaflets at the end of each leafstalk. The plant parts emit a slightly unpleasant scent when bruised (hence the specific name *foetidus)* but are otherwise odorless. In late winter and early spring, clusters of inch-wide green blossoms with purple markings appear atop leafy, 1½-foot stems. Stems, leafstalks, and flower stalks of the selection 'Wester Flisk' have a striking red tint. Once established, *H. foetidus* is also fairly drought tolerant.

Christmas rose, *H. niger* (Zones 1–7, 14–17, 32–45), blooms between December and early spring, depending on the severity of

Helleborus foetidus

the winter. Each leafless, 1½-foot flower stem usually holds one upward-facing blossom to 2 inches across; the blooms open white or greenish white, then turn purplish pink with age. The dark green leaves are divided into seven to nine leaflets. Plants require winter chill to perform well and thus do not succeed in warm-winter climates. Named varieties are sometimes offered; these include **'Potter's Wheel'**, with large white flowers with a green eye, and **'White Magic'**, with large white blossoms that take on a hint of pink as they age.

The easiest hellebore to grow is Lenten rose, **_H. orientalis_** (Zones 2–10, 14–24, 31–41). It begins flowering in late winter and continues into spring. The 15- to 18-inch flowering stems bear a few modified leaves and branched clusters of nodding, 3- to 4-inch-wide flowers in colors varying from white to greenish, purple, rose, or yellow, often spotted on the inside with deep purple. The leaves are glossy, divided into 5 to 11 leaflets.

CULTURE. Although Corsican hellebore *(H. argutifolius)* and *H. foetidus* withstand some drought once established, all hellebores appreciate regular watering and soil enriched with organic matter. Plant them in filtered sun or light to full shade. They do not require division to maintain vigor. You can divide clumps to obtain more plants, but the divisions are slow to reestablish. Most hellebores self-sow, and it's easy to move volunteer seedlings to new locations while they are small.

Effective with Dicentra, Doronicum, Epimedium, Euphorbia, ferns, Mertensia virginica, Primula, Thalictrum.

Helleborus orientalis

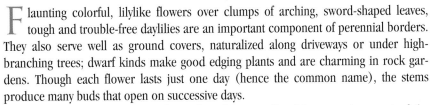

F launting colorful, lilylike flowers over clumps of arching, sword-shaped leaves, tough and trouble-free daylilies are an important component of perennial borders. They also serve well as ground covers, naturalized along driveways or under high-branching trees; dwarf kinds make good edging plants and are charming in rock gardens. Though each flower lasts just one day (hence the common name), the stems produce many buds that open on successive days.

Many daylily species exist, but only a few are offered by nurseries; most of the daylilies sold commercially are hybrids created by amateur and professional breeders. More than 20,000 named varieties have been registered by the American Hemerocallis Society, and hundreds more appear each year. These hybrids are classified in several ways. First, they're categorized as deciduous, evergreen, or semievergreen. Deciduous types go completely dormant in winter and are the hardiest, surviving without protection to about −35°F/−38°C; where winters are very mild, however, they may not get enough chill to perform well. Evergreen kinds grow well in mild-winter regions and colder areas too, but need a protective mulch (such as 4 to 6 inches of hay) where temperatures dip below −20°F/−29°C. Semievergreen sorts may or may not retain their leaves, depending on where they are grown.

Another way hybrid daylilies are grouped is by size and season of bloom. Stems of most standard-size daylilies grow 2½ to 4 feet tall, though a few types reach 6 feet. Miniature and small-flowered varieties grow just 1 to 2 feet tall. And you'll find daylilies that bloom early, midseason, and late; choose some of each to prolong the season of bloom. There are also everblooming and reblooming (remontant) types, such as the well-known dwarf bright gold **'Stella de Oro'** and its lemon yellow offspring **'Happy Returns'**, which blossom for most of the summer.

These plants are also classed by flower size and form. The blossoms range from 3 to 8 inches across (just 1½ to 3 inches in the smaller varieties) and may be lily shaped or chalice shaped; you'll also find double-flowered varieties and spider types with narrow, twisted petals. Some daylilies are fragrant; a familiar example is the old-fashioned favorite **'Hyperion'**, a 4-footer with clear yellow midsummer blooms.

HEMEROCALLIS

DAYLILY

Liliaceae

ZONES VARY

FULL SUN, EXCEPT AS NOTED

REGULAR TO MODERATE WATER

FLOWERS IN SPRING, SUMMER, AUTUMN

Hemerocallis 'Oodnadatta'

Listing continues >

Hemerocallis 'Black-eyed Stella'

Given all these possibilities, you naturally have a multitude of choices when you shop for daylilies. To be sure you get what you want, select plants in bloom or buy from mail-order nursery catalogs with good color photographs.

CULTURE. Though daylilies survive with little attention, they grow and bloom better if given regular water and well-drained soil amended with organic matter. They thrive in full sun except where summers are dry and hot; in these regions, choose a spot in filtered sun or partial shade. Removing spent flowers improves the plants' appearance and helps promote more flowers in the reblooming varieties. Divide clumps when they become crowded, usually after 3 to 6 years; reblooming kinds do best if divided every other year. Divide in summer in cool-summer regions and where the growing season is short. If you garden in a hot-summer area, divide in autumn or early spring.

Effective with Anchusa azurea, Anthemis tinctoria, Canna, Chrysanthemum frutescens, Crambe cordifolia, Lupinus, Monarda.

HEUCHERA
🌿 CORAL BELLS, ALUM ROOT
Saxifragaceae

- 🌿 ZONES VARY
- ☼ ◑ FULL SUN OR LIGHT SHADE
- 💧 REGULAR WATER
- ✳ ✳ ✳ ✳ FLOWERS IN SPRING, SUMMER

Coral bells have long been favorites for their airy spikes of small, bell-shaped blossoms—but in recent years, dozens of new selections have been gaining popularity primarily for their handsome, colorful foliage rather than their flowers. The plants have rounded to heart-shaped leaves on long leafstalks and form low, mounded, slowly spreading clumps. Wiry, 1- to 3-foot flower stalks appear from spring through summer, bearing dainty flowers (to ¼ inch or more across) in open clusters.

Most of the varieties grown for ornamental foliage are listed as **H. americana** (Zones 1–6, 15–17, 32–43), though many are actually hybrids with other species. The basic form grows in a 1- to 2-foot clump of foliage composed of lobed, white-mottled green leaves 1½ to 4 inches wide (or wider); tiny greenish flowers are borne on 2- to 3-foot stems. Among the many cultivars grown for foliage are **'Cascade Dawn'** and the similar **'Pewter Veil'**, both with purplish leaves enhanced by silver netting; **'Persian Carpet'**, bearing 8-inch-wide, metallic silver leaves with purple veins and margins; **'Stormy Seas'**, with dark, ruffled foliage marked with silver, lavender, and pewter; and darkest purple **'Velvet Night'**.

H. × brizoides (Zones 1–10, 14–24, 31–45) covers a group of slender-stemmed hybrids cultivated for their profuse and dainty blossoms. Members include white-flowered **'June Bride'**, raspberry red **'Raspberry Regal'**, and dusty pink **'Weston Pink'**. Native to the western United States, **H. micrantha** (Zones 2–11, 14–24, 31–43) is best known for the 1- to 2-foot-tall forms (which may be hybrids or selections) **'Palace Purple'**, with maplelike leaves in a rich brownish or purplish shade, and **'Ruffles'**, featuring leaves decoratively lobed and ruffled around the edges; both bear spikes of minute white flowers.

Forming neat tufts of round, 1- to 2-inch leaves with scalloped edges, **H. sanguinea** (Zones 1–11, 14–24, 31–45) sends up slender, wiry stems bearing open clusters of nodding bright red or coral pink flowers. Varieties with white, pure pink, or crimson blossoms are available.

CULTURE. Where summers are hot and dry, coral bells (especially those with colored foliage) need light shade, preferably during the afternoon. Elsewhere, they'll tolerate full sun. Provide well-drained soil enriched with organic matter. Clumps become crowded after 3 or 4 years, with the foliage growing at the ends of short, thick, woody stalks. Divide in early spring; when replanting, set the plant's crown even with the soil surface.

Effective with Adenophora, Alstroemeria, Iberis sempervirens, Lupinus, Papaver orientale, Phormium, Platycodon grandiflorus, Sisyrinchium striatum.

Heuchera 'Palace Purple'

Rose-mallow gives the garden a touch of the tropics. Vigorous and robust, it bears large (up to 1-foot-wide!), showy flowers. The oval leaves are large too, from 4 to 10 inches long and 4 to 5 inches wide; they're carried on stems 2 to 8 feet tall, depending on the variety. Seed-grown strains include 4-foot **Southern Belle** and the shorter **Disco Belle** (to just 2 feet); both bear 8- to 12-inch-wide flowers in a range of colors including red, pink, rose, and white, often with a red eye. For specific colors, look for named selections such as 4-foot-high **'Blue River'**, with pure white, 10-inch blossoms, or **'Lord Baltimore'**, featuring 10-inch-wide, deep red flowers on a plant 4 to 6 feet tall.

CULTURE. Plant rose-mallow in good soil, well enriched with organic matter. It needs regular water; mulching helps conserve moisture. Avoid windswept locations, where flowers will burn and plants will lose moisture rapidly. In areas where summers are hot and dry, give plants light shade to prevent wilting. Fertilize every 6 to 8 weeks during the growing season. The stems die to the ground in winter, even in mild climates.

Though clumps increase in size gradually over the years, they do not need division for continued good growth and bloom. Seed-grown strains flower the first year if sown indoors and planted out as early as possible.

Effective with Aruncus, Astilbe, Eupatorium.

HIBISCUS moscheutos
ROSE-MALLOW
Malvaceae

- ZONES 2–21, 26–41
- FULL SUN OR LIGHT SHADE
- REGULAR WATER
- FLOWERS IN SUMMER

Hibiscus moscheutos

Excellent in shady borders, as weed-suppressing ground covers, and in containers, these tough perennials bear spikes of attractive trumpet-shaped flowers—but they're prized chiefly for their exceptionally handsome, varied foliage. The leaves may be lance shaped, heart shaped, oval, or nearly round; they may be smooth or wavy edged, glossy or dusted with a grayish bloom like that on a ripe plum. The texture may be smooth, quilted, or puckered. Colors range from all shades of green to chartreuse to gray and blue, and there are myriad variegations involving white, yellow, or cream markings. In size, hostas vary from tiny dwarfs just 3 to 4 inches high to "giants" that reach 4 to 5 feet. Unsurprisingly, breeders have introduced hundreds of varieties. Names can be confusing and, in some species, have undergone many changes; to be sure you're getting the plants you want, buy them in full leaf or from a mail-order catalog with good photographs. If you're serious about growing hostas or just want to learn more about these plants, you may want to contact the American Hosta Society.

The variable species **H. fortunei** is known mainly for its many selections, which offer a wide range of leaf colors. Plants are typically 1 to 1½ feet high, with lilac blooms and oval leaves to 1 foot long. **'Albo-picta'** changes color with the seasons. In spring, its pointed leaves have light green centers with a darker margin; by late summer, they're solid green. **'Hyacinthina'** has large gray-green leaves thinly edged in white.

Hosta sieboldiana 'Frances Williams'

The term "hosta hybrids" covers many widely grown hostas. The dwarf **'Chartreuse Wiggles'** reaches just 6 inches, featuring lance-shaped, wavy-edged chartreuse-gold leaves. **'Ginko Craig'** forms a 1- to 1½-foot mound of elongated, frosty green leaves with silver margins. **'Hadspen Blue'**, to 1 foot tall, has slightly wavy, broadly oval leaves with a thick, heavy texture that makes them somewhat resistant to slug assault. Also somewhat slug resistant is **'Sum and Substance'**, with textured, shiny yellow leaves to 20 inches long; it forms a mound 3 feet high and 5 feet wide and is fairly sun tolerant.

HOSTA
HOSTA, PLANTAIN LILY, FUNKIA
Liliaceae

- ZONES 1–10, 12–21, 28, 31–45
- LIGHT TO FULL SHADE, EXCEPT AS NOTED
- REGULAR WATER
- FLOWERS IN SUMMER

Hosta fortunei

Listing continues >

TOP: *Hosta* 'Ginko Craig'
BOTTOM: *Hosta sieboldiana* 'Elegans'

Narrow-leafed hosta, **H. lancifolia,** has 6-inch-long, lance-shaped glossy deep green leaves; it forms a foot-high mound and is more tolerant of sunny, dry conditions than many other hostas. Fragrant hosta, **H. plantaginea (H. grandiflora, H. subcordata),** bears large (to 4-inch-long), fragrant, trumpet-shaped white flowers over a 2-foot mound of bright green, 10-inch-long oval leaves with a quilted surface.

H. sieboldiana (H. glauca), to 2½ feet tall, features heart-shaped, 10- to 15-inch-long blue-green leaves that are heavily veined and puckered. Many slender, pale lilac flower spikes nestle close above the foliage early in the season. The leaves of its slug-resistant cultivar **'Elegans'** are covered in a blue-gray bloom. The classic **'Frances Williams'** has round, puckered, blue-green leaves boldly edged in yellow.

CULTURE. In general, hostas are shade lovers, though some will tolerate sun (and most will take considerable sun in cool-summer regions). If planted in sun, a hosta will be more compact than the same variety planted in shade and will produce more flowers; if planted in shade, it may grow taller and wider. You'll get the most luxuriant growth if you plant in good, organically enriched soil and fertilize regularly during the growing season. Be sure plants are kept moist.

Foliage collapses and withers in autumn frosts, then grows anew in spring. Slugs and snails chew the leaves; put out bait or handpick and destroy these pests. As noted above, they are are less attracted to varieties with thick foliage.

Hostas remain vigorous without division; in fact, the clumps become more beautiful as they grow larger. To increase a favorite hosta, carefully remove plants from a clump's perimeter. Or cut a wedge-shaped piece from a clump and transplant it; the clump will fill in quickly.

Effective with Aconitum, Alchemilla mollis, Anemone × hybrida, Astilbe, ferns, Polygonatum, Pulmonaria, Thalictrum, Tricyrtis.

IBERIS sempervirens
EVERGREEN CANDYTUFT
Brassicaceae (Cruciferae)

- ZONES 1–24, 31–45
- FULL SUN, EXCEPT AS NOTED
- REGULAR WATER
- FLOWERS IN SPRING, EXCEPT AS NOTED

Iberis sempervirens

Bright white flowers borne in 2-inch clusters cover evergreen candytuft from early to late spring. These 8- to 18-inch-tall plants also sport good-looking, glossy dark green foliage, making them a handsome choice for the front of the border or for rock gardens.

Available selections include some that are shorter and more compact than the species, among them 6-inch-tall **'Alexander's White'**, with fine-textured foliage; **'Little Gem'**, 4 to 6 inches tall; and **'Pygmaea'**, which reaches only 4 inches. **'Purity'** is a wide-spreading selection that grows 6 to 12 inches tall. Another spreading choice is vigorous, showy **'Snowflake'**, which grows 4 to 12 inches high and 1½ to 3 feet wide. It has broader, more leathery leaves and larger flowers than other evergreen candytuft selections and blooms not only in spring, but also sporadically in summer and fall. **'Autumn Snow'**, reaching 8 to 10 inches tall, also has larger flowers; it blooms in spring and again in fall.

CULTURE. Plant evergreen candytuft in good, well-drained soil. Give full sun except in regions with hot summers, where the plants perform better with a little afternoon shade. In all regions, you can set out plants in spring. In mild-winter areas, you can also plant in fall for a more effective flower show—the plants will establish themselves over winter and be ready to bloom sooner in spring.

After the main bloom period is over, cut or shear plants back to make them more compact. Start new plants by taking stem cuttings in summer.

Effective with Armeria maritima, Aurinia saxatilis, Dianthus, Dicentra, Heuchera, Iris (bearded), Phlox subulata, Veronica.

Irises are choice plants for perennial gardens. Their showy flowers, composed of three true petals *(standards)* and three petal-like sepals *(falls)*, rise above swordlike leaves that form a flat fan of foliage. The irises discussed here grow from rhizomes—thickened modified stems that grow horizontally along or just beneath the soil surface.

BEARDED IRISES

Most widely grown are bearded irises (Zones 1–24, 30–45), so called because of the characteristic caterpillarlike tuft of hairs adorning the falls. Available in a dazzling array of colors and color combinations, these hybrids typically bloom in spring, though you'll also find some rebloomers that flower again later in the season. Most kinds are classified by the height of the plant when in bloom. Most familiar are the *tall* bearded irises; these flower in midspring, carrying their large, broad blossoms on branching stems 2½ to 4 feet high. They bloom in every color but true red and green (and breeders are working on those); many have elaborately ruffled and fringed blossoms. The various types of *median* irises range in height from 8 to 28 inches; many bloom a few weeks earlier in spring than tall bearded iris and have somewhat smaller flowers. *Miniature dwarf* irises, charming planted at the front of the border and in rock gardens, grow just 2 to 8 inches tall and bear a wealth of blossoms in early spring.

Choosing among the hundreds of named cultivars can be tricky. If possible, visit a specialty nursery during bloom season so that you can see color, size, and flower shape; mail-order catalogs with good color photographs are also a fine source of information, as is the American Iris Society.

CULTURE. Bearded irises need good drainage, since the rhizomes may rot if they are too wet. They'll grow in a range of soils, from sandy to claylike—but if you plant in clay, plant in raised beds or on ridges to assure good drainage. Amend any soil with organic matter before planting. Choose a location in full sun in cool and mild climates. In the hottest regions, you can select a spot that receives light shade during the afternoon (too much shade reduces flowering, however). Plant in July or August in cold-winter regions, in September or October where summers are hot; in mild regions, plant any time from July to October. Set the rhizomes with their tops just beneath the soil surface. New growth proceeds from the fan or leafy end of the rhizome, so point that end in the direction you want growth to occur. Bearded irises grow best if watered regularly from the time growth begins until about 6 weeks after the blooms fade; they need less moisture during summer. Clumps become crowded and bloom less freely after 3 or 4 years. When this occurs, dig and divide at the best planting time for your climate.

Bearded irises are effective with Amsonia tabernaemontana, Aurinia saxatilis, Centranthus ruber, Diascia, Dictamnus albus, Iberis sempervirens, Lupinus, Paeonia, Phlox.

BEARDLESS IRISES

Japanese and Siberian irises are widely available types of beardless irises. Both lack beards on their falls and have rhizomes that produce fibrous roots (rather than the fleshy ones typical of bearded irises), but in other respects, they differ considerably from each other.

Japanese irises (Zones 1–10, 14–24, 32–45) are derived solely from *I. ensata* (formerly *I. kaempferi).* They have narrow, graceful upright leaves and sumptuous, relatively flat single to double flowers 4 to 12 inches across, borne on slender stems to 4 feet high. Colors include purple, violet, pink, rose, red, and white, often with contrasting veins or edges. They flower in late spring or early summer.

Listing continues >

IRIS

🌿 IRIS

Iridaceae

🌱 ZONES VARY

EXPOSURE NEEDS VARY

WATER NEEDS VARY

✳ ✳ ✳ ✳ ✳ ✳ FLOWERS IN SPRING, SUMMER

Bearded iris
'Orange Harvest'

Iris ensata 'Caprician Butterfly'

CULTURE. Plant in fall or spring, in acid to neutral soil. Plants grow well in full sun where summers are cool; in hot regions, give dappled sun or light shade. These irises require plenty of moisture; they can be grown in well-watered borders or planted in containers and sunk halfway to the rim in a pond. Divide crowded clumps in late summer or early autumn, replanting the rhizomes immediately so they don't become dry.

Iris ensata

Siberian irises (Zones 1–10, 14–23, 32–45) are for the most part named hybrids derived from *I. sibirica* and *I. sanguinea*. They form clumps of narrow, almost grasslike leaves. In midspring, slender stems to 4 feet tall (depending on the variety) rise from the foliage clumps, each bearing two to five blossoms with upright standards and flaring to drooping falls. Colors include white, light yellow, and shades of blue, lavender, purple, wine, and pink.

CULTURE. Plant in full sun or partial shade, in neutral to acid soil well amended with organic matter. In cold-winter regions, plant in early spring or late summer; in milder regions, plant in autumn. Water liberally from the onset of growth in spring until several weeks after bloom time ends. Division is required infrequently—only when clumps become hollow in the center. Do the job at the best planting time for your region.

Beardless irises are effective with Aruncus, Delphinium, Dictamnus albus, Paeonia, Trollius.

Siberian iris 'Ego'

KNIPHOFIA

🌿 RED-HOT POKER, TORCH-LILY, POKER PLANT

Liliaceae

🌱 ZONES 3–9, 14–24, 28–34

☼ FULL SUN, EXCEPT AS NOTED

💧💧 REGULAR TO MODERATE WATER

❄ ❄ ❄ ❄ FLOWERS IN LATE SPRING, SUMMER

Thick, fountainlike clumps of coarse, grassy foliage topped with tall flowering spikes bring a strong vertical element to the border, providing an effective contrast to the many perennials that have a mounded form. The blossoms are attractive to hummingbirds.

The old-fashioned red-hot poker, **K. uvaria**, blooms in late spring, sending up 4- to 6-foot flower spikes above gray-green, 1½- to 3-foot-long leaves. The blossoms at the bottom of each cluster are yellow, those toward the top orange red. Modern hybrids (with this and other species in their heritage) reach 1½ to 4 feet or taller and may bloom in late spring or summer, depending on the variety. Vigorous **'Bees' Sunset'** is 4 feet tall in bloom, with abundant spikes of yellow-orange summer flowers. **'Little Maid'**, just 1½ to 2 feet tall, features creamy white flowers in summer. **'Percy's Pride'** is a late-spring bloomer with tightly clustered lime to light yellow flowers on 3-foot stems.

CULTURE. These plants require good drainage. Set them in a sunny location, in soil enriched with organic matter; in hot-summer areas, choose a site with some afternoon shade. They tolerate considerable drought but look and bloom better with regular to moderate water. Cut out flower spikes after bloom, both to make the plants more presentable and to encourage more flowers. Cut old foliage to the ground in autumn where winter temperatures remain above 0°F/−18°C. In colder areas, tie the leaves over the clump to protect the growing points; or cover clumps with a loose mulch. Red-hot pokers don't require division, but you can dig and remove young plants from a clump's edge to increase your supply.

Effective with Agapanthus, Diascia, Monarda, Nepeta, Perovskia.

Kniphofia uvaria

With fragrant flowers and silvery gray to gray-green foliage, lavender is equally at home in the perennial border and the herb garden. A number of species and varieties of this beautiful subshrub are available. The hardiest and most widely planted species is English lavender, **L. angustifolia** (Zones 4–24, 30, 32–34, 39), the lavender prized for perfume and sachets. The plant reaches 3 to 4 feet high and wide, bearing narrow, smooth-edged gray leaves to 2 inches long; in late spring or summer, small (½-inch-long) lavender flowers appear, carried in 1½- to 2-foot-high spikes. Selections, many of them lower growing than the species, include the popular **'Hidcote'**, reaching 15 to 20 inches tall and bearing short spikes of deep purplish blue flowers; **'Lavender Lady'**, a fast grower to 10 inches tall that often produces its lavender blossoms the first year from seed; and **'Rosea'**, a 15-inch plant with pink flowers.

French lavender, **L. dentata** (Zones 8, 9, 12–24, 31), forms a dense, billowy plant to 3 feet high, with gray-green, square-toothed leaves. The dark lavender flowers bloom over a long period in spring and summer—or almost all year round, in mild-winter areas.

Lavandin, **L. × intermedia** (Zones 4–24, 30–34, 39), is not a single plant, but a group of vigorous, especially fragrant hybrids that tolerate warm, humid summers better than most lavenders. They bloom in early to midsummer. **'Grosso'** is possibly the most fragrant of all, with compact, 8-inch-high mounds of silvery foliage and 2½-foot-long, arching stems carrying fat spikes of purple flowers. Violet-blossomed **'Fred Boutin'** reaches just 1½ feet high; **'White Spike'** grows 3 feet tall and wide, holding its long spikes of pure white flowers above branches covered with silvery leaves.

Spanish lavender, **L. stoechas** (Zones 4–24, 30, 31, warmer parts of 32), forms a stocky, compact plant 1½ to 3 feet tall, with narrow gray leaves ½ to 1 inch long. The deep purple flowers, showy from midspring to early summer, grow in dense, short spikes, each topped with a big tuft of purple bracts (modified leaves). The cultivar **'Wings of Night'** has especially dark flowers.

CULTURE. Lavenders thrive in average to poor soil, as long it is well drained. Plant them in full sun and water moderately. To keep the plants compact, shear them after flowering or cut back in early spring just as growth begins. When plants decline, start new ones from stem cuttings taken in summer.

Effective with Echinops, Eryngium, Euphorbia, Phlomis, Origanum, Santolina, Thymus.

LAVANDULA
🌿 LAVENDER
Lamiaceae (Labiatae)
- ✿ ZONES VARY
- ☼ FULL SUN
- ◐ MODERATE WATER
- ✳ ✳ ✳ FLOWERS IN SPRING, SUMMER

TOP: *Lavandula angustifolia*
BOTTOM: *Lavandula stoechas*

Showy perennials native to the eastern and central United States, the gayfeathers form basal tufts of narrow, grassy leaves that are topped in summer by leafy stems bearing spikes of small, bright flowers. The plants' upright form stands in pleasing contrast to the more rounded outlines of other perennials. Bloom proceeds from the top of the spike down, with the upper flowers opening before the lower ones—an unusual feature, since blossoms in terminal spikes typically open from the bottom up.

Two species produce stems up to 5 feet high: **L. ligulistylis,** with dark red buds and reddish purple flowers, and Kansas gayfeather **(L. pycnostachya),** with purplish pink flowers in the standard form and white flowers in the selection **'Alba'.** The

Liatris ligulistylis

LIATRIS
🌿 GAYFEATHER
Asteraceae (Compositae)
- ✿ ZONES 1–10, 14–24, 26, 28–45
- ☼ FULL SUN
- ◐◐ REGULAR TO MODERATE WATER
- ✳ ✳ FLOWERS IN SUMMER

Liatris pycnostachya with Rudbeckia

most widely available species, **L. spicata**, grows to about 4 feet high and bears light purple blossoms. Among its cultivars are **'Floristan White'** and dark purple **'Floristan Violet'**, both 3 feet tall; 2- to 2½-foot **'Kobold'**, with bright rosy lilac flowers; and **'Silvertips'**, bearing shimmering silvery lilac flowers on 3-foot stems.

CULTURE. Gayfeathers need moderately fertile, well-drained soil; they are especially prone to rot in soggy soil during their winter dormant period. They're drought tolerant but look and bloom best with moderate to regular watering. After a number of years, when performance declines, divide and reset crowded clumps in early spring.

Effective with Echinacea purpurea, Helenium, Platycodon grandiflorus, Rudbeckia, Stokesia laevis, Veronica.

LIGULARIA

LIGULARIA
Asteraceae (Compositae)

- ✔ ZONES 3–9, 15–17, 32, 34, 36–41
- ◐ ● LIGHT TO FULL SHADE
- ◐ AMPLE WATER
- ✳ ✳ FLOWERS IN SUMMER

Ligularia stenocephala 'The Rocket'

Stately perennials with daisy flowers and clumps of large, handsome leaves, ligularias make a bold statement planted near water, at the edge of a woodland, or in a shady, well-watered border. **L. dentata** is grown primarily for its attractive foliage: leathery, tooth-edged, rounded, medium green leaves that can measure up to 20 inches across. Its branching heads of vivid orange daisies bloom atop strong, 3- to 5-foot stems. The selection **'Dark Beauty'** has especially dark purple foliage. **'Desdemona'** and **'Othello'** have leaves that are green on their upper surfaces, deep purple beneath; the leafstalks and veins are deep purple as well.

Better known for its flower spikes than its foliage is **L. stenocephala,** usually represented by the variety **'The Rocket'** (which is either a selection or a hybrid of *L. stenocephala)*. This plant has clumps of deeply cut green leaves topped by slender, graceful, 5-foot spires of yellow daisies.

CULTURE. Ligularias grow best with rich soil, ample moisture, and some shade; they do not tolerate heat or low humidity, which causes the leaves to wilt. To help hold moisture around the roots, some gardeners line the planting hole with a plastic bag, perforated in a few places to allow some drainage. Be sure to control slugs and snails, which can ravage the leaves. You can leave clumps undisturbed for years; if more plants are needed, divide in early spring.

Effective with Aruncus, Astilbe, Cimicifuga, Eupatorium, Lobelia cardinalis.

LIMONIUM

✂ SEA LAVENDER, STATICE
Plumbaginaceae

- ✔ ZONES VARY
- ☼ FULL SUN
- ◐ MODERATE WATER
- ✳ ✳ ✳ FLOWERS IN SUMMER

Limonium latifolium

Sea lavender's leathery basal leaves contrast nicely with the airy clusters of small delicate flowers it bears on many-branched stems. On established plants, the cloud of blossoms may reach 3 feet high. The flowers have a papery texture and can be dried for use in everlasting arrangements. **L. latifolium** (Zones 1–10, 14–24, 26, 28, 31–43) produces sprays of bicolored blooms in lavender blue and white and forms a basal rosette of smooth-edged leaves 6 to 10 inches long and wide. **L. perezii** (Zones 13, 15–17, 20–27) grows in clumps of broad, wavy-edged leaves to 1 foot long; wiry stems carry large clusters of small purple-and-white flowers. This species is fast growing and can be planted as a summer annual in cold-winter areas.

CULTURE. These tough plants need only well-drained, average soil. They are drought tolerant but bloom more profusely if given moderate water. Clumps can remain in place indefinitely; if more plants are needed, you can take root cuttings in late winter, divide clumps in early spring, or sow seed in early spring.

Effective with Eryngium, Euphorbia, Gaura lindheimeri, Oenothera.

Limonium perezii

Linaria purpurea

A charming perennial with a gentle presence, toadflax is an upright, bushy plant 2 to 3 feet tall, with many slender, vertical stems clothed in narrow blue-green leaves. Small purple flowers resembling tiny snapdragons are carried in graceful spikes. The selection **'Canon Went'** has soft pink flowers; **'Springside White'** features white flowers and gray-green leaves. Dainty **'Antique Silver'** reaches only 6 inches high and bears pinkish silver flowers.

CULTURE. Plant toadflax in well-drained soil of average fertility. It needs only moderate watering. Deadheading helps prolong flowering. To increase a planting, remove rooted portions from the edge of a clump. Toadflax often self-sows.

LINARIA purpurea
TOADFLAX
Scrophulariaceae

- ZONES 2–24, 30–41
- FULL SUN
- MODERATE WATER
- FLOWERS IN SUMMER

Effective with Campanula, Dianthus, Nepeta, Oenothera, Stachys byzantina.

Differing markedly from the familiar low, spreading annual lobelia *(L. erinus),* perennial lobelias have flowering stems that rise 3 to 4 feet above low foliage clumps, bearing narrow spires of brightly colored blossoms. Native to moist meadows and near-boggy pondside conditions, they require a moist site in the garden as well. Their flowers are much appreciated by hummingbirds.

Cardinal flower, *L. cardinalis,* succeeds in Zones 1–7, 12–17, 26 (upper half), 28–45. It forms rosettes of bright green, lance-shaped leaves; from these rise leafy, 3- to 4-foot spikes that bear brilliant red, 1½-inch-wide flowers. Selections with white or pink blooms are also available. Similar in appearance is big blue lobelia, *L. siphilitica* (Zones 2–9, 14–17, 31–43), a 3-footer with vivid blue to blue-purple flowers. A hybrid between these two species is *L. × gerardii* (Zones 2–9, 14–17, 31–43); it's usually offered in the selection **'Vedrariensis'**, which features coppery green foliage and bright royal purple blossoms.

Crossbreeding between various lobelia species has resulted in a number of hybrids of uncertain ancestry; they may be offered as *L. × speciosa, L. cardinalis,* or simply by cultivar name. They're hardy in Zones 2–9, 14–17, 31–43; most have bronze to red stems and leaves. Spectacular **'Bees' Flame'** features beet red foliage and bright scarlet blooms on spikes to 5 feet. The **Compliment** series, available from seed, produces 2½-foot-tall plants with red, pink, purple, or scarlet blossoms. Reaching 3 feet tall, **'Dark Crusader'** has dark purple foliage and deep magenta red flowers; **'Tania'**, another 3-footer, has showy magenta purple blossoms and silvery green foliage.

LOBELIA
LOBELIA, CARDINAL FLOWER
Campanulaceae (Lobeliaceae)

- ZONES VARY
- LIGHT SHADE, EXCEPT AS NOTED
- AMPLE WATER
- FLOWERS IN SUMMER

Lobelia siphilitica

Listing continues >

Lobelia cardinalis

CULTURE. Plant these moisture-loving perennials in soil liberally amended with organic matter; water frequently. Give partial to light shade; in cool-summer climates, plants will also take full sun. These lobelias are not long lived, but you can maintain them by dividing the clumps every year or two right after flowering, then replanting the most vigorous divisions. You can also take stem cuttings just after flowering or layer the stems to start new plants. Volunteer seedlings may appear. Where winter temperatures dip to −10°F /−23°C or below, protect the plants with a layer of mulch; remove it as soon as weather warms in spring.

Effective with Aruncus, Filipendula, Ligularia, Rheum palmatum, Trollius.

LUPINUS
LUPINE
Fabaceae (Leguminosae)

- ✂ ZONES 1–7, 14–17, 34, 36–45
- ☼ FULL SUN
- ◖ REGULAR WATER
- ✳ ✳ ✳ ✳ ✳ ✳ ✳
  FLOWERS IN SPRING, EARLY SUMMER

Their magnificent spires packed with colorful blossoms, hybrid lupines are classic and aristocratic border perennials. Many of these showy plants are known as **Russell Hybrids** and are derived from crosses involving several species. They form a bushy clump of attractive foliage topped by erect, 3- to 4-foot-tall spikes of sweet pea–shaped blossoms. They're usually sold as mixed colors, but some specialty nurseries offer named selections such as yellow **'Chandelier'**, brick red **'My Castle'**, and blue-and-white **'The Governor'**. Other strains, available as single or mixed colors, include the dwarf **Gallery Hybrids** (15 to 18 inches tall) and the somewhat taller **Popsicle Strain** (reaching 1½ to 2 feet tall).

CULTURE. Lupines grow best in regions with fairly cool summers. Humidity combined with heat is harder on them than dry heat; in areas with warm, dry summers, they can be grown with some success if planted in light shade and kept moist. Set them out in spring, in well-drained, neutral to acid soil enriched with organic matter. They are rather short-lived plants and will need to be replaced or revitalized after several years. You can grow new plants from seed or divide established plants in spring, replanting the divisions in well-prepared soil.

Lupinus, Russell Hybrids

Effective with Alchemilla mollis, Delphinium, Geranium, Hemerocallis, Heuchera, Iris (bearded), Paeonia, Thalictrum.

LYCHNIS
CAMPION, ROSE CAMPION, MALTESE CROSS, CROWN PINK, GERMAN CATCHFLY
Caryophyllaceae

- ✂ ZONES VARY
- ☼ ◐ FULL SUN OR LIGHT SHADE
- ◖ ◖ REGULAR TO MODERATE WATER
- ✳ ✳ ✳ ✳ FLOWERS IN SUMMER

The campions are a diverse group of hardy, easy-to-grow perennials with eye-catching flowers. Maltese cross, *L. chalcedonica* (Zones 1–9, 11–24, 31–43), bears its vibrant red, ¾-inch, cross-shaped flowers in large clusters. Leaves and stems are hairy; the plant is loose and open in form, growing 2 to 3 feet high. Its variety **'Alba'** bears white flowers; **'Rosea'** has rose-colored blossoms. A related hybrid, 1½- to 2-foot-tall *L. × arkwrightii* (Zones 2–9, 14–24, 31–41), offers clusters of larger (1½-inch-wide) flowers in a brilliant shade of orange scarlet that is complemented by bronzed purple foliage. The selection **'Vesuvius'** sports vermilion flowers.

Rather different in both foliage and blossom is crown pink or rose campion, sometimes also called dusty miller *(L. coronaria,* Zones 3–9, 14–24, 30–34). Its oblong, 4-inch, grayish white leaves have a feltlike surface and form low clumps; above these, many-branched gray-white stems rise to 2½ feet high, bearing inch-wide, circular flowers of vibrant magenta. **'Alba'** has pure white blooms, while **'Angel's Blush'** bears white blossoms enhanced by a deep pink eye.

German catchfly, *L. viscaria* (Zones 1–9, 11–24, 31–43), is a compact, low-growing plant with tufts of grasslike foliage to 5 inches long. The slender, sticky stems reach 1½ to 2 feet high and bear loose clusters of bright pink flowers, each about ½ inch wide. Selections include **'Splendens Flore Pleno'**, with double magenta blossoms, and white-flowered **'Alba'** and **'Snowbird'**.

CULTURE. All campions need well-drained soil. Maltese cross *(L. chalcedonica)* and *L. × arkwrightii* grow best in good soil with regular watering. Average soil and moderate to regular watering suit German catchfly *(L. viscaria)*. Crown pink *(L. coronaria)* flourishes in poor soil with just moderate watering, though it will also accept ordinary garden conditions. Propagate all but crown pink by dividing crowded clumps in spring. Crown pink is short lived but self-sows abundantly, ensuring that seedlings are always available for transplanting.

Effective with Armeria maritima, Artemisia, Dianthus, Nepeta, Oenothera, Verbascum.

Lychnis chalcedonica

L ong blooming and easy to grow, the mallows are favorites for cottage gardens and perennial borders alike. They're bushier than the related hibiscus and biennial hollyhocks *(Alcea rosea)*, with smaller, more rounded leaves. *M. alcea* (Zones 1–9, 14–24, 31–43) is usually represented by the cultivar **'Fastigiata'**, which forms a many-branched, upright, narrow plant 3 to 4 feet high with intricately lobed foliage and 2-inch-wide pink blossoms. Musk mallow, *M. moschata* (Zones 1–9, 14–24, 31–45) is a more rounded plant to 2½ feet high, with showy, 2-inch rose-colored flowers and leaves finely cut into numerous threadlike segments. The entire plant emits a mildly musky fragrance if brushed or bruised. **'Alba'** has blossoms of pure icy white.

M. sylvestris (Zones 1–9, 14–24, 31–45) is a short-lived perennial often grown as a biennial. It blooms all summer and often until the first frosts, bearing 2-inch mauve blossoms on erect, bushy plants 2 to 4 feet high. The cultivar **'Zebrina'** *(M. zebrina)* has pale lavender pink flowers with pronounced deep purple veins. **'Primley Blue'** bears soft blue flowers with darker veins on lower-growing, somewhat prostrate plants that reach 1½ to 2 feet tall.

CULTURE. Give mallows full sun except in the hottest regions, where they prefer light shade. They grow well in average soil as long as it's well drained. Though short lived, these plants are easy to raise from seed; volunteer seedlings often provide replacement plants.

Effective with Agastache, Artemisia, Centranthus ruber, Echinops, Eryngium, Platycodon grandiflorus.

MALVA
MALLOW
Malvaceae

✿ ZONES VARY
☼ FULL SUN, EXCEPT AS NOTED
● REGULAR WATER
✳ ✳ ✳ FLOWERS IN SUMMER, AUTUMN

Malva moschata 'Alba'

T his charming harbinger of spring is native to the eastern United States. Broadly oval, bluish green leaves form loose clumps that send up leafy, 1½- to 2-foot-tall stems bearing pendent clusters of 1-inch flowers. The buds are usually pink to lavender, but they open to dainty trumpet-shaped blossoms of pure, clear blue. Because the plants go dormant soon after spring flowering is completed, choose a location where the resulting empty space will be covered in summer by annuals or by foliage of other plants (such as hostas or ferns) that leaf out and expand later in the season.

CULTURE. Plant Virginia bluebells in a partially shaded location, in moist soil enriched with organic matter. Give ample moisture from the time growth begins until flowering ends; plants need less water after entering dormancy but should not be allowed to go dry.

Listing continues >

MERTENSIA virginica
VIRGINIA BLUEBELLS
Boraginaceae

✿ ZONES 1–21, 31–45
◑ LIGHT SHADE
● REGULAR WATER
✳ FLOWERS IN SPRING

Clumps can remain in place indefinitely; they will slowly spread. To get more plants, transplant volunteer seedlings or dig and divide clumps in early fall.

Effective with Dicentra, Doronicum, ferns, Helleborus, Primula, Pulmonaria, Trollius.

Mertensia virginica

MONARDA

🐦 🐝 BEE BALM, OSWEGO TEA, HORSEMINT

Lamiaceae (Labiatae)

- ✎ ZONES VARY
- ☼ FULL SUN, EXCEPT AS NOTED
- ● REGULAR WATER
- ❋ ❋ ❋ ❋ FLOWERS IN SUMMER

Lance-shaped, 6-inch leaves with a strong, pleasantly minty odor form a spreading clump that sends up numerous leafy, branching stems crowned with one or two whorls of tubular, two-lipped flowers surrounded by showy bracts (modified leaves). The blossoms are very attractive to hummingbirds. **M. didyma** (Zones 2–11, 14–17, 30–41), native to the eastern United States, bears scarlet flowers on 3-foot-high plants; many selections and hybrids are available, including enduring favorites such as '**Cambridge Scarlet**' and '**Croftway Pink**' (both 3 feet tall). The species and its older cultivars are susceptible to powdery mildew, but some newer cultivars are at least somewhat resistant; these include 4-foot '**Jacob Cline**', with deep red flowers, and '**Gardenview Scarlet**', with extra-large, richly colored blooms on a 2½-foot plant. Two other 2½-footers are '**Marshall's Delight**', bearing clear pink flowers, and purple-blossomed '**Violet Queen**'.

M. fistulosa (Zones 1–24, 28–45) is native from the easternmost United States to the Rocky Mountains; it reaches 2 to 5 feet tall and produces lavender to whitish pink flowers. Because it's not as showy as other bee balms, it's usually planted in wild gardens. A parent of some of the cultivars mentioned above, this species has conferred on its offspring some tolerance of dry conditions and resistance to mildew.

CULTURE. Given good, organically enriched soil and liberal watering, bee balm grows vigorously. Its susceptibility to powdery mildew increases in dry soil and in sites with poor air circulation. In cool- to mild-summer regions, give plants full sun; in hotter areas, partial shade is best. Clumps can spread rapidly, even invasively, and should be divided every 2 to 3 years in early spring.

Effective with Chrysanthemum × superbum, Chelone, Cimicifuga, Delphinium, Filipendula, Hemerocallis, Kniphofia, Phlox, Physostegia virginiana.

Monarda didyma 'Cambridge Scarlet'

NEPETA

🐝 CATMINT

Lamiaceae (Labiatae)

- ✎ ZONES 1–24, 30, 32–43
- ☼ FULL SUN
- ◐ MODERATE WATER
- ❋ ❋ ❋ ❋ FLOWERS IN SPRING, SUMMER

Bearing billowy mounds of blossoms over spreading, aromatic gray-green foliage, catmint is delightful in the border and as an informal edging plant. Carried in loose spikes, the small, tubular flowers nearly cover the plants over a long spring-and-summer season. The oval, slightly rough-textured leaves grow ¾ to 1½ inches long. Many forms of ornamental catmint are as attractive to felines as catnip (*N. cataria*), sending them into a frenzy of rolling; young plants may need protection until they become large and tough enough to withstand such attentions. Selected forms of hybrid **N. × faassenii** include 2-foot-tall

Nepeta × faassenii

'**Dropmore Hybrid**', with rich blue flowers; 1½-foot '**Porcelain**', featuring blue-gray leaves and blossoms in a soft shade of blue; and white-flowered '**Snowflake**', reaching just 12 to 15 inches high. A taller choice is '**Six Hills Giant**', a 2- to 3-foot plant with 9- to 12-inch spikes of dark violet blooms.

N. grandiflora is also fairly large, reaching 2½ to 3 feet; its flowers are lavender blue. Its cultivar '**Dawn to Dusk**' has soft sage green foliage and pink blossoms that open from lavender blue buds. About the same size as *N. grandiflora* is 2- to 3-foot *N. sibirica,* with darker green foliage and 10-inch spikes of bright blue flowers. Its selected form '**Souvenir d'André Chaudron**' ('**Blue Beauty**') is more compact (to 1½ feet tall) and produces larger flowers.

CULTURE. Catmint is easy to grow, needing only well-drained soil and a warm, sunny location. To keep plants more compact and encourage repeat bloom later in summer, shear off spent flowering stems. To propagate, divide clumps in early spring or take stem cuttings in spring or summer.

Effective with Achillea, Agastache, Amsonia tabernaemontana, Chrysanthemum coccineum, Coreopsis, Diascia, ornamental grasses, Kniphofia, Linaria purpurea, Lychnis.

Nepeta sibirica
'Souvenir d'André Chaudron'

OENOTHERA
SUNDROPS, EVENING PRIMROSE
Onagraceae

- ZONES VARY
- ☼ FULL SUN, EXCEPT AS NOTED
- ⬤ MODERATE TO LITTLE WATER
- ✳ ✳ ✳ FLOWERS IN SUMMER

These adaptable, carefree plants produce an abundance of silky, four-petaled flowers with a flattish bowl shape. Some species bloom during the day; others open as sunlight wanes in late afternoon, then close the following morning. Sundrops, *O. fruticosa* (often listed as *O. tetragona),* grows in Zones 1–21, 30–45. A shrubby plant 1½ to 2 feet high, it has green leaves, reddish brown stems and flower buds, and bright yellow, 1½-inch-wide flowers that open in the daytime. Available cultivars include 1½-foot '**Erica Robin**', with bright yellow blossoms and foliage that emerges golden yellow, then turns reddish; foot-tall '**Highlights**', with somewhat larger flowers; and '**Fireworks**', a 1½-footer with purple-tinted foliage that contrasts attractively with its vivid yellow blooms.

Ozark sundrops, *O. macrocarpa (O. missouriensis),* is suited to Zones 2–24, 30, 33–37, 39, 41. Its prostrate, trailing stems reach 10 inches long, bearing soft, velvety, 5-inch leaves and showy, paper-thin, 4- to 5-inch-wide yellow flowers that open in the afternoon. Large winged seedpods follow the blossoms.

Mexican evening primrose, *O. speciosa* (often sold as *O. berlandieri* or *O. speciosa childsii),* succeeds in Zones 3–24, 29, 30, 33. Planted in the right spot, it's a useful garden plant, a good choice for a free-flowering ground cover—especially in difficult locations such as the strip of ground between sidewalk and street. Be cautious about locating it where it can advance on other plantings, though; it spreads briskly by underground stems and can be quite invasive. The slender, 10- to 15-inch-tall stems bear numerous 2-inch-wide pink flowers that open in the daytime. '**Woodside White**' (to 15 inches tall) has white blooms that fade to pale pink; '**Siskiyou**' bears light pink flowers on 8-inch plants.

CULTURE. Plant evening primroses in full sun; sundrops (*O. fruticosa*) also performs well in light shade. These are carefree plants, tolerant of both drought and poor soil, but they do need reasonably good drainage to do their best.

To rejuvenate crowded plantings or obtain new plants, divide in early spring or take stem cuttings in spring.

Effective with Baptisia, Ceratostigma plumbaginoides, Epilobium, Limonium, Linaria purpurea, Lychnis, Verbascum.

TOP: *Oenothera fruticosa*
BOTTOM: *Oenothera speciosa*

ORNAMENTAL GRASSES

Arrhenatherum elatius bulbosum 'Variegatum'

Ornamental grasses bring new dimensions of texture, color, height, and graceful motion to the border, highlighting and enlivening groups of more traditional perennials. Varying in size from low tufts to giants rising to 8 feet or taller, the many choices can serve as edgings, mix with midsize perennials, and provide accents or focal points; most are excellent for containers, as well. Many have variegated or colored leaves as well as interesting blooms, and the foliage and flowering stems often persist into autumn and winter.

Early spring is the best time for both planting and dividing ornamental grasses. This is also the time to tidy up the clumps before new growth begins, cutting back dead foliage.

Note that a few ornamental grasses can be invasive in the garden or nearby wild lands. Before planting a species new to you, ask the supplier if it could become a problem. For example, two species commonly known as pampas grass (*Cortaderia jubata* and, to a lesser extent, *C. selloana*) have become serious weeds along the California coast, crowding out sensitive native plants and threatening coastal ecosystems. Drought-tolerant tender fountain grass, *Pennisetum setaceum*, self-seeds freely and has become a pest in gardens and wild areas in some desert regions. Likewise, some cultivars of *Miscanthus sinensis* selected for their early bloom ('Graziella' and 'Malepartus', for instance) may set seed and spread aggressively when grown in warm, moist regions with long growing seasons.

Described below are some of the most popular ornamental grasses grown today.

Striped bulbous oat grass **(Arrhenatherum elatius bulbosum 'Variegatum'**, Zones 2–7, 32–34, 36–41) forms a graceful foot-tall clump of narrow dark green leaves boldly edged in bright white, making an attractive edging for a perennial border. This grass blooms only in cooler climates, sending up flowering stems to about 3 feet in summer. Bulblike structures form at the base of the clump and root easily to produce new plants, but the plant is not invasive.

Plant in sun to partial shade in cool-summer regions; where summers are hot, choose a location in partial shade. The plant grows and looks best at the cooler times of year, with new leaves appearing in spring and often again in fall; in hot climates, plants may go dormant in midsummer. Give them soil enriched with organic matter; water regularly. Divide and replant whenever vigor decreases.

Calamagrostis × acutiflora 'Karl Foerster'

Feather reed grass, **Calamagrostis × acutiflora** 'Karl Foerster' ('Stricta'), grows in Zones 2–24, 29–41. It has a strong vertical form, with narrow, reedlike 1½- to 4-foot green stems rising over deep green, lustrous foliage. Feathery, purplish flowering stems appear in early summer, growing to 6 feet high; they age to buff and remain attractive throughout most of the winter. **C. × a.** '**Overdam**' is similar but has variegated foliage with a central creamy white stripe. Clumps are compact and expand gradually. Feather reed grass rarely produces volunteer seedlings. It is evergreen in milder climates, partly so in colder regions.

Choose a sunny or partially shaded location. Performance is best with good soil and regular watering, but the plants will grow even in soil that is heavy, damp, and poorly drained.

Members of the genus **Carex** are sedges rather than true grasses, but their long, narrow leaves give them a grasslike appearance. Foliage is striped or unusually colored in some species. The plants described here are hardy in Zones 4–9, 14–24, 28–32, warmer parts of 33. All but Bowles' golden sedge are evergreen. Leatherleaf sedge, **C. buchananii,** forms an upright 2- to 3-foot clump of striking reddish bronze, arching leaves that are slightly curled at the tips; it offers a fine-textured color contrast to other perennials and grasses. New Zealand hair sedge, **C. comans (C. albula),** forms dense, fine-textured clumps of narrow leaves that are usually about a foot long but can reach as much as 6 feet. Leaves of '**Frosty Curls**' are silvery green; '**Bronze**' has coppery brown foliage. Bowles' golden sedge **(C. elata** '**Aurea**') is just 2 feet tall, with an upright yet fountainlike habit. Its narrow leaves are brilliant yellow from spring well into summer, then turn green for the remainder of the growing season. Variegated Japanese sedge, **C. morrowii** '**Variegata**', forms a 1-foot mound of drooping, green-and-white striped leaves; the form '**Gold Band**' has gold-striped leaves.

Grow these plants in full sun in areas where summers are cool; give them partial shade in warmer areas. They need regular water and thrive in the boggy soil at pond and stream margins.

Tufted hair grass, **Deschampsia caespitosa** (Zones 2–24, 28–41), forms a 1- to 2-foot-high clump of narrow dark green leaves; it's evergreen in mild regions but goes dormant in colder climates. Delicate, arching, 3-foot stems bearing clouds of airy flower heads appear in early summer and persist into winter. '**Goldschleier**' ('**Gold Veil**') has golden yellow blossoms, while '**Bronzeschleier**' ('**Bronze Veil**') bears bronzy yellow blooms.

Tufted hair grass prefers partial shade but tolerates full sun in cool-summer regions. Provide regular moisture for the best performance.

The fescues **(Festuca,** Zones 1–24, 29–45) form tight, tufted, evergreen clumps of narrow foliage. Nomenclature is confusing; you may find the following plants sold under different botanical names.

Large blue fescue, **F. amethystina,** forms a clump of foot-tall bluish green foliage, with flowering stems reaching 2 feet high. The selection '**Superba**' has attractive amethyst pink flowers. Common blue fescue, **F. glauca** (also sold as **F. cinerea** and **F. ovina glauca)** is available in a number of similar selections with foliage in various shades of blue; they grow 8 to 12 inches tall, with the flowering stems reaching slightly higher.

Listing continues >

Carex morrowii 'Variegata'

Deschampsia caespitosa

Festuca glauca

Hakonechloa macra 'Aureola'

Imperata cylindrica 'Red Baron'

Miscanthus sinensis 'Cabaret'

The fescues tolerate partial shade in all regions and require it where summers are hot. Plant them in average but well-drained soil and provide moderate water. When clumps become crowded and decline in vigor, divide and replant in spring.

Japanese forest grass, ***Hakonechloa macra*** **'Aureola'** (Zones 3–9, 14–24, 31–35, 37–39), somewhat resembles a tiny bamboo. Its graceful, slender, lax or arching green leaves are striped with gold; they reach about 1½ feet in length. **'All Gold'** is a selection with entirely golden foliage. These grasses spread slowly by underground runners; they go dormant in winter. Plant in partial shade in well-drained soil enriched with organic matter. Water regularly.

Blue oat grass, ***Helictotrichon sempervirens*** (Zones 2–24, 30–41), forms 2- to 3-foot, evergreen fountains of narrow, bright blue–gray leaves. Small flower plumes appear in late spring, held a foot or two above the foliage on slim stems. This grass is a clump-forming species and does not spread. Provide a full-sun location and well-drained soil of average to good quality; water moderately. Poor drainage during the winter months can cause the roots to rot.

Japanese blood grass, ***Imperata cylindrica*** **'Red Baron'** **('Rubra'),** Zones 3–24, 26, 28, 31–35, is one of the most colorful ornamental grasses. Clumps of upright foliage grow 1 to 2 feet high, the top half of each blade colored red; the color is most intense in full sun and is especially striking if plants are located in a spot where the sun can shine through the blades. Japanese blood grass spreads slowly by underground runners. It is dormant in winter. Provide average to good soil and moderate to regular watering.

Eulalia grass ***(Miscanthus sinensis,*** Zones 2–24, 29–41) and its many named selections form tall, robust but graceful clumps with stately flowering stems that rise well above the foliage. The leaves and stems turn golden tan in winter, providing interest until you cut them down at cleanup time in early spring. One of the most compact selections is **'Adagio'**, a 2- to 4-foot plant with narrow green leaves and pink flower heads that turn white with age. Slightly larger, at 3 to 5 feet, is **'Arabesque'**, another narrow-leafed form; its flowers open salmon and fade to white. A taller selection is 6- to 7-foot **'Cabaret'**, with broad green leaves beautifully variegated with cream center stripes; its flowers are pink. **'Morning Light'** is a popular and elegant cultivar featuring silvery leaves with delicate vertical stripes of creamy white; the foliage grows 4 to 5 feet high and is topped at bloom time with showy reddish brown flowers. **'Strictus',** also known as porcupine grass, grows upright to 5 to 6 feet. Its green leaves have horizontal yellow stripes.

The eulalia grasses make dense, noninvasive clumps whether planted in sun or light shade. Given moderate to regular watering, the plants will grow in any well-drained soil. The tallest varieties may need staking if grown in rich soil.

Purple moor grass, **Molinia caerulea** (Zones 2–9, 14–17, 32–41), forms a neat, dense clump 1 to 2 feet high. In summer, narrow spikelike clusters of yellowish to purplish flowers rise 1 to 2 feet or more above the green foliage; the flowering stems are quite numerous, but they have a narrow structure that gives the clump an unusual see-through quality. The blossom clusters turn tan in fall and last late into the season, when both they and the leaves break off and blow away. The 1- to 1½-foot-tall selection **'Variegata'** has purple flowers and green leaves striped lengthwise with creamy white. Selections of **M. c. arundinacea** include **'Skyracer'**, with foliage clumps to 3 feet high and upright flowering stems reaching 7 to 8 feet, and the similar **'Transparent'**, with 6-foot flowering stems that are more arching than those of 'Skyracer'.

Native to wet moorlands, these grasses prefer neutral to acid soil, organically enriched and regularly watered. Plant in full sun or light shade. They are long lived but slow growing, taking a few years to reach their full potential.

Molinia caerulea arundinacea 'Skyracer'

Native to the tall grass prairie of the Midwest, switch grass **(Panicum virgatum,** Zones 1–11, 14–21, 28–43) forms an upright clump of narrow leaves that are topped in summer by slender flower clusters; these open into loose, airy clouds of pinkish blossoms that fade to white, then brown. Clumps reach 4 to 7 feet when in bloom. Foliage turns yellow in fall, gradually fading to beige. Both foliage and flowers persist all winter. The 4-foot-tall selection **'Haense Herms'** is grown for its red fall foliage; **'Prairie Sky'** forms a stiffly upright clump of metallic blue leaves to 5 feet high. **'Warrior'** is an especially vigorous selection that reaches 5 to 6 feet tall; its fall foliage is deep reddish brown, eventually fading to tan.

Switch grasses are easy to grow, tolerating wet or dry soil and sun or partial shade.

The fountain grasses, **Pennisetum** (zones vary), form graceful clumps of broadly arching foliage; slender stems carrying furry, foxtail-like flower plumes rise above the leaves in summer. Hardiest is **P. alopecuroides** (Zones 3–24, 31–35, 37, 39), forming a bright green, 3- to 4-foot clump and bearing pinkish flower plumes. Leaves turn yellow in fall, brown in winter. **'Hameln'** is more compact, with clumps reaching just 1 to 1½ feet; its white plumes are carried on stems to 3 feet tall. **'Little Bunny'**, just 1½ feet tall in bloom, is a dwarf suitable for the front of the border or for rock gardens. **'Moudry'** bears dramatic black plumes that rise to about 3 feet, held above a 1½- to 2-foot clump of glossy foliage. These fountain grasses may self-sow to some extent but are not weedy.

Pennisetum orientale

Oriental fountain grass, **P. orientale** (Zones 3–9, 14–24, 31–35, 37, 39), forms a dense, rounded, 1½-foot clump of narrow gray-green leaves that turn straw colored in fall. The fuzzy pink flower plumes stand a foot or more above the foliage.

Plant fountain grasses in sun or light shade in average garden soil; provide regular water.

Giant feather grass, **Stipa gigantea** (Zones 4–9, 14–24, 29–34), forms clumps of narrow, arching leaves 2 to 3 feet tall. At bloom time, it lives up to its name, producing stems up to 6 feet high that carry large, open, airy sheaves of yellowish flowers that shimmer in summer breezes. This stately grass is evergreen in mild climates.

Give full sun and good soil. Water regularly when young; established plants will take some drought.

Stipa gigantea

ORIGANUM

🌿 🐝 OREGANO

Lamiaceae (Labiatae)

- 🌿 ZONES VARY
- ☀ FULL SUN, EXCEPT AS NOTED
- 💧 MODERATE TO LITTLE WATER
- ✳ ✳ FLOWERS
  IN SUMMER

Origanum laevigatum
'Herrenhausen'

Oregano is probably best known as a culinary herb—but you'll also find forms with ornamental value, well worth planting in borders and containers. **O. vulgare 'Aureum'** (Zones 1–24, 30–45), a variant of wild marjoram, is grown for its golden foliage (which turns green by midsummer), though it also bears pinkish purple flowers. A spreading plant 4 to 6 inches tall, it's excellent as a small-scale ground cover or for edging a bed or border. A related hybrid, **'Norton's Gold'**, forms a 5-inch mound of glossy golden leaves that keep their color all summer long.

A taller choice is **O. laevigatum** (Zones 3–24, 32–34), with arching, 1½- to 2-foot-long stems that bear branched clusters of purple flowers. This species is usually sold in the selected forms **'Herrenhausen'**, with lilac pink flowers and reddish purple foliage, and **'Hopley's'**, featuring large heads of deep purple flowers.

CULTURE. With the exception of 'Norton's Gold', which needs some afternoon shade to keep its leaves from scorching, these oreganos grow best in full sun. They require little water but do need good drainage. Divide crowded clumps in spring.

Effective with Agastache, Artemisia, Lavandula, Penstemon, Ratibida, Santolina.

PAEONIA

🌿 PEONY

Paeoniaceae

- 🌿 ZONES 1–11, 14–16, 32–45
- ☀ FULL SUN, EXCEPT AS NOTED
- 💧 REGULAR WATER
- ✳ ✳ ✳ ✳ FLOWERS IN
  LATE SPRING

Paeonia 'Chief Justice'

Herbaceous peonies are classics for the perennial border, providing interest over three seasons. Strong leaf buds emerge in early spring, eventually developing into rounded, shrublike, 2- to 4-foot-tall clumps of handsome leaves divided into numerous segments; these foliage clumps remain attractive well into autumn. Later in spring, bright flower buds appear, bursting open into silky blossoms with a light, clean fragrance that range in size from 4 to 10 inches across, depending on the variety.

Peonies' beautiful blossoms have naturally attracted the attention of breeders, and specialty catalogs list multitudes of named hybrids in colors ranging from deep red, coral, and all shades of pink to cream, white, and (recently) pure yellow. These hundreds of cultivars are classified by flower form and bloom time. Forms include double, with full flowers composed of many petals; single or semidouble, with one or two rows of petals; and Japanese (sometimes called bomb), with a single row of petals and a large central mass of narrow, petal-like segments called staminodes. And you'll find early, midseason, and late bloomers; by choosing some in each group, you can enjoy flowers over a period of 4 to 6 weeks. Since most varieties require a definite period of winter chill for good performance, gardeners in warm-winter climates should look for peonies recommended for such conditions. Early to midseason bloomers and single or Japanese flower forms are typically the most likely to do well.

CULTURE. In most regions, peonies should be planted in full sun, but in a location sheltered from strong winds that might break stems when they're heavy with blossoms. Where the spring bloom season is hot and dry, however, give plants some afternoon shade. Peonies also require well-drained soil, deeply dug and amended with plenty of organic matter; add lime to highly acid soil. Prepare the soil a few days before planting so it can settle. Peonies are usually planted as bare-root tubers in early fall (though tubers are available in earliest spring in some parts of the West). Planting depth is critical and depends on your climate. In warm-winter regions, position the growth buds (the "eyes" at the top of the root) no more than 1 inch below the soil surface; this exposes the plants to needed winter cold. In colder regions, plant so that the growth buds are 1½ to 2 inches deep. Be aware that, in any area, planting too deeply reduces or eliminates flowering.

Peonies may not bloom the first spring after planting, but they'll hit their stride the following year. Even in windless sites, staking may be needed for double-flowered varieties. During periods of cool, humid weather, the fungal disease botrytis may spot foliage and stems and cause buds to turn brown and fail to open. To help prevent this problem, clean the planting area thoroughly in autumn, disposing of all leaves and stems. As new growth emerges in spring, spray with copper fungicide.

Divide clumps only when absolutely necessary. Dig in early fall, hose off the roots, and divide them into sections, each with at least three eyes. Replant promptly.

Effective with Alchemilla mollis, Baptisia, Chrysanthemum × superbum, Dictamnus albus, Geranium, Iris, Lupinus, Trollius.

Paeonia 'Age of Gold'

Oriental poppies are stars of the late-spring border, flaunting sumptuous bowl-shaped flowers made up of crinkly, tissue-thin petals. Carried on long, leafy flower stalks, the blossoms typically have a dark blotch at each petal base, though many cultivars have blotchless blooms with lighter centers. Flowers reach 4 to 8 inches wide (or wider); plant height varies, too, with some forms attaining 16 inches in bloom, others growing as tall as 4 feet. The foliage clumps are made up of finely divided, very hairy leaves. The entire plant dies to the ground soon after flowering finishes; new leaves emerge in early autumn and remain as a small tuft over winter. Perennials that expand later in summer, such as baby's breath *(Gypsophila paniculata)* and boltonia, are traditionally planted near Oriental poppies to cover the gap they leave in the border.

Hundreds of cultivars are available; just a few are mentioned here to give an idea of the range of colors. Among bicolors, 2- to 3-foot-tall **'Maiden's Blush'** produces silky, 6-inch-wide, ruffled white blooms edged in pink. In the orange tones, **'Prince of Orange'** is noted for orange-scarlet flowers on a 2½-foot plant, while **'Mrs. Perry'** (over 3 feet tall) is a classic salmon pink selection with a black center. **'Allegro'** is a dwarf red form less than 20 inches tall. As the name indicates, **'Black and White'** (2½ feet tall) bears white blossoms with black spots at the petal bases.

CULTURE. Oriental poppies grow best in regions with chilly winters. Plant in well-drained soil amended with organic matter. These plants thrive in light shade (and require it during the heat of afternoon in hot-summer areas), but they'll also take full sun where summers are cool. Water regularly while plants are growing and flowering, less often during the dormant period. You can leave the clumps in place for many years. If you need to divide for increase or to reduce crowding, do so in late summer. Plants may also be propagated by root cuttings taken in late summer.

Effective with Aquilegia, Aurinia saxatilis, Boltonia asteroides, Dianthus, Euphorbia, Gypsophila paniculata, Heuchera.

Bright and cheerful, penstemons produce spikes of long-blooming tubular blossoms that attract hummingbirds throughout the flowering season. The hardiest species, **P. barbatus** (Zones 1–24, 31–43), is also the best bet for humid-summer regions, but it does need some winter chill for best performance. A somewhat sprawling plant to 3 feet high, it features pink or rose flowers and 2- to 6-inch-long green leaves; its cultivar **'Elfin Pink'** has bright pink flowers on a 1- to 2-foot plant. Also adaptable to a wide range of climates is **P. digitalis** (Zones 1–9, 14–24, 29–43), native to much of the eastern and midwestern United States. Growing 3 to 5 feet tall, this species has larger leaves than *P. barbatus* (to 7 inches long) and white or pale pink flowers. Its

PAPAVER orientale
ORIENTAL POPPY
Papaveraceae

- ZONES 1–11, 14–21, 30–45
- LIGHT SHADE, EXCEPT AS NOTED
- REGULAR TO MODERATE WATER
- FLOWERS IN LATE SPRING

Papaver orientale

PENSTEMON
PENSTEMON, BEARD TONGUE
Scrophulariaceae

- ZONES VARY
- FULL SUN, EXCEPT AS NOTED
- REGULAR TO MODERATE WATER
- FLOWERS IN SPRING, SUMMER

Penstemon digitalis

2½- to 3-foot-tall cultivar '**Husker Red**' bears whitish pink blooms, which contrast nicely with its maroon foliage.

The most colorful penstemons are a group of hybrids often referred to as *P.* × *gloxinioides.* These are grown as perennials in regions with dry summers and fairly mild winters (Zones 7–9, 12–24); elsewhere, they're treated as annuals. Compact, bushy, upright plants 2 to 4 feet high, they bloom in almost all colors but orange and yellow; in many, the blossoms have white interiors. Among the many selections are lavender '**Alice Hindley**', deep purple '**Black-bird**', deep red '**Firebird**', wine-colored '**Burgundy**' and '**Garnet**', and dark purple '**Midnight**'. Other choices include '**Stapleford Gem**', with soft blue blooms that age to purple, and '**Thorn**', with bright white flowers tipped in pink. '**Hopley's Variegated**' has medium green leaves with creamy yellow margins and bears lilac blue blossoms with white throats.

CULTURE. Grow these penstemons in well-drained soil of average fertility. They will not tolerate soggy soil, especially in winter. Where summers are hot, give plants a bit of shade during the heat of the day. Cut back plants after the first flush of flowers to encourage a second round of bloom.

After 3 or 4 years, performance declines, at which time it's best to replace the plants. Start new ones from stem cuttings (taken either in spring or in summer) or by layering.

Penstemon × *gloxinioides* 'Firebird'

Effective with Anthemis tinctoria, Ceratostigma plumbaginoides, Origanum, Perovskia, Phlomis, Salvia, Scabiosa.

PEROVSKIA
RUSSIAN SAGE
Lamiaceae (Labiatae)

- ZONES 3–24, 28–35, 37, 39
- FULL SUN
- MODERATE WATER
- FLOWERS IN SUMMER

A fast-growing plant with a light, airy look, Russian sage forms a shrubby, upright clump (to 3 to 4 feet high and wide) of numerous gray-white stems clothed in gray-green foliage. The lower leaves are 2 to 3 inches long and deeply cut; as they ascend the stems, they become smaller and are merely toothed rather than cut. Each stem terminates in a branching spray of small, tubular, lavender blue flowers that seem to float over the foliage.

Although Russian sage is usually sold as *P. atriplicifolia,* the plants in circulation are in fact thought to be hybrids of that species and *P. abrotanoides.* '**Blue Spire**' (sometimes sold as *P. atriplicifolia* '**Superba**' or as *P.* '**Longin**') is a widely grown selection with deep violet blooms; choices with lighter blue blossoms include '**Blue Mist**', which begins to flower earlier in the season than other selections, and '**Blue Haze**'. '**Filagran**' is more delicate in appearance than the others, with silvery, filigree-like foliage and light blue flowers.

CULTURE. Russian sage grows in almost any sort of soil, as long as it is well drained. To keep plants as bushy as possible, cut them nearly to the ground in early spring, leaving just one or two pairs of growth buds on each vigorous stem to provide the new season's growth. This perennial can remain in place indefinitely, without division. To increase your plantings, you can take stem cuttings in summer. Mature plants sometimes produce rooted offshoots near the edge of a clump that can be dug up and moved.

Effective with Agastache, Boltonia asteroides, Epilobium, Gaura lindheimeri, Kniphofia, Lavandula, Penstemon, Phlomis, Sedum.

Perovskia atriplicifolia

These Mediterranean relatives of *Salvia* have bold, coarse-textured foliage and erect stems set with whorls of tubular flowers. Jerusalem sage, **P. fruticosa** (Zones 4–24, 31, warmer parts of 32), is a shrubby, branching plant to 4 feet or taller, with woolly, gray-green, 6- to 8-inch leaves. Inch-long bright yellow flowers are clustered in tight, ball-shaped whorls along the upper parts of the stems. In contrast, **P. russeliana** (Zones 3–24, 30–34, 39) is spreading rather than upright, making an attractive and effective ground cover. It advances (though not invasively) by runners, forming 1- to 1½-foot-tall clumps of heart-shaped, furry leaves to 8 inches long. Blossom spikes set with whorls of soft yellow flowers rise to 3 feet. **P. samia** (Zones 3–24, 30–34, 39) is similar but bears purplish pink flowers.

CULTURE. The various sorts of phlomis are easy to please. They tolerate poor soil as long as it is well drained; they put up with drought, though they do better with moderate water. Most prefer full sun, although Jerusalem sage *(P. fruticosa)* can also grow in light shade. After bloom, cut back flowering stems of Jerusalem sage to encourage repeat bloom; also cut back plants by about a third in fall or early spring to keep them shapely. *P. russeliana* and *P. samia* do not usually rebloom, but since their spent flowering stems are attractive, many gardeners leave them intact through winter. Propagate Jerusalem sage from stem cuttings taken in summer; the others can be divided in spring.

Effective with ornamental grasses, Lavandula, Penstemon, Perovskia, Santolina, Veronica.

PHLOMIS
PHLOMIS, JERUSALEM SAGE
Lamiaceae (Labiatae)

- ◢ ZONES VARY
- ☼ FULL SUN, EXCEPT AS NOTED
- ◓ MODERATE WATER
- ✳ ✳ FLOWERS IN SPRING, SUMMER

Phlomis fruticosa

Ranging from low, spreading plants to taller classics for the border, the many kinds of phlox are a reliable source of garden color. All have blossoms that are quite similar in shape: a slender tube flares out to a flat, five-segmented flower that's circular in outline. In the low-growing phloxes, the segments may be separate, giving the bloom the look of a star or pinwheel; the tall-growing kinds usually have overlapping segments, so each blossom looks like an unbroken circle.

Several low-growing, spring-flowering species are spreaders that are useful as edgings, for ground covers, or in the rock garden. Spreading slowly by creeping rhizomes, sweet William phlox, **P. divaricata** (Zones 1–17, 28–43), grows to 1 foot high, with slender, leafy stems clothed in 1- to 2- inch-long oval leaves; its fragrant lavender blue flowers bloom in open clusters. Varieties include **'Fuller's White'**, icy blue **'Dirigo Ice'**, and compact **'London Grove'**, with deep blue blooms. **P. d. laphamii** has bright blue flowers on 1½-foot stems.

Creeping phlox, **P. stolonifera** (Zones 1–17, 28–45), forms a spreading, mounding, 6- to 8-inch-high plant with narrow evergreen leaves to 1½ inches long. It blooms profusely, bearing lavender flowers in small clusters. Named selections include lavender blue **'Blue Ridge'**, pink **'Melrose'**, deep lavender **'Sherwood Purple'**, and **'Bruce's White'**.

Another low-growing species is moss pink, **P. subulata** (Zones 1–17, 28–45), a favorite for rock gardens and banks. Its creeping stems, clothed in ½-inch, needlelike evergreen to semievergreen leaves, form a 6-inch-high mat that's transformed to a sheet of brilliant color at bloom time in late spring or early summer. Named varieties are available with blossoms in shades of blue, purple, pink, red, and white.

Mainstays of the summer perennial garden for generations, the tall phloxes offer large clusters of flowers in a wide variety of colors. **P. maculata** and **P. carolina** (Zones 1–14, 18–21, 31–45) bloom in early summer, with 15-inch-long clusters of blossoms that range in color from white through all shades of pink to magenta, often with a contrasting eye. The plants grow 3 to 4 feet high and have shiny green, mildew-

PHLOX
PHLOX, MOSS PINK
Polemoniaceae

- ◢ ZONES VARY
- ☼ FULL SUN, EXCEPT AS NOTED
- ◓ REGULAR WATER, EXCEPT AS NOTED
- ✳ ✳ ✳ ✳ ✳ FLOWERS IN SPRING, SUMMER

Phlox subulata with *Aurinia saxatilis*

Phlox maculata 'Alpha'

Phlox paniculata

resistant foliage. Nurseries offer named selections (which may be assigned to either species), including the classic pure white **'Miss Lingard'**, rose pink **'Alpha'**, pink-and-white **'Natascha'**, and deep rose pink **'Rosalinde'**.

Blooming in midsummer, border or summer phlox, *P. paniculata* (Zones 1–14, 18–21, 27–43), carries its fragrant flowers in large dome-shaped clusters up to 8 inches across. Colors include white and shades of lavender, pink, rose, red, and near-orange; blooms of some varieties have a contrasting eye. The plants grow to 2 to 4 feet or more, depending on the particular selection. They are more susceptible to powdery mildew than other tall phloxes, but some of their many cultivars are resistant (though not immune). These include **'Bright Eyes'**, with pale pink blossoms sporting a crimson eye; white-flowered **'David'**; **'Eva Cullum'**, bearing pink blooms with a red eye; and lilac pink **'Franz Schubert'**.

CULTURE. In most climates, low-growing sweet William phlox (*P. divaricata*) and creeping phlox (*P. stolonifera*) prefer light shade, though they'll accept sun in cool-summer regions. Plant these species in well-drained, organically enriched soil. Moss pink (*P. subulata*), however, prefers full sun in all but the hottest-summer regions and grows well in light, well-drained soil. All three species can be divided in spring to increase a planting.

The tall phloxes need regular attention to remain healthy and attractive. They're at their best where summers are cool to mild; in hot-summer regions, they fare better with more shade and a mulch to help retain moisture around the roots. Plant in well-prepared soil enriched with plenty of organic matter, and water regularly throughout the growing season.

To help avert the problem of powdery mildew on border phlox (*P. paniculata*), look for resistant cultivars (see above) and choose a planting location with good air circulation; avoid crowding the plants or setting them next to walls and hedges.

Tall phloxes send up numerous stems in each clump, but you should cut out all but the strongest four to six of these. Regularly cut off spent flower heads; this may encourage a second flowering from side shoots—and, in the case of border phlox, will prevent seed setting and a resultant crop of volunteer seedlings, which generally bloom purplish pink regardless of the parent plant's color. To maintain vigor, divide clumps every 2 to 4 years in early spring.

Low-growing phloxes are effective with Aurinia saxatilis, Dianthus, Iberis semper-virens, Iris (bearded), Sisyrinchium. Tall phloxes are effective with Cimicifuga, Delphinium, Monarda, Physostegia virginiana, Platycodon grandiflorus.

PHORMIUM
NEW ZEALAND FLAX
Agavaceae

- ✿ ZONES 14–28, EXCEPT AS NOTED
- ☼ ◑ FULL SUN OR LIGHT SHADE, EXCEPT AS NOTED
- ♦ ◊ REGULAR TO MODERATE WATER
- ✳ ✲ FLOWERS IN SUMMER

Dramatic accent plants for large borders or containers, these striking evergreen perennials form fanlike clumps of many swordlike leaves. The arching leaves of *P. colensoi (P. cookianum)* grow 2½ inches wide and up to 5 feet long, topped by tubular yellow or amber flowers on stems up to 7 feet high. Selected forms include 1- to 1½-foot-tall **'Cream Delight'**, with variegated cream-and-green foliage, and 3-foot-high **'Tricolor'**, with green-centered leaves margined in cream and red.

P. tenax is a larger, bolder plant, with stiff 5-inch-wide leaves that can reach 9 feet long; erect, reddish brown flower stalks to 10 feet high are crowned with many dark red to yellowish blossoms. Forms of this species selected for their leaf color include purple-red **'Atropurpureum'**; **'Rubrum'**, with very dark purplish red foliage; and **'Variega-tum'**, featuring green leaves striped with creamy white.

Many other cultivars noted for brightly colored foliage have been developed from *P. colensoi* and *P. tenax*. They're smaller than *P. tenax* and tend to be less tolerant of cold and heat than either parent; damage is likely at temperatures below 20°F/−7°C. Among these cultivars are purple-foliaged **'Jack Spratt'**, a dwarf reaching just 1½ feet high; 4-foot-tall **'Yellow Wave'**; 4- to 5-foot **'Maori Chief'** and **'Maori Sunrise'**, both with dazzling pink-and-green leaves; and maroon **'Dark Delight'**, which can reach 6 feet high.

CULTURE. New Zealand flaxes grow best where summers are cool to mild, where they will accept sun or light shade. In hot-summer areas, the plants (especially the hybrid forms) need light shade during the heat of the day. Plant in average, well-drained soil and provide moderate water. Some of the most colorful selections have a tendency to revert to green; to keep this from happening, cut out any solid green leaves you see. In cold-winter areas, New Zealand flaxes are choice plants for large containers, which can be moved to a cool greenhouse over winter. Division isn't necessary to keep plants healthy, but you can increase your supply by dividing large clumps in spring.

Effective with Diascia, Euphorbia, ornamental grasses, Heuchera, Sedum.

Phormium 'Yellow Wave'

Physostegia virginiana 'Variegata'

The blossoms of this North American native resemble snapdragons (hence the name "false dragonhead") and will remain in place if twisted or pushed out of position (hence "obedient plant"). The plants grow in spreading clumps, sending up 3- to 4-foot stems clothed in toothed, lance-shaped leaves to 5 inches long; in summer or early autumn, each stem is topped by a tapering spike of inch-long flowers. Blossoms are typically a bright bluish pink, but named selections offer other colors. **'Bouquet Rose'** has rose pink blossoms, while **'Red Beauty'** offers deeper rose blooms; both grow about 3 feet tall. Two 2-foot selections are **'Summer Snow'**, with clear white flowers, and **'Variegata'**, bearing pink blossoms set off by foliage strikingly variegated in creamy white.

CULTURE. False dragonhead grows best if given good soil and plenty of moisture; it blooms less freely with poorer soil and less water. The flower stalks may need support to remain upright. Plants spread rapidly; to keep them in bounds, divide clumps every 2 years in early spring.

Effective with Anemone × hybrida, Aster, Erigeron, Monarda, Phlox paniculata, Scabiosa.

PHYSOSTEGIA virginiana
⚘ FALSE DRAGONHEAD, OBEDIENT PLANT
Lamiaceae (Labiatae)

- ✿ ZONES 1–24, 26–45
- ☼ ◑ FULL SUN OR LIGHT SHADE
- ⬤ REGULAR WATER
- ✻ ✻ FLOWERS IN SUMMER, EARLY AUTUMN

Physostegia virginiana

The common name comes from the attractive, unusual buds: they're inflated and balloonlike, carried on slender stalks at the ends of upright stems clothed in broadly oval, 3-inch leaves. The blossoms—blue violet with purple veining—are star shaped and 2 inches wide. Cultivars include 3-foot-tall, white-flowered **'Albus'**; **'Hakone Blue'**, which bears double bright blue flowers on 15- to 24-inch plants; 16-inch **'Komachi'**, which produces large blue buds that never open; popular dwarf **'Sentimental Blue'**, reaching 6 to 9 inches tall; and 1½- to 2-foot **'Shell Pink'**.

CULTURE. Balloon flower grows best in well-prepared, fairly light, well-drained soil. Choose a spot in light shade except in cooler regions, where the plant will succeed in full sun. Bloom will last for 2 months or more if you remove individual spent blossoms

PLATYCODON grandiflorus
⚘ BALLOON FLOWER
Campanulaceae (Lobeliaceae)

- ✿ ZONES 1–24, 26, 28–45
- ◑ LIGHT SHADE, EXCEPT AS NOTED
- ⬤ REGULAR WATER
- ✻ ✻ ✻ FLOWERS IN SUMMER

carefully, without damaging the new buds growing nearby along the flowering stem. The plant dies back completely in fall and new growth appears quite late the next year, so mark the plants' location to avoid accidentally digging them up. Balloon flower is slow to establish and does not need division. If you want more plants, divide in spring, taking plenty of soil along with the deep roots.

Effective with Campanula, Heuchera, Liatris, Malva, Phlox.

Platycodon grandiflorus

POLYGONATUM
SOLOMON'S SEAL
Liliaceae

- 🌿 ZONES 1–7, 14–17, 28–43
- ☼● LIGHT TO FULL SHADE
- 💧 REGULAR WATER
- ✳ FLOWERS IN SPRING

Polygonatum biflorum

Spreading underground rhizomes send up stems that grow upright for a distance, then arch outward; broadly oval bright green leaves are arranged in nearly horizontal planes on either side of the stems. Where the leaves join the stems, small bell-shaped blossoms are suspended on threadlike stalks. Small blue-black berries may follow the flowers. Both leaves and stems turn an attractive bright yellow in autumn.

Among the available species of these elegant plants, small Solomon's seal, **P. biflorum,** bears 4-inch leaves on stems that grow to 3 feet; the flowers are usually in pairs or threes. Great Solomon's seal, **P. commutatum** (sometimes sold as **P. canaliculatum),** is a larger plant requiring a sizable amount of garden space. Clothed in 7-inch leaves, its stems normally grow 4 to 5 feet tall, though they have been known to attain 7 feet. The flowers are borne in groups of 2 to 10. Two- to 3-foot-tall **P. odoratum 'Variegatum',** with attractive variegated foliage margined in creamy white, is a bright addition to a shady area; its stems are a contrasting dark red until the plant is fully grown. The flowers come in pairs or singly.

CULTURE. Although these plants grow best in the moist, organically rich soil typical of woodlands, they perform reasonably well in drier soils, even in competition with tree roots. They can remain in place for years without division. If you want to increase your planting, remove and replant rhizomes (each with at least one bud) from the edge of the clump in early spring.

Effective with Acanthus mollis, Alchemilla mollis, Aquilegia, Bergenia, Epimedium, ferns, Hosta, Pulmonaria.

PRIMULA
PRIMROSE
Primulaceae

- 🌿 ZONES VARY
- ☼ LIGHT SHADE, EXCEPT AS NOTED
- 💧 REGULAR WATER, EXCEPT AS NOTED
- ✳ ✳ ✳ ✳ ✳ ✳ FLOWERS IN WINTER, SPRING, EARLY SUMMER

Whether planted along a shaded path, in a border, or near a pond or stream, primroses are enchanting in bloom. Above their foliage rosettes rise stems bearing circular, five-petaled flowers; each petal is indented at the apex. The blossoms may be borne individually, in clusters at the stem tips, or in tiered, candelabralike clusters along the stem. Primroses are often considered a symbol of spring, and most are in fact spring blooming—but some start flowering in mid- to late winter in mild climates, and a few bloom in early summer.

The genus is a complex one, comprising hundreds of species and hybrids. The primroses described here are relatively common and easy to grow, as long as they receive the conditions they need.

Polyanthus primroses, **P. × polyantha** (Zones 2–10, 12–24, 32–41), are generally considered the most adaptable. They form clumps of fresh green, tongue-shaped leaves to 8 inches long; 1- to 2-inch-wide flowers in an array of colors including everything but black and true green appear from winter to early or midspring. The blossoms are carried in terminal clusters on stocky, 8- to 12-inch stems. Many strains are available, usually in mixed colors; one such strain is **Pacific Giant,** bearing extra-large flowers in white and shades of blue, yellow, red, and pink.

Similar in form is English primrose, *P. vulgaris* (Zones 2−6, 14−17, 21−24, 32−41); its light yellow, fragrant flowers appear in early spring, borne on individual stems held above 6-inch clumps of leaves. The flowers appear singly in the species, but garden strains may have two or three flowers per stem. Colors include white, yellow, red, blue, bronze, and wine; there are many double-flowered varieties, such as '**Miss Indigo**', with blooms of a deep, rich purple.

Sometimes called drumstick primrose, *P. denticulata* (Zones 1−6, 34−43) carries its dense, ball-shaped clusters of flowers atop foot-high, stout stems. Colors range from blue violet to purple; there are also white forms. When the plants bloom in very early spring, the spatula-shaped leaves are about 6 inches long; they later expand to about 1 foot. Cultivars include white-flowered '**Alba**' and red-purple '**Rubra**'.

P. sieboldii (Zones 2−6, 17, 34, 36−40) has downy, wrinkled, 2- to 4-inch leaves on long, slender leafstalks; the leaves are arrow shaped, with scalloped edges. In late spring, slender 4- to 8-inch stems bear clusters of 1- to 1½-inch-wide lilac flowers with a white eye. Named selections include white-flowered '**Snowflake**'; '**Sumina**', with large flowers of lavender blue; and '**Wine Lady**', bearing white blossoms flushed with purple red. The foliage dies down after flowering, helping the plants endure hotter summers better than other primroses.

The most widely available of the so-called Candelabra primroses, *P. japonica,* succeeds in Zones 2−6, 17, 32 (cooler parts), 34, 36−40. It reaches 2½ feet high during its bloom time in late spring to early summer. The tongue-shaped leaves are 9 inches long; flower colors include purple, red, pink, and white. '**Miller's Crimson**' is an excellent red variety; '**Postford White**' features large white blossoms. These plants need lots of water; grow them at the edge of a pond, in a boggy area, or even in very shallow water.

CULTURE. The primroses described here flourish in moist, organically enriched soil; as noted above, *P. japonica* requires even damper conditions. In cool-summer areas, especially those where foggy, overcast weather is common, you can plant primroses in nearly full-sun locations. In sunnier regions, however, they need protection from afternoon sun; filtered or dappled sunlight or high shade are preferred. Primrose plants form tight clumps; when performance eventually declines, divide the clumps right after flowering finishes.

Effective with Aquilegia, Corydalis, Epimedium, ferns, Helleborus, Mertensia virginica.

Primula vulgaris

Primula denticulata

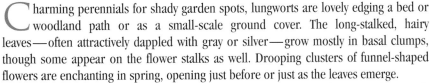

Charming perennials for shady garden spots, lungworts are lovely edging a bed or woodland path or as a small-scale ground cover. The long-stalked, hairy leaves—often attractively dappled with gray or silver—grow mostly in basal clumps, though some appear on the flower stalks as well. Drooping clusters of funnel-shaped flowers are enchanting in spring, opening just before or just as the leaves emerge.

Blue lungwort, *P. angustifolia,* has bright blue flowers that open from pink buds; the plants grow 8 to 12 inches high, bearing dark green, unspotted foliage. Selections include '**Blaues Meer**', with larger, brighter blue flowers than the species, and sky blue '**Azurea**'.

P. longifolia bears slender, silver-spotted deep green leaves to 20 inches long. Its purplish blue flowers, carried on 8- to 12-inch stalks, open a little later in spring than

PULMONARIA
LUNGWORT, BETHLEHEM SAGE
Boraginaceae

✿ ZONES 1–9, 14–17, 32–43
◐ ● LIGHT TO FULL SHADE
● REGULAR WATER
✳ ✳ ✳ ✳ FLOWERS IN SPRING

TOP: *Pulmonaria longifolia*
BOTTOM: *Pulmonaria 'Excalibur'*

those of the other species. The selection **'Bertram Anderson'** has deep blue flowers. One of the earliest-blooming species is *P. montana (P. rubra)*, with light green, unspotted leaves and coral red blossoms on flowering stems to 16 inches tall. The cultivar **'David Ward'** bears rich coral flowers that beautifully enhance its foliage—unusually large olive green leaves with an irregular, creamy margin.

Reaching about 1½ feet tall, Bethlehem sage, *P. saccharata*, has blue flowers and silvery-spotted leaves. Catalogs usually offer named selections, including early-blooming **'Highdown'**, with rich blue blossoms; pink-flowered **'Pierre's Pure Pink'**; **'Mrs. Moon'**, an old favorite with large, silver-spotted leaves and light blue flowers that unfurl from pink buds; and **'Janet Fisk'**, also featuring flowers that turn from pink to blue and leaves that are silvery almost all over.

Many hybrid lungworts are also sold, most featuring especially beautiful foliage. **'Excalibur'** has striking silvery white foliage margined in dark green; its flowers are violet blue. Leaves of **'Roy Davidson'** are long and narrow, evenly marked with silver; the blossoms are sky blue. **'Spilled Milk'** features foliage of an almost solid silver white, with just a few flecks of dark green.

CULTURE. Lungworts need soil that is well drained but always moist. Incorporate plenty of organic matter before planting. Choose a spot in partial to full shade; leaves tend to wilt in full sun even if the soil is moist. Crowded clumps will need dividing after a number of years. Do the job in early autumn, and be sure to keep the newly planted divisions well watered.

Effective with Acanthus mollis, Brunnera macrophylla, Dicentra, Epimedium, ferns, Hosta, Mertensia virginica, Polygonatum.

RATIBIDA
🌱 MEXICAN HAT,
PRAIRIE CONEFLOWER
Asteraceae (Compositae)

- ✴ ZONES 1–24, 26–43
- ☀ FULL SUN
- ●● REGULAR TO MODERATE WATER
- ✳ ✳ FLOWERS IN SUMMER, EARLY AUTUMN

I deal for natural-looking borders and wildflower gardens, these natives of prairie and western states are branching, stiffly erect plants with deeply divided leaves and flower heads featuring raised central cones. Two-foot-tall Mexican hat, *R. columnifera*, bears distinctive blooms with a narrow brown cone up to 2 inches long; the drooping yellow petals (ray flowers) are about the same length. Its form *R. c. pulcherrima* has especially attractive mahogany red blossoms. Prairie coneflower, *R. pinnata*, is a taller plant (to 4 feet), and its flowers are a bit different: they feature a rounded brown cone and yellow ray flowers that are longer than the cone.

Ratibida pinnata

CULTURE. These adaptable plants grow well in average, well-drained soil and are tolerant of some drought. Propagate by seed sown in spring.

Effective with Achillea, Coreopsis, ornamental grasses, Origanum, Yucca.

RHEUM palmatum
ORNAMENTAL RHUBARB
Polygonaceae

- ✴ ZONES 2–9, 14–24, 31–41
- ☀ ◑ FULL SUN OR LIGHT SHADE
- ● AMPLE WATER
- ✳ FLOWERS IN SUMMER

A n imposing addition to the perennial garden, this highly ornamental relative of culinary rhubarb (which is an attractive plant in its own right) has dark green, deeply incised basal leaves 2 to 3 feet across. In early summer, thick stalks shoot up to 6 feet or higher, bearing fluffy panicles of red flowers. The cultivar **'Atrosanguineum'** is even showier than the species; its leaves are dark red when they emerge in spring and remain reddish into summer, then gradually turn to green by summer's end. The flowers are deep red, followed (as is the case for other ornamental rhubarbs) by attractive seeds. Note that these plants are not edible—and their leaves, like those of culinary rhubarb, are poisonous.

CULTURE. Ornamental rhubarb does well in full sun to partial shade; in hot climates, it needs shade in the afternoon. Plant in well-drained soil enriched with plenty of organic matter, and provide regular moisture during the growing season. Propagate by division in early spring.

Effective with Geum, ornamental grasses, Lobelia.

Rheum palmatum 'Atrosanguineum'

Showy and carefree plants for the summer garden, these coneflowers—all with golden yellow blossoms—are descendants of North American natives, chosen by breeders for their more compact growth habit and long bloom season. The common name refers to the dark, raised cone that centers each flower. Most widely grown and (deservedly) most popular of the coneflowers is ***R. fulgida sullivantii*** 'Goldsturm' (Zones 1–24, 28–43), a long bloomer that flowers from midsummer through fall. Its clumps of broadly lance-shaped, hairy dark green leaves send up many 2- to 2½-foot stems bearing 3-inch-wide flowers with a nearly black cone. Also suited to Zones 1–24, 28–43 is summer-blooming ***R. laciniata.*** Its form 'Golden Glow' ('Hortensia') bears 2- to 3½-inch double blossoms on vigorous, spreading plants that reach 6 to 7 feet; clump-forming 'Goldquelle' also has double blooms, but it grows only 2½ to 3 feet tall.

Reaching 4 to 6 feet high, ***R. nitida*** 'Herbstsonne' ('Autumn Sun') succeeds in Zones 3–9, 14–24, 28–35, 37, 39. It blooms from late summer to fall, producing 4- to 5-inch flowers with a bright green central cone. The bold, bluish gray basal leaves of giant coneflower, ***R. maxima*** (Zones 28–35, 37, 39), reach 2 feet long and 8 inches wide, forming a mound of foliage 2 to 3 feet tall and wide. Flowering stems rise 5 to 6 feet in midsummer, topped by 3½-inch-wide blossoms with a prominent brown to black cone and drooping petals (ray flowers).

CULTURE. Coneflowers are easy to grow, requiring only average to good soil and moderate to regular water. To maintain good performance, divide clumps every 2 to 4 years in spring. *(R. laciniata* 'Golden Glow' may spread aggressively, requiring more frequent division to keep clumps in bounds.)*

Effective with Asclepias tuberosa, Echinacea purpurea, Echinops, Eupatorium, Helianthus, Liatris, Salvia, Yucca.

RUDBECKIA
☙ ✿ CONEFLOWER
Asteraceae (Compositae)

✿ ZONES VARY

☼ ◐ FULL SUN OR LIGHT SHADE

● ◖ REGULAR TO MODERATE WATER

✳ FLOWERS IN SUMMER, AUTUMN

Rudbeckia fulgida sullivantii 'Goldsturm'

The many salvias combine attractive spikes of two-lipped flowers with aromatic foliage. Perennial salvias include hardy sorts, among them attractive selections of culinary sage, and tender species (often grown as annuals in cold regions).

The most widely planted hardy perennial sage is ***Salvia × superba (S. nemorosa, S. × sylvestris),*** successful in Zones 2–11, 14–24, 30–41. It forms a low (1½- to 2-foot), dense plant with lance-shaped green leaves; branching flower spikes appear in summer and fall. Among its many selections are 'Blue Hill', noted for true blue flowers; 'East Friesland', with deep purple blooms; 'May Night', bearing larger deep indigo flowers on a compact plant to 1½ feet high and wide; and pink 'Rose Queen', another compact grower to 1½ feet tall and wide.

Blue sage, ***S. azurea grandiflora (S. pitcheri),*** grows in Zones 2–11, 14–24, 26 (northern part), 27–43. It's a narrow-leafed, upright plant to 5 feet high, more open in structure than *S. × superba,* with gentian blue blossoms from midsummer until frost.

Listing continues >

SALVIA
✿ SALVIA, SAGE
Lamiaceae (Labiatae)

✿ ZONES VARY

☼ FULL SUN, EXCEPT AS NOTED

● REGULAR WATER, EXCEPT AS NOTED

✳ ✳ ✳ ✳ ✳ ✳ FLOWERS IN LATE SPRING, SUMMER, AUTUMN

TOP: *Salvia × superba* 'East Friesland'
BOTTOM: *Salvia verticillata* 'Purple Rain'

S. pratensis (S. haematodes), Zones 2–11, 14–24, 30–41, forms a loose, 1½-foot-wide rosette of wrinkled 6-inch leaves, above which rise branching 2- to 3-foot stems bearing lavender blue flowers in late spring and summer. ***S. verticillata* 'Purple Rain'** (Zones 2–11, 14–24, 30–41) reaches a compact 1½ to 2 feet tall, with broad, hairy, heart-shaped leaves and long, arching spikes of purple flowers in summer and autumn.

Considered an essential component of the herb garden, common sage, ***S. officinalis*** (Zones 2–24, 26, 28–41), also offers attractive selections well suited to the perennial border. Most grow 1½ to 2 feet high. **'Berggarten'** has wide, handsome gray-green leaves and deep blue late-summer flowers. Among varieties with colored foliage are yellow-and-green **'Icterina'**; **'Purpurascens'**, with purplish leaves; and **'Tricolor'**, with foliage marked in gray, white, and purplish pink.

The following five salvias are more tender. Fast-growing mealy-cup sage, ***S. farinacea*** (Zones 8, 9, 14–24, 26–31, warmer parts of 32), is a rounded, somewhat shrubby plant 2 to 3 feet high, with lance-shaped gray-green leaves and spikes of ½-inch flowers. Selections include **'Blue Bedder'**, **'White Porcelain'**, and **'Strata'**, which has blue flowers with white calyces. Autumn sage, ***S. greggii*** (Zones 8–24, 26–31), is a drought-tolerant Texas native reaching about 3 feet tall; despite the common name, it blooms from late spring to fall. The species has bright red blossoms, but you can also find forms in yellow, purple, pink, and white.

S. guaranitica (Zones 8, 9, 14–24, 26–31, warmer parts of 32) is a large, lush plant that grows 4 to 5 feet tall and bears long spikes of dark blue flowers in summer and fall. In hot, dry climates, give it light shade. Another large salvia that appreciates light shade is ***S. involucrata*** (Zones 8–24, 27–30), a velvety-leafed plant that reaches an impressive 6 feet high. It bears spires of rose pink flowers in late summer and fall. Bog sage, ***S. uliginosa*** (Zones 6–9, 14–24, 27–31, warmer parts of 32) blooms in late summer to fall, carrying sparkling sky blue blossoms with white markings on upright stems to 6 feet tall. It spreads by rhizomes to make big clumps of bright green leaves and (common name notwithstanding) is somewhat drought tolerant, though it happily accepts ample watering.

CULTURE. Salvias need good drainage, moderately fertile soil, and—in most cases—regular water. As noted above, *S. greggii* can manage with little water, and *S. uliginosa* tolerates fairly dry or damp soil. All salvias can be propagated by stem cuttings taken in spring or summer. Spreading kinds such as *S. × superba*, *S. azurea grandiflora*, and *S. uliginosa* can also be divided in spring.

Effective with Asclepias tuberosa, Centaurea, Gaillardia × grandiflora, Gaura lindheimeri, Penstemon, Rudbeckia.

SANTOLINA
LAVENDER COTTON
Asteraceae (Compositae)

- ✿ ZONES 3–24, 27, 29, 30, 32–35, 39, EXCEPT AS NOTED
- ☼ FULL SUN
- ◖ MODERATE WATER
- ✳ FLOWERS IN SPRING, EARLY SUMMER

Mounds of attractive, fragrant foliage and a profusion of small, buttonlike flower heads make lavender cotton a favorite for ground covers and edgings for borders or herb gardens, but it's also a good choice for planting within the border to contrast with heavier-textured perennials.

S. chamaecyparissus (S. incana) is a spreading, 2-foot plant with finely divided gray–white foliage and bright yellow flower heads. The cultivar **'Lemon Queen'** is more compact—just 8 to 12 inches tall—with blossoms of a delicate creamy yellow. ***S. pinnata neapolitana* 'Edward Bowles'** forms a rounded plant to 20 inches tall, with feathery gray-green leaves and pale primrose yellow blooms. Green lavender cotton, ***S. rosmarinifolia (S. virens),*** succeeds in Zones 4–24, 27, 29, 30, 32. It's a 2-foot-tall plant with bright yellow blossoms and narrow green leaves much like those of rosemary.

Santolina chamaecyparissus

CULTURE. Give these plants average, well-drained soil. Though they'll survive considerable drought, they perform best with moderate water. To keep plants compact, shear or cut them back after flowering; cutting back to just a few inches tall in early spring also helps maintain compactness. Plants may die to the ground in the coldest zones but usually come back from the roots. Propagate by layering stems or by stem cuttings taken in spring and summer.

Effective with Epilobium, Lavandula, Origanum, Phlomis.

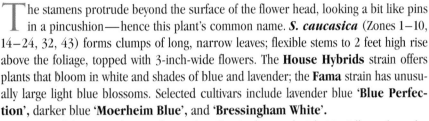

The stamens protrude beyond the surface of the flower head, looking a bit like pins in a pincushion—hence this plant's common name. *S. caucasica* (Zones 1–10, 14–24, 32, 43) forms clumps of long, narrow leaves; flexible stems to 2 feet high rise above the foliage, topped with 3-inch-wide flowers. The **House Hybrids** strain offers plants that bloom in white and shades of blue and lavender; the **Fama** strain has unusually large light blue blossoms. Selected cultivars include lavender blue '**Blue Perfection**', darker blue '**Moerheim Blue**', and '**Bressingham White**'.

Two well-known cultivars of *S. columbaria* (Zones 4–24, 32–34) are lavender blue '**Butterfly Blue**' and lavender pink '**Pink Mist**'; both of these bloom throughout the growing season in cold-winter regions, nearly year-round where winters are mild. The plants have finely cut gray-green leaves and carry their 2-inch-wide flowers on foot-tall stems.

CULTURE. Pincushion flowers grow best in soil enriched with organic matter; add lime to strongly acid soils. Be sure that soil is well drained, and keep in mind that plants are particularly sensitive to wet soil in winter. *S. caucasica* is best suited to regions with cool to mild summers, where it accepts full sun. In other areas, it performs better if given light shade during the heat of the day—but *S. columbaria* is a better choice for hot-summer climates. During the bloom season, remove spent blossoms to prolong flowering. Propagate by seed, division in early spring, or basal cuttings taken in spring.

Effective with Diascia, Geranium, Penstemon, Physostegia virginiana, Stokesia laevis.

SCABIOSA
PINCUSHION FLOWER
Dipsacaceae

- ZONES VARY
- FULL SUN, EXCEPT AS NOTED
- REGULAR WATER
- ✳ ✳ ✳ ✳ FLOWERS IN SUMMER, EXCEPT AS NOTED

Scabiosa columbaria 'Butterfly Blue'

SEDUM
SEDUM, STONECROP
Crassulaceae

- ZONES VARY
- FULL SUN
- MODERATE WATER
- ✳ ✳ ✳ FLOWERS IN LATE SUMMER, AUTUMN

Many sedums are low growers that are well suited to the rock garden. The following choices, however, are larger plants reaching 1½ to 2 feet high; their attractive fleshy foliage and showy late-season flowers make them an interesting addition to borders or container gardens.

S. spectabile (recently renamed *Hylotelephium spectabile*) grows well in Zones 1–24, 28–43. Starting growth in early spring from a low foliage rosette, it sends up erect or slightly spreading, 1½-foot-high stems set with 3-inch, roundish blue-green leaves. The dense, dome-shaped, 6-inch-wide clusters of pink flowers mature into brownish maroon seed clusters; many gardeners leave these atop the bare stems for winter interest. Cultivars include deep rose red '**Brilliant**', soft rose '**Carmen**', and white '**Iceberg**'. Similar in growth habit is *S. telephium (Hylotelephium telephium)*, suited to Zones 1–24, 29–43; it has somewhat narrower leaves on stems to 2 feet tall. The cultivar '**Atropurpureum**' features burgundy leaves and dusky pink flowers, while '**Munstead Red**' has bronzy purple leaves and deep red blooms.

Among the various hybrid sedums (which may be listed under either of the above species), the most widely known and grown is *S.* '**Autumn Joy**' ('**Herbstfreude**'). Its fleshy, toothed blue-green leaves reach 2 to 3 inches long; 1½- to 2-foot flower stems are topped with broad, rounded clusters of blossoms that emerge pink, then age to cop-

Sedum spectabile 'Brilliant'

pery pink and finally to rust. Foot-tall **'Frosty Morn',** another hybrid sedum, has white-bordered mint green foliage that effectively sets off its white to light pink flowers. **S. 'Matrona'** also has beautiful foliage: its leaves are dark gray with a deep pink border. The 2-foot stems are topped by large heads of soft pink flowers.

CULTURE. Sedums need well-drained soil but are not particular about fertility. When floppy stems and a decline in flowering indicate overcrowding, divide clumps in early spring. You can also take stem cuttings in late spring and early summer.

Effective with Armeria maritima, Ceratostigma plumbaginoides, Chrysanthemum × morifolium, Echinacea purpurea, ornamental grasses, Perovskia, Phormium, Stachys, Verbascum.

SEMPERVIVUM tectorum
HEN AND CHICKS, HOUSELEEK
Crassulaceae

- ✂ ZONES 2-24, 29-41
- ☀ FULL SUN
- ◐◒ REGULAR TO LITTLE WATER
- ✳ FLOWERS IN SUMMER

Forming low, spreading mats of tightly packed leaf rosettes, hen and chicks is a good choice for an edging, especially when used along paths and around rocks. It's also an easy-to-grow, effective container choice. Succulent gray-green leaves with red-brown tips form rosettes 4 to 6 inches across; the flowers are red, borne in clusters on thick, hairy stems up to 2 feet tall. The rosettes die after blooming and setting seed, but new offset rosettes ("chicks") formed around each one carry on the show. Specialty nurseries offer dozens of named cultivars and hybrids, many with attractive reddish foliage.

Sempervivum tectorum

CULTURE. Plant hen and chicks in full sun. It tolerates poor soil but must have good drainage. Propagate by removing and planting the offsets.

Effective with Armeria maritima, ornamental grasses, Thymus.

SISYRINCHIUM
BLUE-EYED GRASS
Iridaceae

- ✂ ZONES VARY
- ☀◑ FULL SUN OR LIGHT SHADE
- ◐ REGULAR WATER
- ✳✳✳✳ FLOWERS IN SPRING, SUMMER

Sisyrinchium striatum

These plants resemble their iris relatives in their narrow, swordlike leaves, but their flowers are quite different—they're flat and circular in outline, with six segments. **S. angustifolium** (Zones 1–6, 32–43), native to the eastern United States, has dark green foliage and bears clustered blue flowers, usually with a yellow eye, in late spring or early summer. It grows 6 to 18 inches tall. A similar plant is 4- to 16-inch-tall **S. bellum** (Zones 4–11, 14–24), a native of coastal California. It blooms in early to mid-spring, carrying purple to bluish purple blossoms on short stems above green or bluish foliage. Its form **'Album'** has milky white blooms, while blue-flowered **'Wayne's Dwarf'** grows only 3 to 5 inches tall.

Blooming in spring to early summer, **S. striatum (Phaiophleps nigricans,** Zones 4–11, 14–24, 29–31) is larger than the other species, with attractive gray-green leaves to 1 foot long and 1 inch wide and 2- to 2½-foot flowering stems. The inch-wide blossoms, set close to the stems, are creamy yellow with brown streaks. The form **'Aunt May' ('Variegata')** has particularly handsome leaves that are margined in creamy white; they provide garden interest even when the plant is not in flower.

CULTURE. Set out plants in ordinary garden soil, in full sun or light shade; provide regular water. The leaves of *S. striatum* turn black as they age and should be removed to keep the plants attractive. The various blue-eyed grasses seldom need dividing; if you want to increase your planting, you can dig and transplant portions of the clumps. Most provide plenty of volunteer seedlings.

Effective with Heuchera, Phlox, Thymus, Veronica.

From mid- or late summer into fall, goldenrods brighten the garden with large, branching clusters of small yellow flowers carried on leafy stems that rise from tough, woody, spreading rootstocks. But for all their ease of care and flamboyant color, they're not as widely planted as they deserve—largely because their pollen is incorrectly thought to cause hay fever. The actual culprit is usually ragweed, which blooms at the same time.

Solidago rugosa reaches 5 feet tall, bearing burnished yellow autumn flowers on arching, widely branching stems. The cultivar '**Fireworks**' is a bit more compact, growing to just 4 feet; its fluffy golden blossom sprays appear on nearly horizontal branches. Still smaller is 1½- to 2-foot **S. sphacelata** '**Golden Fleece**' (Zones 2–11, 14–21, 28–41), a suitable choice for a tough, fast-growing ground cover. It blooms in late summer and fall, producing many sprays of golden yellow flowers.

A number of hybrid goldenrods are available, sometimes listed under one of the parents, **S. virgaurea. '**Cloth of Gold**',** just 18 to 20 inches high, has a long bloom season beginning in midsummer or early fall. Stiffer and more erect is '**Strahlenkrone**' ('**Crown of Rays**'), a 2-footer with wide, flat, branched flower clusters. Three-foot '**Goldenmosa**' produces very large flower clusters reminiscent of florists' mimosa; '**Peter Pan**' grows 2 to 3 feet tall.

A hybrid of goldenrod and a perennial aster, × **Solidaster luteus** resembles goldenrod, but its late-summer blossoms are larger, reminiscent of small primrose yellow asters. The plants grow 2 feet high and, unlike goldenrods, require staking to stay upright.

CULTURE. These undemanding plants grow well in wild gardens or in borders; in either case, they accept average soil and are fairly drought tolerant. To control spreading and rejuvenate the clumps, divide them every 3 to 4 years in early spring.

Effective with Anthemis tinctoria, Boltonia asteroides, Echinacea purpurea, Eupatorium, Gaillardia × grandiflora, Helenium, Helianthus.

SOLIDAGO AND SOLIDASTER

GOLDENROD
Asteraceae (Compositae)

- ZONES 1–11, 14–21, 28–45, EXCEPT AS NOTED
- FULL SUN
- MODERATE WATER
- FLOWERS IN SUMMER, AUTUMN

Solidago sphacelata 'Golden Fleece'

The garden plants known by the name "betony" share certain features—square stems and aromatic foliage, for example—but beyond that, they differ considerably from each other.

Lamb's ears, **S. byzantina (S. lanata, S. olympica),** is a favorite gray-leafed perennial for Zones 1–24, 29–43. Grown as an accent plant and small-scale ground cover, it forms dense, ground-hugging rosettes of soft, thick, 4- to 6-inch-long, elliptical, woolly white leaves that do indeed look something like a lamb's ears. It's quick to increase: one plant will spread into a clump as the stems root where they touch soil. In most varieties, 1- to 1½-foot flowering stems bearing small leaves and whorls of small purple flowers appear in late spring and early summer. Many gardeners enjoy the blossoms, but others feel they detract from the foliage and cut off the stems when they appear. Cultivars include '**Countess Helene von Stein**' ('**Big Ears**'), with leaves twice as big as those of the species and few flowering stems; '**Silver Carpet**', which flowers only rarely; and '**Primrose Heron**', another seldom-blooming sort with foliage that is primrose yellow in spring, then turns to gray green as summer progresses.

Listing continues >

STACHYS

BETONY, LAMB'S EARS
Lamiaceae (Labiatae)

- ZONES VARY
- FULL SUN, EXCEPT AS NOTED
- MODERATE WATER
- FLOWERS IN LATE SPRING, SUMMER

Quite different in appearance is **S. macrantha (S. grandiflora),** suited to Zones 1–24, 31–45. It forms a dense, foot-high clump of long-stalked, dark green, heart-shaped leaves with scalloped edges; wrinkled and roughly hairy, they reach 3 inches across. The plants spread rapidly in rich, moist soil. Slender stems to 1½ to 2 feet tall rise above the leaves, bearing tiered whorls of showy purplish pink flowers. **'Robusta'** and **'Superba'** offer larger flowers; **'Alba'** is a white-flowered form.

Common betony, **S. officinalis** (Zones 1–24, 29–45), has elongated green leaves and 1½- to 2-foot stems bearing small reddish purple or lilac pink flowers in densely packed whorls. Cultivars include **'Grandiflora Rosea'**, with larger soft pink blossoms, and white-flowered **'Grandiflora Alba'**.

CULTURE. The betonies are undemanding perennials, growing well in average soil with moderate watering. The two green-leafed species require some shade where summers are hot; lamb's ears will tolerate light shade but does not require it. When clumps show bare spots or vigor declines, divide and replant in spring (lamb's ears will require division more frequently than the other betonies).

Effective with Achillea, Armeria maritima, Ceratostigma plumbaginoides, Chrysanthemum frutescens, Dianthus, Diascia, Linaria pupurea, Sedum, Verbena.

Stachys macrantha

STOKESIA laevis
STOKES' ASTER
Asteraceae (Compositae)

- ZONES 2–9, 12–24, 26, 28–43
- ☼ FULL SUN
- ⬥ REGULAR WATER
- ✳ ✳ ✳ ✳ FLOWERS IN SUMMER, AUTUMN

Stokesia laevis 'Klaus Jellito'

Stokes' aster blooms over a long period, bearing large, colorful blossoms enhanced by good-looking dark green leaves 2 to 8 inches long. Native to the southeastern United States, it's a much-branched plant 1½ to 2 feet high. The asterlike, 3- to 4-inch-wide flowers emerge from tight flower buds enclosed in leafy, curved, prickly bracts (modified leaves). Each blossom has a central button of small flowers surrounded by a ring of larger ones. Seed is available for blue and white Stokes' asters; you'll also find a number of named cultivars. Among the latter are **'Alba'** and **'Silver Moon'**, both 1½-foot plants with white flowers; popular **'Blue Danube'**, with lavender blue blooms; and **'Klaus Jelitto'**, with somewhat larger lavender flowers. A new twist in the world of Stokes' asters is offered by 15- to 18-inch-tall **'Mary Gregory'**: its blossoms are a soft yellow. Unique because of its large size is 3- to 4-foot **'Omega Skyrocket'**, with pale blue flowers.

CULTURE. These plants are tolerant of average soils, but they must have good drainage, especially in winter. In the coldest regions, provide winter protection with a covering of evergreen boughs or straw. When declining performance indicates overcrowding, divide clumps in early spring. You can also start new plants by sowing seed in early spring.

Effective with Achillea, Coreopsis, Liatris, Scabiosa.

THALICTRUM
MEADOW RUE
Ranunculaceae

- ZONES VARY
- ☼ LIGHT SHADE, EXCEPT AS NOTED
- ⬥ REGULAR WATER
- ✳ ✳ ✳ FLOWERS IN LATE SPRING, SUMMER

With their graceful, fernlike leaves and branching, open blossom clusters, the airy-looking meadow rues are choice perennials for a shaded border or the edge of a wooded spot. Their foliage is similar to that of columbine *(Aquilegia)*, to which they are related, but they're generally larger than columbines, with leafy flower stems that rise 2 to 6 feet high, depending on the species. Flower shape is different, too: the profuse small, petal-less blossoms have four segments (sepals) and a prominent cluster of stamens.

Earliest to bloom each year is **T. aquilegifolium,** successful in Zones 2–10, 14–17, 32 (cooler parts), 33–41. It reaches 2 to 3 feet tall, with blue-tinted foliage; the flowers consist of clouds of fluffy stamens (the white or greenish sepals drop off) followed by attractive, long-lasting seed heads. The species has rosy lilac blooms; '**Album**' has white flowers, while '**Thundercloud**' produces larger heads of deep purple.

Chinese meadow rue, *T. delavayi (T. dipterocarpum),* is suited to Zones 2–10, 14–17, 31–41. It has especially delicate green foliage and thin, dark purple stems that reach 3, 4, or even 6 feet high; these are topped by open, airy clusters of flowers with lavender sepals and yellow stamens. The cultivar '**Hewitt's Double**' has double lilac blossoms that last longer than those of the species.

T. flavum glaucum (T. speciosissimum) succeeds in Zones 2–10, 14–17, 31–41. Bearing blue-green foliage and pale yellow flowers, it grows vigorously to 3 to 5 feet tall. One of the most popular meadow rues is *T. rochebrunianum* (Zones 1–10, 14–17, 32–43). Its intricately branched, 4- to 6-foot stems rise above green foliage clumps, bearing clouds of small blossoms with lilac sepals and pale yellow stamens. '**Lavender Mist**' is a superior selection.

CULTURE. Meadow rues thrive in good, well-drained, organically enriched soil. They do well in light shade or dappled sunlight anywhere; in cool-summer regions, they'll also take full sun. Chinese meadow rue *(T. delavayi)* and *T. flavum glaucum* generally need staking to remain upright. Divide clumps every 4 to 5 years in early spring.

Effective with Aconitum, Brunnera macrophylla, Cimicifuga, Digitalis, Helleborus, Hosta, Lupinus.

TOP: *Thalictrum aquilegifolium* 'Album'
BOTTOM: *Thalictrum delavayi* 'Hewitt's Double'

Thymus × citriodorous

These fragrant, low-growing perennial herbs are ideal for edging borders and planting between stepping-stones. Lemon thyme, *T. × citriodorus* (Zones 1–24, 26, 28–43), grows 4 to 12 inches high, clothed in oval, ¼-inch-wide green leaves that do indeed have a lemon fragrance. Tiny pale purple flowers are borne in dense, oblong flower heads. Cultivars include '**Argenteus**', with silver-splashed leaves, and green-foliaged, lime-scented '**Lime**'; both have pale purple flowers. The main stems of creeping thyme, *T. praecox arcticus* (Zones 1–24, 29–43), form a flat mat; the flowering stems rise 2 to 6 inches high, bearing purplish white blossoms. Among the many cultivars are white '**Albus**' and dark pink '**Dorothy Klaber**'.

CULTURE. Given well-drained soil and a sunny location, thyme is easy to grow. To help prevent rot, take care to avoid overwatering. Shear as needed to restrain the plants and encourage new growth. Propagate by division in early spring.

Effective with Dianthus, Lavandula, Sempervivum tectorum, Sisyrinchium.

THYMUS
THYME
Lamiaceae (Labiatae)

- 🌿 ZONES VARY
- ☼ FULL SUN
- 💧 MODERATE WATER
- ✳ ✳ ✳ FLOWERS IN SUMMER

Easy-to-grow spiderworts bloom over a long season, carrying their three-petaled flowers above clumps of glossy, grasslike foliage. Variously classified as *T. virginiana* or *T. × andersoniana,* the plants produce 1½- to 3-foot stems with arching, straplike green leaves on either side; clusters of flower buds appear atop each stem. Though each blossom lasts only a day, the buds are numerous enough to ensure a prolonged show. Cultivars include '**Innocence**', with creamy white flowers; magenta pink '**Red Cloud**'; and '**Blue Stone**', with blossoms in medium blue. '**Concord Grape**' has purple flowers and blue-green foliage, while '**Purple Profusion**' features violet blossoms set off by purplish leaves.

Listing continues >

TRADESCANTIA
SPIDERWORT
Commelinaceae

- 🌿 ZONES 1–24, 26, 28–43
- ☼ ◑ FULL SUN OR LIGHT SHADE
- 💧💧 REGULAR TO AMPLE WATER
- ✳ ✳ ✳ ✳ FLOWERS IN LATE SPRING, SUMMER

Tradescantia 'Concord Grape'

CULTURE. Spiderworts appreciate organically enriched soil and plenty of water, though they're tough plants that will survive with poorer soil and less water. They tolerate poor drainage better than most other perennials. As summer progresses, clumps often become leggy or sprawling; when they reach this stage, cut them back almost to the ground. New foliage will appear quickly, sometimes giving a second show of flowers. To rejuvenate the plants or increase your supply, dig and divide in early spring.

Effective with Amsonia tabernaemontana, Chelone, Digitalis, Trollius.

TRICYRTIS
TOAD LILY
Liliaceae

- ✂ ZONES VARY
- ◐ ● LIGHT TO FULL SHADE
- ♦ REGULAR WATER
- ✳ ✳ ✳ ✳ FLOWERS IN AUTUMN, EXCEPT AS NOTED

The orchidlike blossoms of toad lilies are unusual and fascinating, worthy of careful inspection; place the plants along a pathway or on a shaded bank to invite close-up viewing. Each waxy, inch-wide flower consists of three petals and three sepals; a column of decorative stamens and styles rises from the center. The upright to arching stems are clasped in broadly oval leaves; the flowers appear at the leaf bases (axils) and in terminal clusters. The blooms are typically spotted in red or purple, and the common name "toad lily" may come from this mottled appearance—though some believe it's related to the Philippine Tasaday people's practice of wiping their hands with juice from the flowers before setting out to collect frogs.

Formosa toad lily, *T. formosana* (Zones 3–9, 14–17, 31–34, 39), has fairly upright, 2- to 2½-foot stems clothed in glossy leaves with darker green mottling. The plants spread by stoloniferous roots but are not invasive. The brown to maroon buds open to blooms of white to pale lilac, densely spotted in dark red. 'Alba' has white flowers with crimson spots; 'Amethystina' is an early-blooming cultivar that begins flowering in late summer, bearing lavender blue blossoms spotted in dark red.

Common toad lily, *T. hirta* (Zones 2–9, 14–17, 32–41), grows to 3 feet tall. The arching stems bear softly hairy foliage; the flowers are white to pale lilac, spotted with purple. 'Hatatogisa' has purple-spotted blooms of dusky dark blue. 'Miyazaki' bears pink to white flowers with crimson spots; 'Miyazaki Gold' is similar but has gold-edged leaves. 'White Towers' is a vigorous cultivar with pure white blossoms.

Two hybrid toad lilies with extra-showy blossoms are 'Sinonome', with white flowers boldly splashed with purple, and 'Togen', featuring unspotted pale lavender flowers with darker petal and sepal tips. Both grow in Zones 3–9, 14–17, 31–34, 39.

Tricyrtis hirta 'Miyazaki'

CULTURE. Toad lilies are woodland plants and appreciate moist, organically enriched soil with good drainage. They seldom need division, but if you want to increase your planting, you can remove rooted pieces from a clump's perimeter in early spring. Plants may self-sow, producing abundant volunteer seedlings.

Effective with Anemone × hybrida, Chelone, Epimedium, ferns, Hosta.

TROLLIUS
✤ GLOBEFLOWER
Ranunculaceae

- ✂ ZONES 1–6, 32–43
- ◐ LIGHT SHADE, EXCEPT AS NOTED
- ♦♦ AMPLE WATER
- ✳ ✳ ✳ FLOWERS IN SPRING, SUMMER

The large, rounded flowers make the common name easy to understand. Carried on 1½- to 3-foot stems above clumps of attractive, shiny, finely cut leaves, they're typically bright yellow or orange, creating a cheery patch of color at bloom time. Because they require cool, moist soil, globeflowers are good candidates for planting near a pond or stream.

Plants grown under the name *T. × cultorum* are hybrids among several species; most bloom in late spring. Cultivars include 2-foot-tall, cream-blossomed 'Alabaster', a more pastel choice than other globeflowers; 2-foot-high 'Earliest of All', bearing pale orange-yellow blooms in midspring; and 3-foot 'Etna', with dark orange flowers.

Growing 1½ to 2 feet tall, **T. europaeus** blooms in spring, producing 1- to 2-inch-wide flowers of lemon yellow. It's somewhat more tolerant of dry soil than other globe-flowers. The cultivar **'Superbus'** is a 2-foot plant with extra-large (4-inch-wide) sulfur yellow blossoms.

Globeflowers sometimes listed in catalogs as *T. ledebourii* are probably really a different species, **T. chinensis.** The summer flowers are cup shaped, with an outer ring of broad, spreading sepals surrounding inner upright petals and showy stamens. The most widely available cultivar is **'Golden Queen'**, with large yellow-orange flowers on 3-foot stems.

CULTURE. Plant globeflowers in soil amended with plenty of organic matter, and water them liberally. In all but the coolest-summer regions, locate the plants in a shady part of the garden. They generally do not require division for many years; divide only when clumps decline in vigor or become thin in the center, doing the job in early spring. Plants are slow to reestablish after division and may bloom sparsely the following year.

Effective with Astilbe, Iris (Japanese), Lobelia, Mertensia virginica, Paeonia, Tradescantia.

Trollius chinensis 'Golden Queen'

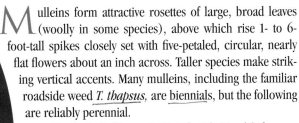

Verbascum 'Helen Johnson'

Mulleins form attractive rosettes of large, broad leaves (woolly in some species), above which rise 1- to 6-foot-tall spikes closely set with five-petaled, circular, nearly flat flowers about an inch across. Taller species make striking vertical accents. Many mulleins, including the familiar roadside weed *T. thapsus,* are biennials, but the following are reliably perennial.

V. chaixii (Zones 2–11, 14–24, 31–41) forms a 1½-foot-wide rosette of hairy green or slightly gray foliage; the flowering spikes (branched in older plants) arise in late spring, reaching 3 feet high and bearing light yellow flowers centered in red. **'Album'** has white blooms with purple centers. Imposing **V. olympicum** (Zones 3–10, 14–24, 32–34, 39) produces a 3-foot-wide rosette of large white leaves covered in soft, downy hairs. The branched stems appear in summer, growing as tall as 5 feet and carrying bright yellow flowers. Purple mullein, **V. phoeniceum** (Zones 1–10, 14–24, 32–43), forms a 1½-foot-wide rosette of dark green leaves that are smooth on top, hairy beneath. It blooms in spring, carrying slender spikes of blossoms in purple, rose, white, or yellow on 2- to 4-foot stems.

Other appealing mulleins include hybrids of the above and other species, such as **'Helen Johnson'** (Zones 3–10, 14–24, 32–34, 39), with coppery pink flowers on 3-foot stems, and **'Pink Domino'** (Zones 3–10, 14–24, 32–34, 39), which bears rose pink flowers on 3- to 3½-foot stems.

CULTURE. Tough and undemanding, the mulleins do best with well-drained, relatively poor soil and only moderate watering. Cut off spent flower spikes both to induce a second round of bloom from new stems and to prevent seed setting, which can result in numerous volunteer seedlings. If you want to increase your planting, let a few plants produce seeds. Remember, though, that seedlings of hybrid selections won't be the

VERBASCUM
MULLEIN
Scrophulariaceae

🌱 ZONES VARY
☀ FULL SUN
💧 MODERATE WATER
✳ ✳ ✳ ✳ FLOWERS IN LATE SPRING, SUMMER

Verbascum chaixii

same as the parents; to propagate hybrids, take root cuttings in early spring or separate rooted young rosettes from the clump.

Effective with Artemisia, Lychnis coronaria, Oenothera, Sedum, Verbena.

VERBENA

🌸 VERBENA

Verbenaceae

🌱 ZONES VARY

☼ FULL SUN

💧 MODERATE TO LITTLE WATER

❋ ❋ ❋ ❋ ❋ FLOWERS IN SPRING, SUMMER

Verbena bonariensis

Easy to grow and long blooming, the perennial verbenas described below perform best where summers are sunny and warm; in regions where they're not hardy, they're often grown as annuals. (The familiar bedding verbenas, *V. hybrida* and *V. peruviana*, are typically also treated as annuals and replaced each year, even in the mild-winter regions where they are perennial.)

A large, dramatic-looking plant with branching stems 3 to 6 feet tall, **V. bonariensis** is a South American native hardy in Zones 8–24, 28–31, warmer parts of 32. Many clusters of purple flowers appear at the stem tips. Though the plant is fairly sturdy, it has an open, airy look, a see-through quality that makes it suitable for the front of the border as well as the middle or back. *V. bonariensis* has naturalized in warmer regions of the United States—as has another South American verbena, **V. rigida** (Zones 3–24, 28–33). Growing 10 to 20 inches high and spreading by underground stems, this species carries its small, circular purple flowers in tight clusters at the ends of stiff, upright stems. Cultivars include scarlet-flowered **'Flame'**, which grows only 6 inches tall but spreads vigorously; pale lilac **'Lilacina'**; and lavender blue **'Polaris'**.

Native from Virginia to Florida and west to Colorado and Mexico, **V. canadensis** (Zones 2–24, 28–41) reaches 1½ feet high and bears clusters of rosy purple flowers. The stems root as they spread along the ground, making an excellent ground cover. Many cultivars (which may be hybrids with other species) are offered, including warm pink **'Silver Anne'**, purple **'Homestead'**, and white **'Snowflurry'**.

CULTURE. Verbenas need good air circulation (to avoid mildew) and well-drained soil, especially in winter. They tolerate drought and fairly poor soil. Propagate *V. canadensis* and *V. rigida* by removing and replanting rooted shoots from the outsides of clumps. *V. bonariensis* readily self-sows, giving you an ongoing supply of volunteer plants.

Effective with Alstroemeria, Canna, Coreopsis, Gaura lindheimeri, Stachys, Verbascum.

VERONICA

🌿 SPEEDWELL, VERONICA

Scrophulariaceae

🌱 ZONES VARY

☼ FULL SUN, EXCEPT AS NOTED

💧 REGULAR WATER

❋ ❋ ❋ FLOWERS IN SPRING, SUMMER

Their tapering bloom spikes packed with tiny flowers, speedwells are a showy choice for the border. Most bloom in midsummer, but a few begin flowering as early as spring (particularly in mild-winter regions). Shopping for these plants is often confusing: because taxonomists frequently rename species, different nurseries may list the same cultivar (most cultivars are hybrids) under two or three different species. When you choose speedwells for your garden, pay attention not only to botanical names, but also to any descriptions of growth habit and flower color.

V. alpina (Zones 1–7, 14–17, 32–45) forms a low rosette of shiny green leaves; foot-tall stems bearing clusters of blue flowers appear in spring and early summer. The cultivar **'Alba'** is a 10-inch plant with white flowers, while the related long-blooming hybrid **'Goodness Grows'** reaches 1 to 2 feet and bears violet blue blossoms. **V. austriaca teucrium 'Crater Lake Blue'** (Zones 1–9, 14–21, 28, 31–43) is a popular speedwell with short spikes of bright blue flowers in midsummer on a 12- to 15-inch-tall plant.

Reaching 2½ feet high, long-leaf veronica, *V. longifolia* (Zones 1–9, 14–21, 32–43), is taller than many other species; its leafy stems carry deep blue flowers in midsummer. One cultivar is upright, bushy **'Blaureisen'**, with bright blue blossoms. Recently introduced *V. peduncularis* **'Georgia Blue'** (Zones 2–9, 14–24, 29–34) is a charming spring bloomer with white-eyed blue flowers dotting a spreading foot-high mat of foliage. It's a first-rate front-of-the-border plant or small-scale ground cover.

V. spicata (Zones 1–9, 14–21, 28, 31–43) blooms over a long summer season, its clusters of blue flowers rising to 2 feet high above rounded clumps of glossy green foliage. Among its cultivars (which are hybrids with other speedwells) are 3-foot-tall, medium blue **'Blue Charm'**; compact, 8- to 10-inch **'Heidekind'**, with rosy pink blooms; and **'Nora Williams'**, with white-margined foliage and white flowers. *V. incana* (Zones 1–7, 14–17, 32–43) offers gray-white, felted leaves that complement the 1½-foot spires of violet blue blossoms.

CULTURE. Speedwells appreciate average soil with good drainage. They grow best in full sun in most climates, but appreciate some afternoon shade in hot-summer regions. Remove spent flower spikes to encourage further bloom on secondary spikes. When clumps show declining vigor, dig and divide them in early spring. You can also increase plants from stem cuttings taken in spring and summer.

Effective with Campanula, Catananche caerulea, Chrysanthemum × rubellum, C. × superbum, Iberis sempervirens, Liatris, Phlomis, Sisyrinchium.

Veronica austriaca teucrium 'Crater Lake Blue'

Thanks to their strong form, yuccas are the ideal "sculptural" accent plants; the famous English garden designer Gertrude Jekyll often used them to anchor the ends of long perennial borders. Though some yuccas have tall, treelike stems, the kinds most often chosen for perennial gardens are stemless or nearly so, forming rosettes of tough, sword-shaped leaves. Leafless blossom stalks rise from the clump's center, bearing large clusters of bell-shaped flowers.

Adam's needle, *Y. filamentosa* (Zones 1–24, 26–43), is native to the southeastern United States. Its stiff, spiny-tipped gray-green leaves grow 1 to 2 inches wide and 2½ feet long; narrow, threadlike fibers decorate the margins. Creamy white flowers appear on a stalk that rises 4 to 7 feet or even higher. Nurseries offer named cultivars, many with variegated leaves; some may be hybrids with other yucca species. These include **'Bright Edge'**, with yellow-edged foliage; **'Color Guard'**, with striking gold-centered leaves; and **'Variegata'**, with white leaf margins.

Soapweed, *Y. glauca* (Zones 1–24, 29, 30, 33, 35, 41, 43), is native to the central and southwestern United States. It's a somewhat smaller plant than *Y. filamentosa*, with stiff, pointed pale green leaves 1 to 2 inches wide and 1 to 2½ feet long. The greenish white flowers are borne on a 4- to 5-foot bloom spike.

CULTURE. These undemanding plants need only well-drained soil and a full-sun location to thrive. Many gardeners clip off the pointed leaf tips (especially the very sharp daggers of Adam's needle) to protect themselves and others from accidental skewering. Propagate by root cuttings taken in early spring, by seed, or by removing small offsets from the edges of established clumps in spring.

Effective with Asclepias tuberosa, Euphorbia, Sedum, Ratibida, Rudbeckia.

YUCCA
YUCCA, ADAM'S NEEDLE, SOAPWEED
Agavaceae

- ZONES VARY
- FULL SUN
- REGULAR WATER
- FLOWERS IN LATE SPRING, EARLY SUMMER

Yucca filamentosa 'Variegata'

SUNSET'S GARDEN CLIMATE ZONES

A plant's performance is governed by the total climate: length of growing season, timing and amount of rainfall, winter lows, summer highs, humidity. *Sunset's* climate zone maps take all these factors into account—unlike the familiar hardiness zone maps devised by the U.S. Department of Agriculture, which divide the U.S. and Canada into zones based strictly on winter lows. The U.S.D.A. maps tell you only where a plant may survive the winter; our climate zone maps let you see where that plant will thrive year-round. Below are brief descriptions of the 45 zones illustrated on the map on pages 124–125. For more information, consult *Sunset's National Garden Book* and *Western Garden Book*.

ZONE 1. Coldest Winters in the West and Western Prairie States

Growing season: early June through Aug., but with some variation—the longest seasons are usually found near this zone's large bodies of water. Frost can come any night of the year. Winters are snowy and intensely cold, due to latitude, elevation, and/or influence of continental air mass. There's some summer rainfall.

ZONE 2. Second-coldest Western Climate

Growing season: early May through Sept. Winters are cold (lows run from –3° to –34°F/–19° to –37°C), but less so than in Zone 1. In northern and interior areas, lower elevations fall into Zone 2, higher areas into Zone 1.

ZONE 3. West's Mildest High-elevation and Interior Regions

Growing season: early May to late Sept.—shorter than in Zone 2, but offset by milder winters (lows from 13° to –24°F/–11° to –31°C). This is fine territory for plants needing winter chill and dry, hot summers.

ZONE 4. Cold-winter Western Washington and British Columbia

Growing season: early May to early Oct. Summers are cool, thanks to ocean influence; chilly winters (19° to –7°F/–7° to –22°C) result from elevation, influence of continental air mass, or both. Coolness, ample rain suit many perennials and bulbs.

ZONE 5. Ocean-influenced Northwest Coast and Puget Sound

Growing season: mid-April to Nov., typically with cool temperatures throughout. Less rain falls here than in Zone 4; winter lows range from 28° to 1°F/–2° to –17°C. This "English garden" climate is ideal for rhododendrons and many rock garden plants.

ZONE 6. Oregon's Willamette Valley

Growing season: mid-Mar. to mid-Nov., with somewhat warmer temperatures than in Zone 5. Ocean influence keeps winter lows about the same as in Zone 5. Climate suits all but tender plants and those needing hot or dry summers.

ZONE 7. Oregon's Rogue River Valley, California's High Foothills

Growing season: May to early Oct. Summers are hot and dry; typical winter lows run from 23° to 9°F/–5° to –13°C. The summer-winter contrast suits plants that need dry, hot summers and moist, only moderately cold winters.

ZONE 8. Cold-air Basins of California's Central Valley

Growing season: mid-Feb. through Nov. This is a valley floor with no maritime influence. Summers are hot; winter lows range from 29° to 13°F/–2° to –11°C. Rain comes in the cooler months, covering just the early part of the growing season.

ZONE 9. Thermal Belts of California's Central Valley

Growing season: late Feb. through Dec. Zone 9 is located in the higher elevations around Zone 8, but its summers are just as hot; its winter lows are slightly higher (temperatures range from 28° to 18°F/–2° to –8°C). Rainfall pattern is the same as in Zone 8.

ZONE 10. High Desert Areas of Arizona, New Mexico, West Texas, Oklahoma Panhandle, and Southwest Kansas

Growing season: April to early Nov. Chilly (even snow-dusted) weather rules from late Nov. through Feb., with lows from 31° to 24°F/–1° to –4°C. Rain comes in summer as well as in the cooler seasons.

ZONE 11. Medium to High Desert of California and Southern Nevada

Growing season: early April to late Oct. Summers are sizzling, with 110 days above 90°F/32°C. Balancing this is a 3½-month winter, with 85 nights below freezing and lows from 11° to 0°F/–12° to –18°C. Scant rainfall comes in winter.

ZONE 12. Arizona's Intermediate Desert

Growing season: mid-Mar. to late Nov., with scorching midsummer heat. Compared to Zone 13, this region has harder frosts; record low is 6°F/–14°C. Rains come in summer and winter.

ZONE 13. Low or Subtropical Desert

Growing season: mid-Feb. through Nov., interrupted by nearly 3 months of incandescent, growth-stopping summer heat. Most frosts are light (record lows run from 19° to 13°F/–7° to –11°C); scant rain comes in summer and winter.

ZONE 14. Inland Northern and Central California with Some Ocean Influence

Growing season: early Mar. to mid-Nov., with rain coming in the remaining months. Periodic intrusions of marine air temper summer heat and winter cold (lows run from 26° to 16°F/–3° to –9°C). Mediterranean-climate plants are at home here.

ZONE 15. Northern and Central California's Chilly-winter Coast-influenced Areas

Growing season: Mar. to Dec. Rain comes from fall through winter. Typical winter lows range from 28° to 21°F/–2° to –6°C. Maritime air influences the zone much of the time, giving it cooler, moister summers than Zone 14.

ZONE 16. Northern and Central California Coast Range Thermal Belts

Growing season: late Feb. to late Nov. With cold air draining to lower elevations, winter lows typically run from 32° to 19°F/0° to –7°C. Like Zone 15, this region is dominated by maritime air, but its winters are milder on average.

ZONE 17. Oceanside Northern and Central California and Southernmost Oregon

Growing season: late Feb. to early Dec. Coolness and fog are hallmarks; summer highs seldom top 75°F/24°C, while winter lows run from 36° to 23°F/2° to –5°C. Heat-loving plants disappoint or dwindle here.

ZONE 18. Hilltops and Valley Floors of Interior Southern California

Growing season: mid-Mar. through late Nov. Summers are hot and dry; rain comes in winter, when lows reach 28° to 10°F/–2° to –12°C. Plants from the Mediterranean and Near Eastern regions thrive here.

ZONE 19. Thermal belts around Southern California's Interior Valleys

Growing season: early Mar. through Nov. As in Zone 18, rainy winters and hot, dry summers are the norm—but here, winter lows dip only to 27° to 22°F/–3° to –6°C, allowing some tender evergreen plants to grow outdoors with protection.

ZONE 20. Hilltops and Valley Floors of Ocean-influenced Inland Southern California

Growing season: late Mar. to late Nov.—but fairly mild winters (lows of 28° to 23°F/–2° to –5°C) allow gardening through much of the year. Cool and moist maritime influence alternates with hot, dry interior air.

ZONE 21. Thermal Belts around Southern California's Ocean-influenced Interior Valleys

Growing season: early Mar. to early Dec., with the same tradeoff of oceanic and interior influence as in Zone 20. During the winter rainy season, lows range from 36° to 23°F/2° to –5°C—warmer than in Zone 20, since the colder air drains to the valleys.

ZONE 22. Colder-winter Parts of Southern California's Coastal Region

Growing season: Mar. to early Dec. Winter lows seldom fall below 28°F/–2°C (records are around 21°F/–6°C), though colder air sinks to this zone from Zone 23. Summers are warm; rain comes in winter. Climate here is largely oceanic.

ZONE 23. Thermal Belts of Southern California's Coastal Region

Growing season: almost year-round (all but first half of Jan.). Rain comes in winter. Reliable ocean influence keeps summers mild (except when hot Santa Ana winds come from inland), frosts negligible; 23°F/–5°C is the record low.

ZONE 24. Marine-dominated Southern California Coast

Growing season: all year, but periodic freezes have dramatic effects (record lows are 33° to 20°F/1° to –7°C). Climate here is oceanic (but warmer than oceanic Zone 17), with cool summers, mild winters. Subtropical plants thrive.

ZONE 25. South Florida and the Keys

Growing season: all year. Add ample year-round rainfall (least in Dec. through Mar.), high humidity, and overall warmth, and you have a near-tropical climate. The Keys are frost-free; winter lows elsewhere run from 40° to 25°F/4° to –4°C.

ZONE 26. Central and Interior Florida

Growing season: early Feb. to late Dec., with typically humid, warm to hot weather. Rain is plentiful all year, heaviest in summer and early fall. Lows range from 15°F/–9°C in the north to 27°F/–3°C in the south; arctic air brings periodic hard freezes.

ZONE 27. Lower Rio Grande Valley

Growing season: early Mar. to mid-Dec.. Summers are hot and humid; winter lows only rarely dip below freezing. Many plants from tropical and subtropical Africa and South America are well adapted here.

ZONE 28. Gulf Coast, North Florida, Atlantic Coast to Charleston

Growing season: mid-Mar. to early Dec. Humidity and rainfall are year-round phenomena; summers are hot, winters virtually frostless but subject to periodic invasions by frigid arctic air. Azaleas, camellias, many subtropicals flourish.

ZONE 29. Interior Plains of South Texas

Growing season: mid-Mar. through Nov. Moderate rainfall (to 25" annually) comes year-round. Summers are hot. Winter lows can dip to 26°F/–3°C, with occasional arctic freezes bringing much lower readings.

ZONE 30. Hill Country of Central Texas

Growing season: mid-Mar. through Nov. Zone 30 has higher annual rainfall than Zone 29 (to 35") and lower winter temperatures, normally to around 20°F/–7°C. Seasonal variations favor many fruit crops, perennials.

ZONE 31. Interior Plains of Gulf Coast and Coastal Southeast

Growing season: mid-Mar. to early Nov. In this extensive east-west zone, hot and sticky summers contrast with chilly winters (record low temperatures are 7° to 0°F/–14° to –18°C). There's rain all year (an annual average of 50"), with the least falling in Oct.

ZONE 32. Interior Plains of Mid-Atlantic States; Chesapeake Bay, Southeastern Pennsylvania, Southern New Jersey

Growing season: late Mar. to early Nov. Rain falls year-round (40" to 50" annually); winter lows (moving through the zone from south to north) are 30° to 20°F/–1° to –7°C. Humidity is less oppressive here than in Zone 31.

ZONE 33. North-Central Texas and Oklahoma Eastward to the Appalachian Foothills

Growing season: mid-April through Oct. Warm Gulf Coast air and colder continental/arctic fronts both play a role; their unpredictable interplay results in a wide range in annual rainfall (22" to 52") and winter lows (20° to 0°F/–7° to –18°C). Summers are muggy and warm to hot.

ZONE 34. Lowlands and Coast from Gettysburg to North of Boston

Growing season: late April to late Oct. Ample rainfall and humid summers are the norm. Winters are variable—typically fairly mild (around 20°F/–7°C), but with lows down to –3° to –22°F/–19° to –30°C if arctic air swoops in.

ZONE 35. Ouachita Mountains, Northern Oklahoma and Arkansas, Southern Kansas to North-Central Kentucky and Southern Ohio

Growing season: late April to late Oct. Rain comes in all seasons. Summers can be truly hot and humid. Without arctic fronts, winter lows are around 18°F/–8°C; with them, the coldest weather may bring lows of –20°F/–29°C.

ZONE 36. Appalachian Mountains

Growing season: May to late Oct. Thanks to greater elevation, summers are cooler and less humid, winters colder (0° to –20°F/–18° to –29°C) than in adjacent, lower zones. Rain comes all year (heaviest in spring). Late frosts are common.

ZONE 37. Hudson Valley and Appalachian Plateau

Growing season: May to mid-Oct., with rainfall throughout. Lower in elevation than neighboring Zone 42, with warmer winters: lows are 0° to –5°F/–18° to –21°C, unless arctic air moves in. Summer is warm to hot, humid.

ZONE 38. New England Interior and Lowland Maine

Growing season: May to early Oct. Summers feature reliable rainfall and lack oppressive humidity of lower-elevation, more southerly areas. Winter lows dip to –10° to –20°F/–23° to –29°C, with periodic colder temperatures due to influxes of arctic air.

ZONE 39. Shoreline Regions of the Great Lakes

Growing season: early May to early Oct. Springs and summers are cooler here, autumns milder than in areas farther from the lakes. Southeast lakeshores get the heaviest snowfalls. Lows reach 0° to –10°F/–18° to –23°C.

ZONE 40. Inland Plains of Lake Erie and Lake Ontario

Growing season: mid-May to mid-Sept., with rainy, warm, variably humid weather. The lakes help moderate winter lows; temperatures typically range from –10° to –20°F/–23° to –29°C, with occasional colder readings when arctic fronts rush through.

ZONE 41. Northeast Kansas and Southeast Nebraska to Northern Illinois and Indiana, Southeast Wisconsin, Michigan, Northern Ohio

Growing season: early May to early Oct. Winter brings average lows of –11° to –20°F/–23° to –29°C. Summers in this zone are hotter and longer west of the Mississippi, cooler and shorter nearer the Great Lakes; summer rainfall increases in the same west-to-east direction.

ZONE 42. Interior Pennsylvania and New York; St. Lawrence Valley

Growing season: late May to late Sept. This zone's elevation gives it colder winters than surrounding zones: lows range from –20° to –40°F/–29° to –40°C, with the colder readings coming in the Canadian portion of the zone. Summers are humid, rainy.

ZONE 43. Upper Mississippi Valley, Upper Michigan, Southern Ontario and Quebec

Growing season: late May to mid-Sept. The climate is humid from spring through early fall; summer rains are usually dependable. Arctic air dominates in winter, with lows typically from –20° to –30°F/–29° to –34°C.

ZONE 44. Mountains of New England and Southeastern Quebec

Growing season: June to mid-Sept. Latitude and elevation give fairly cool, rainy summers, cold winters with lows of –20° to –40°F/–29° to –40°C. Choose short-season, low heat-requirement annuals and vegetables.

ZONE 45. Northern Parts of Minnesota and Wisconsin, Eastern Manitoba through Interior Quebec

Growing season: mid-June through Aug., with rain throughout; rainfall (and humidity) are least in zone's western part, greatest in eastern reaches. Winters are frigid (–30° to –40°F/–34° to –40°C), with snow cover, deeply frozen soil.

Sunset's Garden Climate Zones

Climate Zones ☒ 1 2 3 4 5 6 7 8 9 10 11 12 13 14 15 16 17 18 19 20 21 22

27

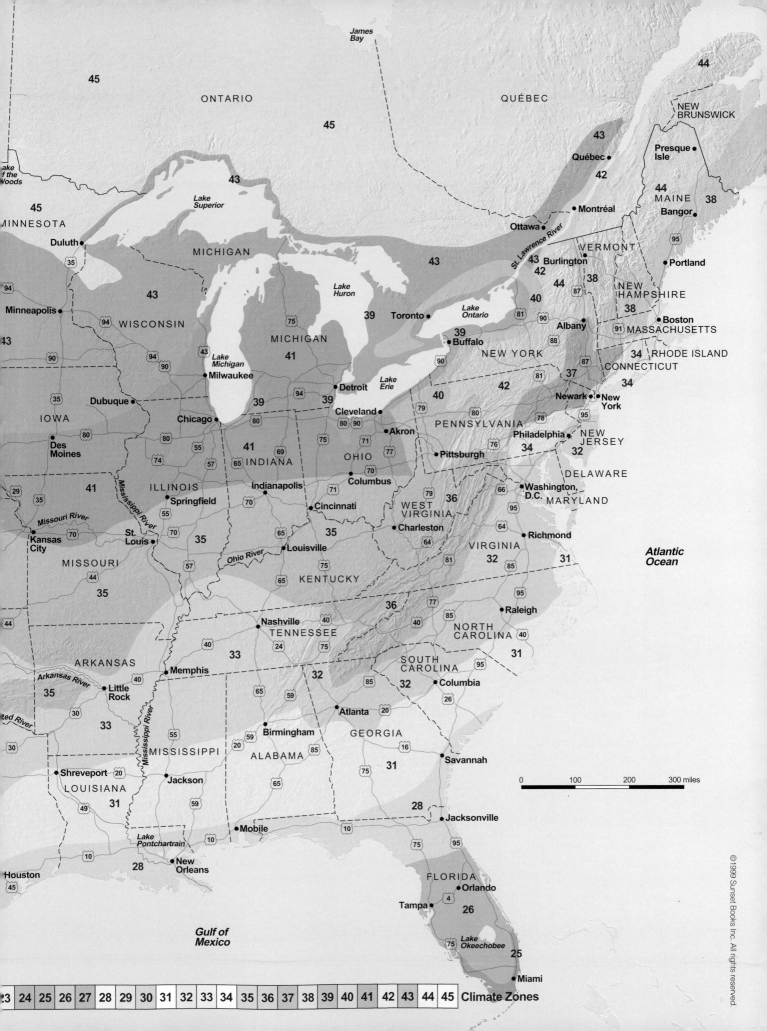

Climate Zones

23 24 25 26 27 28 29 30 31 32 33 34 35 36 37 38 39 40 41 42 43 44 45

RESOURCES

As perennials gain in popularity, local nurseries offer ever wider selections. However, mail-order suppliers are often still the only source for unusual, newly introduced, or hard-to-find varieties. The following list includes some of the growers who publish catalogs of perennial plants and seeds (some charge a small fee). An extensive list of mail-order suppliers and plant societies can be found in Gardening by Mail, *5th edition, by Barbara J. Barton, Mariner Books, 1997.*

ANDRÉ VIETTE FARM AND NURSERY
P.O. Box 1109
Fisherville, VA 22939
(540) 943-2315
www.viette.com

BLUESTONE PERENNIALS
7211 Middle Ridge Road
Madison, OH 44057
(800) 852-5243
www.bluestoneperennials.com

BUSSE GARDENS
5873 Oliver Avenue SW
Cokato, MN 55321-4229
(800) 544-3192

CANYON CREEK NURSERY
3527 Dry Creek Road
Oroville, CA 95965
(530) 533-2166

CARROLL GARDENS
444 East Main Street
Westminster, MD 21157
(800) 638-6334

THE CROWNSVILLE NURSERY
P.O. Box 797
Crownsville, MD 21032
(410) 849-3143
www.crownsvillenursery.com

DIGGING DOG NURSERY
P.O. Box 471
Albion, CA 95410
(707) 937-2480

FORESTFARM
990 Tetherow Road
Williams, OR 97544-9599
www.forestfarm.com

GARDEN PLACE, INC.
6780 Heisley Road
Mentor, OH 44061-0388
(440) 255-3059

HERONSWOOD NURSERY
7530 NE 288th Street
Kingston, WA 98346-9502
(360) 297-4172

HIGH COUNTRY GARDENS
2902 Rufina Street
Santa Fe, NM 87505-2929
(800) 492-7885
www.highcountrygardens.com

MILAEGER'S GARDENS
4838 Douglas Avenue
Racine, WI 53402-2498
(800) 669-9956

NICHE GARDENS
1111 Dawson Road
Chapel Hill, NC 27516
(929) 967-0078
www.nichegdn.com

SHADY OAKS NURSERY
1101 South State Street
P.O. Box 708
Waseca, MN 56093-0708
(800) 504-8006
www.shadyoaks.com

WAYSIDE GARDENS
1 Garden Lane
Hodges, SC 29695-0001
(800) 845-1124
www.waysidegardens.com

WHITE FLOWER FARM
P.O. Box 50
Litchfield, CT 06759-0050
(800) 503-9624
www.whiteflowerfarm.com

WOODSIDE GARDENS
1191 Egg and I Road
Chimacum, WA 98325
(360) 732-4754
www.woodsidegardens.com

MAIL-ORDER SOURCES FOR PERENNIAL SEEDS

J. L. HUDSON, SEEDSMAN
Star Route 2, Box 337
La Honda, CA 94020

SEEDS OF DISTINCTION
P.O. Box 86, Station A (Etobicoke)
Toronto, ON
Canada, M9C 4V2
(416) 255-3060
www.seedsofdistinction.com

THOMPSON & MORGAN
P.O. Box 1308
Jackson, NJ 08527-0308
(800) 274-7333

SUBJECT INDEX

Acid soil, 32
Alkaline soil, 32
Aphids, 41

Bare-root plants, 34
Basal cuttings, 45
Beds, 7
Borders, 7

Caterpillars, 41
Clay, 32, 33
Climate zones, about, 122–125
Cold hardiness and planting sites, 10
Color, 15–17
  flower, by season, 26–29
Color schemes, 16–17
  contrasting, 16
  harmonious, 16
  monochromatic, 17
Containers
  growing perennials in, 25
  planting from, 35
Contrasting color schemes, 16
Cool colors, 15
  sunny garden with, 19
Cutting back, 38
Cuttings, 42, 45

Deadheading, 38
Diseases, 40
Division, 43–44

Drought-tolerant garden, plan for, 22
Drought-tolerant plants, 23

Fertilizer, 37
  adding to soil, 33
Fertilizing, 37
Flower color by season, 26–29
Foliage, using in garden design, 11
Form and size of plants, using in garden design, 11–13

Grouping perennials, tips for, 14

Harmonious color schemes, 16
Hot colors. See Warm colors

Japanese beetles, 41

Layering, 43
Leaf miners, 41
Loam, 32, 33

Mail-order sources for plants and seeds, 126
Mites, 41
Moist soil, perennials for, 35
Monochromatic color schemes, 17
Mulching, 36

Nitrogen, 37

Organic matter, 33

Perennials
  defined, 6
  designing with, 9–24
  mail-order sources for, 126
  permanent (do best without dividing), 14
  selecting, 34
Pests, 40, 41
pH, soil, 32
Phosphorus, 37
Pinching, 38
Planting, 34–35
  bare-root plants, 34
  container-grown plants, 35
  grouping perennials in plantings, 14
  sites, 7, 9–10
  spacing, 14
  timing of planting, 34
Planting bed, how to to prepare, 33
Planting plans
  sample, 18–23
  sketching, 24
Potassium, 37
Powdery mildew, 40
Propagation, 42–45
  cuttings, 42, 45
  division, 43–44
  layering, 43
  from seeds, 42
Pruning, 38

Root cuttings, 42
Root rot, 40
Rust, 40

Sand, 32, 33

Seeds, 42
  mail-order sources for, 126
Selecting perennials, 34
Shade
  garden, plan for, 20
  and planting sites, 9
  plants for, 21
Silt, 32
Size and form of plants, using in garden design, 11–13
Slugs, 41
Snails, 41
Soil, 32–33
  amending, 33
  pH of, 32
  and planting sites, 9
  types of, 32–33
Spacing perennials in plantings, 14
Staking perennials, 39
Stem cuttings, 45
Sunny locations
  garden plans for, 18–19
  and planting sites, 9

Tarnished plant bugs, 41
Texture, 10
Thinning, 38
Thrips, 41

Warm colors, 15
  sunny garden with, 18
Watering, 36
Water-loving perennials, 35
Weed control, 33
Whiteflies, 41
Winter protection, 39

PLANT INDEX

Acanthus mollis, 48
Achillea, 49
Aconite (Aconitum), 49
Aconitum, 49
Adam's needle (Yucca filamentosa), 121
Adenophora, 50
Adiantum pedatum, 78
Agapanthus, 50
Agastache, 51
Alchemilla mollis, 51
Alstroemeria, 52
Alum root (Heuchera), 86
Alyssum saxatile. See Aurinia saxatilis, 59
Amsonia tabernaemontana, 52
Anchusa azurea, 53
Anemone × hybrida, 53
Anise hyssop (Agastache foeniculum), 51
Anthemis tinctoria, 54
Aquilegia, 54
Argyranthemum frutescens. See Chrysanthemum frutescens, 65
Armeria maritima, 55
Arrhenatherum, 98
Artemisia, 55
Aruncus, 56
Asclepias tuberosa, 56
Aster, 57
Aster, Stokes' (Stokesia laevis), 116
Astilbe, 58
Astrantia major, 59
Athyrium, 78

Aurinia saxatilis, 59
Autumn fern (Dryopteris erythrosora), 78
Avens (Geum), 82

Baby's breath (Gypsophila paniculata), 83
Balloon flower (Platycodon grandiflorus), 107
Baptisia, 59
Barrenwort (Epimedium), 74
Basket-of-gold (Aurinia saxatilis), 59
Beard tongue (Penstemon), 103
Bear's breech (Acanthus mollis), 48
Bee balm (Monarda), 96
Bellflower (Campanula), 61
Bergenia, 60
Bethlehem sage (Pulmonaria saccharata), 110
Betony (Stachys), 115
Bishop's hat (Epimedium), 74
Blanket flower (Gaillardia × grandiflora), 80
Bleeding heart (Dicentra), 71
Blue-eyed grass (Sisyrinchium), 114
Blue fescue (Festuca), 99
Blue oat grass (Helictotrichon sempervirens), 100
Blue star (Amsonia tabernaemontana), 52
Boltonia asteroides, 60
Brunnera macrophylla, 61
Bugbane (Cimicifuga), 67

Bugloss, Italian (Anchusa azurea), 53
Bugloss, Siberian (Brunnera macrophylla), 61
Bulbous oat grass (Arrhenatherum), 98
Burning bush (Dictamnus albus), 72
Butterfly weed (Asclepias tuberosa), 56

Calamagrostis, 99
California fuchsia (Epilobium), 74
Campanula, 61
Campion (Lychnis), 94
Candytuft (Iberis sempervirens), 88
Canna, 62
Cardinal flower (Lobelia cardinalis), 93
Carex, 99
Catananche caerulea, 63
Catmint (Nepeta), 96
Centaurea, 63
Centranthus ruber, 64
Ceratostigma plumbaginoides, 64
Chelone, 64
Christmas fern (Polystichum acrostichoides), 79
Christmas rose (Helleborus niger), 84
Chrysanthemum, 65–67
Cimicifuga, 67
Cinnamon fern (Osmunda cinnamomea), 79
Colewort (Crambe cordifolia), 68
Columbine (Aquilegia), 54
Coneflower (Rudbeckia), 111
Coneflower, prairie (Ratibida), 110
Coneflower, purple (Echinacea purpurea), 73
Conoclinium coelestinum. See Eupatorium coelestinum, 76

Coral bells (Heuchera), 86
Coreopsis, 67
Corydalis, 68
Crambe cordifolia, 68
Cranesbill (Geranium), 81
Crown pink (Lychnis coronaria), 94
Cupid's dart (Catananche caerulea), 63

Daylily (Hemerocallis), 85
Delphinium, 69
Dendranthema × grandiflorum. See Chrysanthemum × morifolium, 66
Dendranthema × zawadskii. See Chrysanthemum × rubellum, 67
Deschampsia caespitosa, 99
Dianthus, 70
Diascia, 71
Dicentra, 71
Dictamnus albus, 72
Digitalis, 72
Doronicum, 73
Dropwort (Filipendula vulgaris), 80
Dryopteris, 78
Dusty miller (Artemisia), 55
Dusty miller (Centaurea), 63
Dusty miller (Lychnis), 94
Dwarf plumbago (Ceratostigma plumbaginoides), 64

Echinacea purpurea, 73
Echinops, 73
Epilobium, 74
Epimedium, 74
Erigeron, 75
Eryngium, 76